Language Education During the Pandemic

Wissia Fiorucci
Editor

Language Education During the Pandemic

Rushing Online, Assessment and Community

Editor
Wissia Fiorucci
University of Kent
Canterbury, UK

ISBN 978-3-031-35854-8   ISBN 978-3-031-35855-5 (eBook)
https://doi.org/10.1007/978-3-031-35855-5

© The Editor(s) (if applicable) and The Author(s), under exclusive licence to Springer Nature Switzerland AG 2023

This work is subject to copyright. All rights are solely and exclusively licensed by the Publisher, whether the whole or part of the material is concerned, specifically the rights of translation, reprinting, reuse of illustrations, recitation, broadcasting, reproduction on microfilms or in any other physical way, and transmission or information storage and retrieval, electronic adaptation, computer software, or by similar or dissimilar methodology now known or hereafter developed.

The use of general descriptive names, registered names, trademarks, service marks, etc. in this publication does not imply, even in the absence of a specific statement, that such names are exempt from the relevant protective laws and regulations and therefore free for general use.

The publisher, the authors, and the editors are safe to assume that the advice and information in this book are believed to be true and accurate at the date of publication. Neither the publisher nor the authors or the editors give a warranty, expressed or implied, with respect to the material contained herein or for any errors or omissions that may have been made. The publisher remains neutral with regard to jurisdictional claims in published maps and institutional affiliations.

Cover illustration © YAY Media AS / Alamy Stock Photo

This Palgrave Macmillan imprint is published by the registered company Springer Nature Switzerland AG.
The registered company address is: Gewerbestrasse 11, 6330 Cham, Switzerland

Paper in this product is recyclable.

Notes on Anonymity and Confidentiality

All participants in the case studies presented in this collection were informed of the scope and goals of the research study. Where necessary, research ethics and permissions have been sought and obtained by all researchers from their institutions. All data collection presented in this edited volume has been conducted anonymously. When it was not possible to maintain anonymity or the researcher needed for research purposes information which could lead to the identification of participants, all volunteered information has been kept completely confidential. Where possible, the names of Higher Education institutions where the studies have been conducted have been withheld. Where this was either impossible or irrelevant, said institutions have been named, but participants' anonymity and privacy have been maintained at all times.

Acknowledgements

I would like to thank all the authors in this volume for their commendable professionalism. I would also like to express my most sincere gratitude to all the teachers and students who accepted to be part of the research projects discussed and analysed in the chapters. Finally, I am extremely grateful to Dr Krista Bonello Rutter Giappone and Dr Alvise Sforza Tarabochia for going above and beyond in lending their expertise to take this project across the finish line.

Contents

1 Introduction: Rushing Online   1
Wissia Fiorucci
  1   Note on Nomenclature   6
  2   Assessment   7
  3   (Learning) Community   9
  4   Summary of Chapters   12
  References   20

Part I   English as a Foreign Language: Italian Case Studies   27

2 Authentic and Continuous Assessment During the Pandemic: Teachers' and Students' Perspectives   29
Antonella Giacosa
  1   Introduction   29
  2   Background of the Study   33
  3   Methodology   36
  4   Findings on Experimenting with ACA During the Pandemic   38
  5   Conclusions   51
  References   55

3 Computer-Based Self-Assessment as a Customised Tool for the Strategic Implementation of an Updated Circular Teaching Model   61
Roxanne Barbara Doerr and Annalisa Zanola
1. Introduction: Academic Customised Assessment and Evaluation in the Post-pandemic Era   61
2. The Context of the Study   66
3. Instrument: The Computer-based Self-Assessment Test   69
4. Dataset and Results of 2020–2021 and 2021–2022   73
5. Relevance and Remaining Limitations of the Computer-based Self-Assessment Test   78
6. Conclusions   79
References   81

Part II   Practices in the Virtual Classroom   85

4 Revisiting the Language Lab in the Age of Online Learning: Videoconferencing, Teacher Feedback, and Learner Self-Correction   87
Tobias Heinrich
1. Introduction   87
2. The Language Lab   90
3. Videoconferencing and Corrective Feedback   92
4. Self-Correction   96
5. Working with Recorded Videoconferences: Three Sample Scenarios   98
6. Conclusions   103
References   106

5 Teaching Translation into Spanish Asynchronously: Assessment and Engagement in the Times of COVID   109
Nazaret Pérez-Nieto
1. Introduction   109
2. Research Context   112
3. The Introduction of 'Mediation' into the CEFR   115

4	Changes to the Academic Landscape: Blended Learning and Learning Outcomes	118
5	Methodology	125
6	Presentation of the Activities	126
7	Students' Perspectives: Data Analysis	136
8	Conclusions	144
	References	146

6 Loops, Sayings, and Tongue-Twisters: How to Enhance Foreign Language Communicative Skills in Online Learning Environments   151
Livia Manzini

1	Introduction	151
2	The Participants	154
3	The Selection of Teaching Materials	155
4	The First Experimental Phase (March 2021–April 2021)	157
5	The Second Experimental Phase (March 2022–April 2022)	161
6	Analysis of the Summative Oral-Aural Assessments	163
7	The Students' Feedback	173
8	Conclusions	175
	Appendix	178
	References	202

Part III   Intercultural Competence and Community in Online Settings   205

7 Developing an Online Community and Intercultural Competence: Travelling Virtually to China   207
Wissia Fiorucci, Ru Su, and Alvise Sforza Tarabochia

1	Introduction	207
2	The Project	210
3	Analysis of End of Project Survey	219
4	Conclusions	221
	References	228

8 Developing a Sense of Community Online Through Intercultural Communication: A Gamified Approach — 233
Patricia Díaz-Muñoz and Laura Stecca
1 Introduction — 233
2 Theoretical Background — 235
3 Methodology — 242
4 Results and Findings — 247
5 Conclusions — 252
Appendices — 254
References — 261

Part IV Conclusions — 265

9 The Future of Assessment in Language Education: What Have We Learnt from the Pandemic? — 267
Marion Coderch
1 Introduction — 267
2 The Notion of Continuous Assessment — 268
3 A Holistic Approach to Assessment — 270
4 Flexibility and Choice — 272
5 Inclusive Assessment — 273
6 Academic Integrity in the New Landscape — 276
7 Practical Recommendations — 278
References — 282

Index — 287

Notes on Contributors

Marion Coderch is an assistant professor at the School of Modern Languages and Cultures at Durham University (United Kingdom), where she coordinates the institution-wide Spanish language programme. She has a background in mediaeval studies and has published extensively on attitudes towards women in late mediaeval literature and culture. Alongside her research activity, Marion has taught languages throughout her career. Her scholarship interests in this area include the integration of assessment for learning in university curricula and the professional development of modern foreign language teachers in Higher Education.

Patricia Díaz-Muñoz is a PhD candidate in Linguistics at the Complutense University of Madrid (Spain). Her PhD focuses on (im)politeness and cross-linguistic studies. After finishing her BA degree in English Studies and her MA degree in English Linguistics, Patricia worked as Spanish Language Lector at the University of Kent (United Kingdom). Over the past few years, she has participated in research projects on corpus linguistics and digital discourse conducted by the University of Verona (Italy) and Pablo de Olavide University (Seville, Spain), respectively.

Roxanne Barbara Doerr is a researcher in English Language and Linguistics at the Department of Economics and Management of the University of Brescia (Italy). She holds a PhD in English, the title of

DPhil from the University of Köln, and the title of Doctor Europaeus. Her areas of research and publication include English for specific and academic purposes, military discourse, distance learning and teaching, online discourse communities, corpus assisted discourse studies, and corpus stylistics. Her most recent publications include the book *Academic Style Proofreading: An Introduction* (2022) and essays on the abovementioned research areas in national and international peer-reviewed journals and volumes.

Wissia Fiorucci is Director of Education and Undergraduate Student Experience in the Division of Arts and Humanities at the University of Kent (United Kingdom). She is also the Director of the Language Centre. She is a Senior Fellow of the Higher Education Academy. Over the last ten years Wissia has designed and convened modules and programmes across a range of languages, including French, German, Italian, and Spanish. Her research, teaching, and scholarship practices focus on language education as well as on representations of gender in the media. Wissia is also the co-founder of the Modern Languages Teaching Forum, a network designed to bring together teachers of languages at all levels to share good practices and discuss the challenges facing the sector. She has established several exchange programmes between the University of Kent and universities across the world.

Antonella Giacosa has been an English for Specific Purposes (ESP) teacher in Italian High Schools for more than 20 years and a subject expert at the Foreign Language Department of the University of Turin (Italy). She is completing her PhD in Digital Humanities on interaction during the pandemic in EFL and ESP university classes at the University of Turin. Her research focuses on innovative and transdisciplinary approaches to teaching and learning English and digital classroom interaction competence (e-CIC). Antonella is a member of international projects dealing with internationalisation at home, at the level of tertiary education. She collaborates with the *European Scientific Journal* editorial board for humanities and distance learning. She has recently published different contributions on emergency remote teaching during the COVID-19 pandemic.

Tobias Heinrich is Lecturer in German at the University of Kent (United Kingdom). Tobias studied at the University of Vienna and the Humboldt University of Berlin. Before joining the Department of Modern Languages at the University of Kent in 2017, he taught at the University of Oxford and the University of Vienna. From 2012 to 2014, he was Deputy Director of the Boltzmann Institute for the History and Theory of Biography. Tobias has published on German literature from the eighteenth to the twenty-first century. He is particularly interested in questions of life writing, which are addressed in a monograph on *Theories of Biography circa 1800* (Leben lesen. Theorien der Biographie um 1800) that appeared with Böhlau in 2016. He is also a member of the editorial board for the *European Journal of Life Writing*.

Livia Manzini has just finished her PhD (2022) on the role of pronunciation and intonation in teaching Italian as a foreign language through blended learning at the University of Birmingham (United Kingdom). She holds a BA in Modern Languages and Literatures from the University of Bologna (2014) and an MA in Teaching Italian as a Foreign Language cum laude from the University of Bologna (2017). Her thesis focused on the observation and validation of e-learning and blended learning in teaching Italian as a foreign language. She has been a Fellow of the Higher Education Academy (FHEA) since 2021, and she has worked as Teaching Fellow in Italian at the University of Birmingham from 2019 to 2022.

Nazaret Pérez-Nieto is Lecturer in Spanish at the School ofW Modern Languages at Cardiff University (United Kingdom), where she teaches Spanish language and translation modules at undergraduate and postgraduate levels. Sworn Translator for the English language and Fellow of the Higher Education Academy, she holds the roles of Academic Director for the outreach collaborative project Routes into Languages Cymru, Assessment and Feedback Lead, and Programme Director of Spanish and Portuguese for the Languages for All programme. Her research interests lie in the fields of translation in language teaching and learning, second language acquisition and teaching Spanish as a foreign language. Her more recent publications include the use of task-based projects for transition from university to placements abroad, the development of academic, sociocultural, and employability skills for students of Spanish as a foreign language, and how to teach languages to Generation Z students analysing the impact of the use of audiovisual materials in the Spanish classroom.

Laura Stecca is a freelance teacher of Italian and Spanish and independent researcher. Previously, she taught Italian and Spanish at the University of Kent, where she also co-taught modules on teaching pedagogy and practices. Laura gained experience in teaching Italian as a second language and Italian culture by working in the fields of immigration, international diplomacy, and private education in Italy and abroad. She is also employed as a teaching content creator and moderator at mi.o: Modern Italian Network, and she works remotely for several universities located in the United States through TalkAbroad. Recently, Laura has started a collaboration with *Vivere l'Italiano*, a language school based in central London, where she is responsible for teacher training.

Ru Su is Language Tutor and Head of Mandarin at the University of Kent (United Kingdom). She is a Senior Fellow of the Higher Education Academy (SFHEA) and holds a Certificate in Higher Education (PGCHE). She graduated from QuFu Normal University, located in the hometown of Confucius, in China. Before moving to Canterbury, Ru was a Chinese tutor at the University of Leicester, and she also served as the Mandarin External Examiner at Kingston University London, Leeds Beckett University, and the University of Bath. She was recently appointed as the Chinese External Examiner at De Montfort University, Leicester (2020). She specialises in technology enhanced learning in Chinese language education, as well as in developing material to train and increase intercultural competence. In 2022 she was awarded the University of Kent Teaching Prize for her project *Travelling Virtually in Xi'an, China, the Ancient Capital of 13 Dynasties*.

Alvise Sforza Tarabochia is Senior Lecturer in Italian and Head of the School of Cultures and Languages at the University of Kent (United Kingdom). He has published extensively on cross- and interdisciplinary matters such as biopolitics, psychoanalysis, and especially visual culture.

He is working on the visualisation of mental disorders across history and cultures. He has co-founded the Modern Languages Teaching Forum and promotes the advancement of the teaching of intercultural communication at all levels.

Annalisa Zanola is full Professor of English Language and Linguistics (University of Brescia, Italy) and Director of Unibs Language Teaching Centre. Annalisa is a Delegate and Unibs Representative at 'European Language Council' (ELC) and member of the Formal Consultation team for the Common European Framework of Reference for Languages (CEFR) (Education Department, Council of Europe, and Eurocentres Foundation). She is the author of internationally recognised contributions on the latest trends in English as an international language in professional communication and on English for scientific purposes. She has been teaching English as a foreign language and English linguistics in different academic contexts in Europe for several decades, with particular attention to the implementation of teaching activities in remote mode.

List of Tables

Table 2.1	Assignments of Lecturer A's course	41
Table 2.2	Assignments of Lecturer B's course	41
Table 2.3	Assignments of Lecturer C's course	41
Table 2.4	Authentic assessment: challenges and suggestions	46
Table 2.5	Authentic assessment: challenges and suggestions	48
Table 3.1	Division of 50 multiple-choice questions for the 2020–2021 self-assessment test	71
Table 3.2	Division of 53 multiple-choice and short answer questions for the 2020–2021 self-assessment test	72
Table 3.3	Results of the 2020–2021 self-assessment tests (21–29 September 2020)	75
Table 3.4	Results of the 2021–2022 self-assessment tests (20–29 September 2021)	77
Table 5.1	Module learning outcomes	120
Table 5.2	Skills that students will practise and develop within the module	120
Table 6.1	Linguistic analysis of the Core II Beginners' recordings – Group 1 and Group 2, Term 2 – Academic Year 2020/2021	178
Table 6.2	Linguistic analysis of the Core IV Intermediate's recordings – Group 1 and Group 2, Term 2 – Academic Year 2020/2021	179

Table 6.3	Linguistic analysis of the Core IV Advanced's recordings – Term 2 – Academic Year 2020/2021	179
Table 6.4	Core II Beginners (group 1)—segmentals trained during training sessions 1 and 2 – Term 2 – Academic Year 2020–2021	180
Table 6.5	Core II Beginners (group 1)—results for the segmentals trained during training sessions 1, 2, and 3 – Term 2 – Academic Year 2020–2021	181
Table 6.6	Core II Beginners (group 1)—tongue-twisters used during training sessions 1 and 2 – Term 2 – Academic Year 2020–2021	181
Table 6.7	Core II Beginners (group 1)—results for the tongue-twisters used during training sessions 1 and 2 – Term 2 – Academic Year 2020–2021	182
Table 6.8	Core II Beginners (group 2)—segmentals trained during training sessions 1 and 2 – Term 2 – Academic Year 2020–2021	182
Table 6.9	Core II Beginners (group 2)—results for the segmentals trained during training sessions 1 and 2 – Term 2 – Academic Year 2020–2021	183
Table 6.10	Core II Beginners (group 2)—tongue-twisters used during training session 3 – Term 2 – Academic Year 2020–2021	183
Table 6.11	Core II Beginners (group 2)—results for the tongue-twisters used during training session 3 – Term 2 – Academic Year 2020–2021	184
Table 6.12	Comparison between the results of Core II Beginner's (Group 1 and Group 2) and Core IV Intermediate's (Group 1 and Group 2) – training sessions 1 and 2 – Term 2 – Academic Year 2020–2021	184
Table 6.13	Core IV Intermediate (Group 1 and Group 2)—segmentals trained during training sessions 1, 2, and 3 – Term 2 – Academic Year 2020–2021	185
Table 6.14	Comparative analysis of the results of Core IV Intermediate (GRoup 1 and GRoup 2) and Core IV Advanced—training session 1 – Term 2 – Academic Year 2020–2021	186

Table 6.15	Comparative analysis of the results of Core II Beginner (Group 1 and Group 2), Core IV Intermediate (Group 1 and Group 2), and Core IV Advanced—all training sessions – Term 2 – Academic Year 2020–2021	186
Table 6.16	Comparative analysis of the results of Core II Beginner (Group 1 and Group 2) and Core IV Intermediate (Group 1 and 2) – training sessions 1, 2, and 3 – Term 2 – Academic Year 2020–2021	187
Table 6.17	Core IV Intermediate (Group 1 and Group 2)—results for the segmentals trained during training sessions 1, 2, and 3 – Term 2 – Academic Year 2020–2021	188
Table 6.18	Comparative analysis of the results across the two academic years for Core II Beginner (Group 1 and Group 2, 2020–2021) and Core IV Intermediate (Group 1 and Group 2, 2021–2022)	188
Table 6.19	Core IV Intermediate (Group 1 and GRoup 2)—results across the two academic years 2020–2021 and 2021–2022	189
Table 6.20	Core IV Intermediate (Group 1 and Group 2) and Core II Beginner (Group 1 and Group 2) results across the two academic years 2020–2021 and 2021–2022	189
Table 6.21	Core II Beginners (Group 1)—comparative analysis of each student's performance during training sessions 1 and 2 – Term 2 – Academic Year 2020–2021	190
Table 6.22	Core II Beginners (Group 2)—comparative analysis of each student's performance during training sessions 1, 2, and 3 – Term 2 – Academic Year 2020–2021	191
Table 6.23	Core II Beginners (Group 1)—comparative analysis of each student's summative oral-aural assessment – Academic Year 2020–2021	192
Table 6.24	Core II Beginners (Group 2)—comparative analysis of each student's summative oral-aural assessment – Academic Year 2020–2021	192
Table 6.25	Core IV Intermediate (Group 1 and Group 2)—comparative analysis of each student's performance during training sessions 1, 2, and 3 – Term 2 – Academic Year 2020–2021	193

List of Tables

Table 6.26	Core IV Intermediate (Group 1 and Group 2)—comparative analysis of each student's summative oral-aural assessment – Academic Year 2020–2021	194
Table 6.27	Core IV Advanced—comparison between the results of each student's performance during training sessions 1 and 2, and each student's summative oral-aural assessment – Term 2 – Academic Year 2020–2021	196
Table 6.28	Core IV Intermediate (Group 1, former Core II Beginners)—comparative analysis of each student's performance during training sessions 1 and 2 (Term 2, Academic Year 2020–2021) and training sessions 1, 2, and 3 (Term 2, Academic Year 2021–2022)	197
Table 6.29	Core IV Intermediate (Group 2, former Core II Beginners)—comparative analysis of each student's performance during training sessions 1, 2, and 3 (Term 2, Academic Year 2020–2021) and training sessions 1, 2, and 3 (Term 2, Academic Year 2021–2022)	198
Table 6.30	Core IV Intermediate (Group 1 and Group 2)—comparative analysis of each student's summative oral-aural assessment (–Academic Year 2021–2022	199
Table 6.31	((Core II Beginner (Group 1) and Core IV Intermediate (Group 1, former Core II Beginner)—comparative analysis of each student's oral-aural assessment results across the two academic years 2020–2021 and 2021–2022	200
Table 6.32	Core II Beginner (Group 2) and Core IV Intermediate (Group 2, former Core II Beginner)—comparative analysis of each student's oral-aural assessment results across the two academic years 2020–2021 and 2021–2022	201

1

Introduction: Rushing Online

Wissia Fiorucci

The COVID-19 pandemic forced 1.38 billion learners to rush from the physical classroom to emergency remote teaching and learning (UNESCO 2020). Hodges et al. (2020) coined the term emergency remote teaching (ERT) to define 'a branch of distance education' that arises out of 'a temporary shift of instructional delivery to an alternate delivery mode due to crisis circumstances'[1] (see also Bond et al. 2021). As the situation evolved and ERT became the prevalent means of instruction around the world, issues with motivation and student engagement—and, crucially, accessibility—were forced to the surface.[2] The picture that emerged worldwide, in various ways and depending on varying circumstances, was that educational infrastructures were, by and large, not resilient. Established systems, which had arguably outlived their usefulness, were faced with an unprecedented crisis for which no blueprint existed, and the ensuing issues emerged particularly in areas such as assessment and community.

W. Fiorucci (✉)
University of Kent, Canterbury, UK
e-mail: w.firoucci@kent.ac.uk

© The Author(s), under exclusive license to Springer Nature Switzerland AG 2023
W. Fiorucci (ed.), *Language Education During the Pandemic*,
https://doi.org/10.1007/978-3-031-35855-5_1

Well before the pandemic, it had been widely recognised that in today's globalised world, skills and knowledge honed through 'repetition, pattern-prediction and recognition, memorization', or those 'connected to collecting, storing, and retrieving information' (Zhao and Watterston 2021, p. 5), are becoming redundant. In sharp decline for some time due to artificial intelligence and associated technologies, it had already become clear prior to 2020 that they would soon be supplanted by other skills and competences, like 'creativity, curiosity, critical thinking, entrepreneurship, collaboration, communication, […] global competence' (Zhao and Watterston 2021; see Pink 2006; Wagner 2009; Barber et al. 2012; Florida 2012; Wagner and Dintersmith 2016; Zhao et al. 2019). Before 2020, innovation in assessment practices had been hampered by different factors, such as widespread conservative tendencies (Sambell 2016), lack of institutional funding and support for staff who wanted to modernise (McLean 2018), and restrictions on teachers' autonomy imposed by institutional red tape (Carless 2015). Thus, a sustained focus on skills that should have been recognised as obsolete had meant, inevitably, also a persistence of outdated teaching approaches and assessment methods. Differences notwithstanding, this was true for schools as much as for Higher Education (HE), which is the focus of this collection.

Prior to spring 2020, the prevailing assessment practices in HE around the world had consisted of summative written exams (Ministero dell'Istruzione, dell'Università e della Ricerca 2014; Popkova 2018; Villarroel et al. 2018; Oli and Olkaba 2020). When these had to be delivered remotely, in spring 2020 and in the following academic year, educators found themselves pondering whether they should reproduce at a distance what they had been doing in exam halls or, rather, try to identify other methods to assess their students—the crisis 'stimulated innovation within the education sector' (United Nations 2020, p. 2). On the one hand, within the immediate circumstances of imposed ERT, educators and institutions tended to opt for a conservative approach due to a variety of reasons (e.g. lack of time or lack of knowledge and/or experience with online practices). On the other hand, attempts at change—in teaching delivery and hence in assessment—grew in number as both educators and students adapted to their new settings as the 2020–2021 Academic Year (AY) unfolded: the pandemic 'turned […] teaching and learning upside down, with considerable impact on students in all levels of education' (Bond et al. 2021). For instance, tools once only navigated by those who were tech savvy came to be utilised daily by previously sceptical educators, de facto rendering outdated what up until then had seemed almost perennial and immutable (e.g. in language teaching and in situ listening tests). Yet it quickly became patent that if technology could give 'the student much access to information [promoting] the creation and sharing of knowledge', the ensuing challenge was 'to find ways of increasing students' motivation and engagement' (Nieto-Escamez and Roldán-Tapia 2021, p. 2).

By 'motivation and engagement', we intend two separate but intertwined concepts: while 'motivation is linked to psychological elements that drive behavior', engagement 'indicates the passion and emotional involvement in participating and completing learning activities' (Alsawaier 2018, pp. 12–13 and 14). Motivation and engagement from individuals are crucial to achieving a sense of community, something that was felt to be lost within the new—remote—education environment, presenting itself as another great challenge for teachers and students. Learning in a remote setting within a context of forced social isolation threw into relief the alienating side of the tools (such as videoconferencing) that were being utilised to replace the physical classroom. Such tools would otherwise be effective instruments for enhancing learning and teaching provision, for instance, in distance and blended teaching and learning.

Regarding languages specifically, it was known long before spring 2020 to what extent and in what ways technology could greatly improve and assist language education (Lai et al. 2016, 2018; Zhang and Pérez-Paredes 2021). The online learning experience can help develop 'students' independent learning skills such as the ability to search for [...] out-of-class learning sites and resources', which leads to 'self-initiated, self-constructed, and self-monitored learning experiences' (Zhang and Wu 2022).[3] Zhang and Wu focus, therefore, on the advantages of online delivery for the development of autonomy in learning. Yet the move to an improvised setting such as that of ERT implied the sudden loss of the human relationships that had—up until a few days before the first lockdowns—defined and upheld learning and teaching. Internet technologies cultivate autonomous learning, but they do not necessarily allow for a reliable teaching presence (see Anderson and Krathwohl 2001, Yuan and Kim 2014) or a visible learning community—both of which are crucial catalysts for the development of the 'communicative' component of language instruction, very broadly understood. Poluekhtova et al. (2020) state, for instance, that the communicative environment of the traditional language instruction process cannot be transported into an online environment, certainly not in its traditional forms. The lack of a reliable communicative environment producing constant stimuli can be seen as one reason why—among the range of emotions potentially associated with online language learning—boredom seems to be the most discussed. Pawlack et al.'s survey of an Iranian university's students and teachers (as qtd. in Tao and Xuesong 2022), for instance, shows that both regarded remote classes as more boring than offline classes. Although dealing with negative feelings is something teachers do as a matter of course, learning how to do it online was an entirely different matter: suddenly, teachers were developing new content for online delivery, or adapting old material, as they were also teaching students how to engage with the online tools while managing their feelings. As Klimova summarises it: 'All these changes impose […] on teachers […] different roles in this process of online teaching: pedagogical and intellectual role, social role, managerial and organizational role, and technical role' (2021, p. 1788). Focusing on foreign language (FL) learning at a Faculty of Informatics and Management in the Czech Republic, Klimova's small study reveals that '53% of students feel motivated to study online, while 47% of students do not'. Lack of motivation derived mostly from 'a lack of social contact, especially with their peers, difficulties with concentration, and a need for having more time to respond' (p. 1788). On the other hand, students 'who feel motivated stated that the main driving force was their desire to improve their language skills and knowledge' (p. 1791)—they were moved, that is, by intrinsic motivation. Intrinsically motivated students will more easily adapt to a context of remote learning by deploying their propensity towards autonomous learning: autonomous learners are intrinsically motivated learners (Ushioda 2011) and vice versa. This is not to say that intrinsic motivation cannot be cultivated or elicited—Ushioda claims that teachers can do so precisely by developing their students' autonomy

(2011). Yet, within the context of ERT, the difficulties normally encountered in developing students' autonomy, and thus their motivation and engagement, were conspicuously heightened. And if technology, as aforesaid, has great potential to further autonomous learning, at the same time—as I will explore in more detail in Sect. 3—it could do very little when the notion of 'community' was not the focus of the contingent measures adopted in the emergency.

In spring 2020 and its immediate aftermath, the focus around the world and across all education levels was firmly on compensating for the lack of the physical dimension of learning and teaching (by and large, because of widespread anxiety regarding assessments), rather than its social one. This determined the prevalence of an identifiable series of recurring issues. With Zhang and Wu, whose study was conducted in the context of a Chinese university and its English as a foreign language (EFL) course, we can recognise four main strands of challenges connected with synchronous online language learning during the pandemic: 'The lack of learning climate, the cultivation of learner autonomy, changes of interaction patterns, and the adaptation to remote assessment' (2022). Similarly, Bozkurt et al. (2020), who evaluated both the K-12 and higher educational settings within 31 countries, explored the challenges in ERT language learning and identified psychological pressure and anxiety, assessment, and teaching methods as the main ones (as well as concerns surrounding surveillance and data privacy, an issue that also occurred, for instance, in Italy with the adoption of online proctoring services in HE).[4]

In this volume, the authors will present and analyse crucial elements of the worldwide renegotiation of strategies in language education throughout the pandemic and beyond. Our two main topics—assessment and community—will lead us to explore interconnected and equally important themes, such as motivation and engagement, the relationships at play within the learning context, and academic misconduct and intercultural communication and competence. We will do so through a variety of approaches: from case studies involving hundreds of students, to small-scale experimentations with teaching and learning approaches, to our concluding chapter that provides suggestions for ways forward. While each chapter will address and explain its individual scope and methodology, the collection as a whole reflects on ERT and the subsequent gradual adoptions of (new and existing) online teaching strategies, focusing on the themes above and looking to the future. Through different approaches drawing from both the social sciences and the humanities, the variety of our chapters intends to capture both the highly subjective nature of students' and teachers' experiences, as well as the issues that have recurred worldwide. We will both contextualise the former within the latter and make sense of the latter through the former. Authors explore foreign language (FL) teaching across England and in Wales, but we also look at EFL teaching abroad. There is no claim of a systematic approach to international education, but we have placed our collection within the context of a global pandemic that has affected us all, with difficulties and challenges in assessment and community presenting themselves—albeit to different degrees and in a variety of ways—inevitably and repeatedly, across the world.

In the next section, I will provide clarifications on how we use definitions of distance, remote, and online learning and teaching. Then, I will explain and clarify the two main concepts this collection explores, namely, assessment and community. What do we mean by 'assessment'? What do we mean by 'community'? And how were these terms understood within remote and online learning? These reflections will lay the foundation for reading the chapters in this collection as a whole, whose individual content I will then anticipate at the end of the Introduction.

1 Note on Nomenclature

Throughout this volume, we will refer to distance education as a process that purposely utilises online classes and video recordings and conferencing, among others, to deliver instruction to students. Distance education existed well before the pandemic, and it usually implies no face-to-face (F2F) component and very little or no contact between teachers and students. When referring to the years affected by the pandemic, we will use ERT when speaking specifically of teaching delivery that was shifted online without pedagogy-informed planning. When speaking more generally of teaching delivered online with a degree of planning that implied the consideration of relevant pedagogies, we will utilise the term 'online'.

Authors will thus not utilise the definitions of 'remote' or 'online' interchangeably: remote learning happens indeed online, but we understand it as a result of emergency social distancing measures during the pandemic. Online learning involves, instead, classes and activities specifically meant to be delivered in that format that are also underpinned by theoretical considerations and relevant research. Obviously, the line between ERT and online teaching, especially during the academic year 2020–2021, will not always be easy to untangle, and though we have attempted to respect the boundaries of the above definitions, sometimes the author's choice of one term or the other will inevitably be open to a different interpretation by the reader.

Finally, with blended learning we intend a combination of F2F and online activities, which are complementary to one another. Hybrid learning, on the other hand, is here understood as an educational approach that implies a choice for the student to attend classes either in person or online. In this scenario, therefore, teachers deliver their classes both remotely and in person at the same time; they should do so using technology such as video conferencing, accompanied by relevant apposite devices, for instance, to diffuse sound across the physical classroom in ways that would allow all participants equal participation in seminars.

2 Assessment

When we speak of assessment, what we generally mean is an activity or a group of activities/tasks used to evaluate learners' performance. Assessment may also consist of practices educators use to monitor progress in terms of learning outcomes; it can moreover be an instrument for providing feedback and generating an action plan for a class or a specific individual. The most important question in preparing an assessment is about what learning goals the educator has in mind for that activity (Kyriacou 2006, p. 105). In this respect, high-stakes and end-of-year summative assessments are in a category of their own, as their main purpose is not to 'feed-back' to students or to the teacher as an instrument for progress, but to 'feed-out'—that is, they are mostly utilised to 'identify the standard of attainment [at] a particular point in time. Such attainment may form the basis of certification, or a formal statement' (106). Of course, preparation for an assessment, and the formative components leading up to it, should be designed to address specific learning outcomes and provide the necessary platform to monitor progress and aid learning through feedback and practice. Yet, a summative end-of-year assessment in itself almost exclusively exists to provide grades.

As soon as the pandemic forced education to go online, the foremost immediate concern for both education providers and students revolved around 'feed-out' assessments and how they could be run to ascertain whether students could progress to the next stage of studies, graduate, and so on. Higher Education providers, unlike secondary schools,[5] received no centrally issued guidance or instruction and could thus operate with a degree of flexibility. Yet, this flexibility and freedom, intrinsic as they are to the HE system, had historically caused 'difficulty in managing student expectations around assessment and feedback, particularly on the [...] fairness of outcomes' (Zhao et al. 2022, p. 586). Students, used to unchanging assessment patterns and traditional pen-and-paper exams in schools, understandably struggle to adapt to a structure where a lot is left to the individual lecturer, hence allowing for variety in assessment. As Zhao puts it, in HE 'students have a strong investment in a positive outcome from a process that they evidently do not fully understand or trust' (p. 586). This perceived lack of clarity, in the UK, has been highlighted time and time again by nationwide results for the 'Assessment and Feedback' theme in the National Students Survey even well before the pandemic (Office for Students 2019). Students 'have strong emotions linked to the process' (Zhao et al. 2022, p. 586), all the more (negatively) amplified during ERT. That is, a historic distrust of assessment was coupled with heightened, but pre-existing, negative emotions during the pandemic. This meant that, in the spring of 2020 and at the beginning of the 2020–2021 academic year, the educational world was, by and large, focused on terminal, high-stakes assessments and how best to deliver them in a way that assuaged students' concerns while providing consistent graded outcomes or mitigating for the absence of final exams altogether. Throughout 2020–2021, however, practices evolved in a different direction, and education went through a momentous phase of innovation.

Looking at specific examples from language classes and courses, the authors in this volume will show how the pandemic encouraged teachers to go beyond improvising remote delivery of previously face-to-face (F2F), pen-and-paper exams. The teaching community was quickly led to re-evaluate the importance of assessment from other angles (looking at authentic, continuous, formative, peer assessment), a shift that we believe will have a long-lasting impact on practices, not in the least because, arguably, it had been overdue for some time before the pandemic. By presenting a variety of case studies and examples, authors illustrate this shift, testifying to a much-needed change of perspective in assessment delivery. As we will see, rethinking assessment is also crucial to students' engagement and motivation (Ushioda 2011) and hence to community: assessment practices can be at the heart of a learning community, given how collaborative work and opportunities for feedback create favourable conditions for the relationships at play within it to flourish.

3   (Learning) Community

The immediate reaction to COVID-19 closures was almost invariably to embrace education technologies across the world (Holmes 2020). Distance-learning solutions, that is, were the first port of call, in response to the closure of buildings and the restrictions imposed on physical interactions. The focus at first was very much on transferring online what had previously been delivered F2F—seminars and feed-out assessments. The rushed move to the remote setting happened without immediate changes in format or method, as the attention was on minimising the disruption caused by restrictions and delivering graded outcomes. Regardless of strategies or means, the vision across different countries 'was the same— to build learning environments that did not depend upon [physical] buildings' (Holmes 2020). In other words, the notion of 'community' (within both Higher and Secondary Education) was secondary to more 'immediate' concerns, revealing how both universities and schools were seen primarily not as 'people' (e.g. the teaching and learning community of staff and students), but rather as 'space' (e.g. the buildings where teaching happens). Responses to closures were thus material and technological, and they did not immediately prioritise human relationships or give consideration to how these would be very severely affected by social distancing.

Participation in a learning community can promote students' engagement through a sense of belonging, leading to higher retention rates as well as greater achievement of learning outcomes (Zhao and Kuh 2004; Arbaugh et al. 2008; Akyol and Garrison 2011). Yet as West and Williams (2017) note, the term 'learning community' is riddled with controversy, as no unifying definition exists. For some, learning community entails a space for enhancing and understanding best practices through sharing (e.g. Tosey 2006). For others, a learning community is defined by the processes and acts that lead to working together collaboratively (Davies et al. 2005). For Carlén and Jobring (2004, p. 273), it is an 'atmosphere […] from which sustainable learning processes are gained through a dialogue and collaborative construction of knowledge'. 'Learning community' has also been described with reference to the several pedagogical and social means that facilitate it, such as 'social presence', 'sense of belonging' (e.g. McMillan and Chavis 1986; West and Williams 2017), and 'teaching presence' (Anderson et al. 2001; Yuan and Kim 2014). These definitions, though close, do not offer a unified vision. This lack of consensus and clarity has historically been an issue, for example, in the UK, where students rate the learning community of their institution in the National Student Survey,[6] which then influences policy. It was an even bigger issue with the pivot to ERT, because—first—trying to recreate remotely something that, even within business-as-usual conditions, meant different things to different people was extraordinarily problematic. Secondly, this was almost entirely left to individual teachers, as institutions were—at least initially—mostly focused on delivering feed-out assessments and recreating virtually the physical space of the classroom. As aforementioned, the move to ERT meant that lecturers suddenly found themselves encumbered with a heightened responsibility, as Klimova (2021) puts it: the lack of a visible learning community meant increased pressure on single modules, lessons, and assessment, which overnight became for many the almost exclusive defining elements of university life.

Prodgers et al. (2022) investigated how undergraduate students understood and related to the concept of learning community in Higher

Education in the context of ERT. Their analysis of first-hand accounts produced three main themes, highlighting students' desire for inclusion, connection, and togetherness. These themes, generated through a reflexive thematic analysis, generally align with West and Williams' model of pre-pandemic learning communities (2017).[7] Prodgers et al.'s work, then, extends their framework to an online context. The underlying principle, for them, is that while online environments may unsettle the dynamics that foster a learning community in a physical setting, by cultivating the aspects highlighted by those themes, a meaningful sense of learning community can likewise be provided online. In focusing on pedagogic notions such as 'sense of belonging', they also identify other underpinning crucial aspects of the learning community, 'for example, visibility and accessibility of academic teaching staff' (Prodgers et al. 2022)—the reliable teaching presence. This, or the lack thereof, may affect the sense of belonging, just as much as the chance to share experiences with other students (see Bailey et al. 2021). Belonging in an academic setting can be defined 'as an individual's conceptualization of connectedness to the campus community' (Keyser et al. 2022 p. 2). This connectedness usually results from the web of social interactions and/or the learning environment of a given institution. 'Sense of belonging' can thus be defined and theorised in terms of students' feelings (Maestas et al., 2007) and/or their integration within the institution or parts of it (Hoffman and Morrow 2022).

This collection embraces the many nuances that exist within the definition of 'learning community' by approaching it from a variety of angles and looking at questions of belonging, visibility, and accessibility of teaching staff, which we will refer to also as 'reliability'. In so doing we will explore, for instance, how assessment and feedback can facilitate the formation of a community by tapping into students' motivation and engagement. To capture the several nuances attributed to the notion of 'community' within education, in this volume we refer to 'learning community' when speaking about the human interactions that form a community of staff and students, including a sense of belonging, togetherness, teacher's visibility, and so on. Then, when using the word 'community', we refer both to a learning community and to the space (virtual or otherwise) that shapes and affects those relationships that take place within it. On many occasions, those terms will be interchangeable, which testifies to the fact that separating interactions from the space that allows them to happen will not always be possible. This is due to their indissoluble interconnectedness, both within ERT/online learning and with the face-to-face, physical spaces of learning.

4 Summary of Chapters

4.1 EFL in Italian Case Studies

Antonella Giacosa's Chap. 2 which opens the present collection, argues that the abrupt transition to remote teaching brought with it opportunities to modernise assessment. Drawing on previous research on ERT, she focuses on assessment during the pandemic, claiming that both scholars and educators around the world had expressed a need for modernisation long before the COVID-19 emergency hit. Giacosa's chapter offers, first, an introduction to education and assessment from a global perspective, referring to studies that explore this topic on both national and international scales. Subsequently, she zooms in on the context of two northern Italian universities as a case study, where she conducted research to retrieve and analyse empirical data, focusing on authentic and continuous assessment (ACA) in English as a foreign language (EFL) modules. To explore ACA, both staff and student participants in the study were asked to comment on their experiences with end-of-course assessment in comparison to emergency ACA. Giacosa also investigates the topic of ACA in connection with students' motivation and engagement to gauge the extent to which these may help in addressing the issue of online academic integrity.

Taking our cue from Giacosa's work, we turn our attention to other studies that prompt us to think outside the box. Chapter 3 focuses again on EFL in Italy. Roxana Doerr and Annalisa Zanola's study involves an online self-assessment test of English language that they devised to be implemented at the beginning, and not at the end, of the language course. Their study covers the academic years 2020–2021 and 2021–2022.

The test was conceived as a substitute for the previously implemented additional learning requirements (OFA) exam that is commonly found in the Italian university system, which could not be delivered in its conventional form due to social restrictions. Finding a workable solution was especially important given the number of students enrolled (ca. 700–800) and the remote learning context. On the one hand, as the authors explain, the test allowed students to gain awareness of their overall level and of weaknesses in language competence instantly and ahead of the course. At the same time, students realised that their learning experience would be personalised and mapped out for them from the very beginning, thus supporting intrinsic motivation (Knowles and Dennis 2007). The test itself also gave the authors insight into students' previous experience with languages and language learning, which helped them to identify areas of English grammar that needed attention (Cocea 2006; Conrad and Openo 2018). This enabled them to challenge the traditional progression in grammar teaching within lesson and course planning, as they also assessed the role of self-assessment within it.

In his Chap. 4 Tobias Heinrich similarly offers a brief history of a crucial element of language education, namely the language lab. He explains how the language lab first came to the fore as a welcome innovation after World War II, to then fall into disuse as obsolete with the rise of CLT: the language lab aimed at eliciting proficiency through individual practice, but not in communication more broadly, and thus started to diverge from modern trends. In the 1960s, learners in a lab would sit in individual stations, each utilising a set of devices such as a tape recorder, a microphone, and a headset. The stations, or cubicles, would be laid out in rows and then the teacher's console table would be situated at the top of the room, facing the cubicles (Hayes 1963, pp. 2–4). This arrangement allowed for individual practice and simultaneous feedback, as Heinrich will explain—the language lab, in other words, stimulated autonomous learning in a way that could be seen as similar to that made possible by modern technologies. While these aspects are highly desirable, the elements of isolation and disconnection from others entailed by this layout are not. Yet, as Heinrich points out, the pandemic allowed us to reconsider not the language lab in itself but rather its underlying principles and the possibilities that student-controlled devices offer for self-improvement and progression through stimulating autonomous learning. Using modern technology, we can now avoid the alienating effects produced by the layout of the language lab, returning to its promises of technologically enhanced learning (TEL) whilst allowing communicative cooperation and group work—hence, encouraging a sense of learning community.

4.2　Lessons Learnt: From the Past to the Future of Language Education

In Chap. 5 'Nazaret Pérez-Nieto comments on several recent studies reviewing the role of translation within foreign language (FL) pedagogy. She reminds us of how the long-lasting connection of translation with the grammar-translation method prevented it from appearing in innovative methodologies after communicative language teaching became the umbrella and go-to term to define teaching approaches in the second half of the twentieth century. Yet despite the challenging scrutiny, translation into FLs is still, to these days, part of HE language syllabi. Its validity and role having been questioned and reviewed (Cook 2010; Leonardi 2010; Malmkjaer 2010; Carreres 2014; Laviosa 2014), translation has once more gained interest and attention after the concept of 'mediation' was clarified by the Common European Framework of Reference (CEFR) in 2018 (see North and Piccardo 2016), with *Companion Volume with New Descriptors*, reinforced in the CEFR *Companion Volume* in 2020. This positive re-evaluation, as Pérez-Nieto explains, preceded the pandemic emergency by only a few years. As many educators moved from ERT to adopting online teaching strategies and practices between 2020 and 2021, an opportunity presented itself, Pérez-Nieto argues, to revisit translation utilising an online learning tool that also promotes collaboration and dialogue among students: the Interactive Discussion Board (IDB). The author presents a case study undertaken during 2020–2021, conducted with a group of Year 2 Intermediate Spanish students (B2). Pérez-Nieto's analysis investigates how IDBs can be utilised for the effective monitoring of students' progress, for assessment, and for community building.

Livia Manzini, in Chap. 6 continues the retrospective on the history of language teaching to explain how techniques that were already popular in the last century have been revived by technology within the pandemic emergency. She does so by focusing especially on 'speaking' (on pronunciation and intonation). From the advent of CLT in the second half of the twentieth century, Manzini explains, drama activities have been commonly incorporated into modern language teaching. CLT requires espousing techniques that favoured communicative skills over translation abilities (as we will also see in Pérez-Nieto's chapter), as the latter were traditionally understood (Piazzoli 2011). Accordingly, language teaching methods were elaborated, which scholars (e.g. Way 1967; Heathcote 1984) centred on the use of creative drama (e.g. role-plays and improvisations), which privilege spontaneity and freedom of expression (e.g. fluency) over content, hence aiming at the development of concentration skills and creativity. Based on these premises, the chapter goes on to analyse the use of creative forms of drama to train pronunciation and intonation. Manzini investigates different case studies conducted over two academic years at the University of Birmingham in modules where drama activities were employed for the attainment of communicative skills in both F2F and online language teaching: in her chapter, she specifically analyses the use of tongue-twisters and nursery rhymes in online classes delivered via Zoom and utilising the online recording platform Vocaroo. The data Manzini presents will show that, thanks to the technological devices and virtual learning environments (VLEs) we can utilise nowadays, it is possible to successfully practise speaking online in different communicative contexts—hence agreeing with Heinrich's statements in the previous chapter. Her focus on tongue-twisters and nursery rhymes will show how, more specifically, through technology it is possible to work on students' phonological skills from the very first day of language tuition, hence avoiding the fossilisation of errors that, over time, would hinder the possibility of attaining near-native levels of pronunciation.

4.3 Intercultural Competence, from ERT to Online Practices

In Chap. 7 Wissia Fiorucci, Ru Su, and Alvise Sforza Tarabochia illustrate and analyse the outcomes of an online exchange cultural programme that took place between 2020–2021 and 2021–2022 between the University of Kent (UK) and the KeDaGaoXin University of Xi'an, in Western China. British student participants were learners of Mandarin at different levels, while Chinese participants were advanced learners of English and aspiring EFL teachers. The aim of the programme was, first, to facilitate intercultural communication training and subsequent acquisition of new language skills and competences. The virtual exchange, in turn, was conceived to also mitigate the impact of restrictions imposed on travelling. The success of the programme was assessed via mixed methods.

Fiorucci, Su, and Sforza Tarabochia explain that, through this collaborative project, students from both universities felt that they had achieved and increased intercultural competence, which contributed towards a sense of (international) community during the pandemic whilst enhancing their communicative skills. They also make recommendations for the successful running of similar initiatives based on their own evaluation of the programme, as well as on students' responses to feedback surveys.

Patricia Diaz Munoz and Laura Stecca in Chap. 8 analyse the findings of a small study conducted at an undisclosed Higher Education provider in Europe, which focused on two intermediate language modules (Italian and Spanish). In conducting their study, their aim was twofold: they engaged with ERT to develop online tools for the advancement of students' intercultural competence through the gamified activities they had designed for the study; at the same time, the authors aimed to establish whether gamification would help foster a sense of (intercultural) community at the time of lockdowns and social restrictions. Considering language education during the pandemic, they argue that students' motivation and engagement play a significant role in their achievements (Denden et al. 2021). In other words, 'if students have fun, […], and are motivated during the foreign language learning process, the lesson content would become more meaningful and permanent for them' (Betoncu et al. 2021, p. 1). Yet, stimulating 'fun' to aid motivation and engagement was certainly a most prominent challenge during ERT, something that many language educators tried to counter using gamified activities. In their chapter, Diaz and Stecca, drawing on Alsawaier (2018), show that 'gamification can boost students' motivation and engagement in online lessons due to the component of fun it borrows from video games' and through competition (Tulloch 2014). Gamification also facilitates an increased sense of community, especially if utilised on a systematic basis. Their study thus confirms that 'gamified videoconferences' can help students 'connect with their classmates during isolation time', providing 'effective social support' (Nieto-Escamez and Roldán-Tapia 2021), when conducted using relevant techniques and strategies. They show how, as Cassany notes, 'the cooperative nature of […] gamification may encourage understanding among students from different cultural backgrounds' (2004). The authors also indicate that the gamified activities must be very carefully designed to facilitate the desired outcomes (see Redondo Juárez 2021)—commenting specifically on identifying what type of 'gamers' our students are, following Marczewski's model (2015).

4.4 To Conclude

In our final Chap. 9 Marion Coderch provides final recommendations from lessons learnt during the pandemic. Summarising the views expressed in this collection, and examining relevant research on the topics, Coderch determines that if the pandemic has taught us something, it is that, once and for all, we need to see assessment as an opportunity to learn. Language teachers (and students) must adopt a mentality of perceiving and thus implementing assessment as an occasion for both teachers and students to work together: be it summative or formative, assessment *for learning* can be a powerful tool for enhancing a sense of community and should become the default way forward in assessment practices.

Technologies, Coderch claims, will be fundamental in this mentality shift and crucial in moving towards a more inclusive language provision. As noted throughout this collection, online resources can provide an arrangement of possibilities to implement flexible practices to the advantage of all students. As we are moving and adjusting to a new normality, debates are focusing more on lessons learnt and what needs to be jettisoned or restored from the previous order. Having established the perils of a rushed move to remote education, Coderch concludes, the newly acquired knowledge regarding assessment and online delivery should guide practitioners and institutions towards implementing assessment that is more authentic, relevant, and more aligned with the practical needs of students in today's world.

Notes

1. Another expression used was, for instance, 'pandemic pedagogy' (Hodges et al. 2020; Milman 2020).
2. Accessibility falls outside the scope of this volume, though references to it will be made, given the interconnected nature of issues of digital equity with motivation and engagement. A study by Adnan and Anwar (2020), looking at Pakistani Higher Education during the pandemic, illustrates how online learning cannot produce desired results in underprivileged countries such as Pakistan. Most students do not have access to the internet due to technical and/or financial constraints. This precarious situation then goes on to aggravate other issues they identify, which we have seen are also common to different settings across the globe. Among them, the absence of F2F interaction with the educator and of traditional classroom socialisation—in other words, a perceived lack of a learning community of students and educators—appears as the most problematic one.
3. In this volume, we are not distinguishing English as a second language (L2) from the other languages considered by the individual chapters (German, Italian, Spanish), and thus, when we refer to L2, we also mean English and EFL teaching. That said, while a proliferation of research exists on ERT and the teaching and learning process throughout social distancing and its immediate aftermath, works that focus specifically on modern languages are still scarce, though many have focused on EFL, possibly due to the widespread presence of courses across the world, within and without HE.

4. Other studies focusing on online assessment tools in spring 2020 cited specific concerns about not completing tests or online quizzes in time and the rigidity of the answers required or permitted (Dietrich et al. 2020); unreliable internet connections during tests (Means and Neisler 2020); and educators' concerns about online proctoring services (Cutri et al. 2020).
5. To give an example, in both the Italian and UK systems, for end-of-year high school exams (*Esame di Stato* and A-Levels, respectively), pupils are required to sit tests that have been centrally and externally devised. Teachers have no say in the choice of what the pupils they have known for years will be evaluated on. In Higher Education in both countries, on the other hand (leaving aside subjects that lead to accreditation), lecturers devise their own assessments and assessment patterns. Regardless of the degree of freedom they enjoy within this process (which depends on internal institutional policies), they can tailor these to the cohorts for which they are intended. Within ERT, this provided a level of resilience and agility that schools did not have, as demonstrated by the controversy surrounding school exams in 2020 and 2021. In the UK, all secondary education examinations were cancelled and an alternative method to establish qualification grades had to be devised and effected at short notice. In Italy, comparable disruption and controversy characterised the 2020 delivery of 'Esami di Stato'. The format of the final exams underwent substantial changes with respect to what had been more or less stable and unchanged since 1999 (the year the new *Esame di Stato* format came into being): written tests were abolished and replaced by a 'maxi-oral' lasting one hour and divided into five parts. The evaluation system itself had to change: 13,000 examination boards were dismantled, and new ones were created with exclusively internal members (to avoid travelling for those involved), with only the president being external. Particular attention was given to the security measures to prevent the spread of the infection, which caused further distress and difficulties that might have been avoided with the use of an online platform. Students and commissioners had to always wear a mask, sanitise their hands, and present self-certification confirming they had not had a fever in the three days prior to the test. In Italy, that is, the focus was firmly placed on avoiding online cheating, hence the choice of oral as the main assessment method and in-person delivery for which, however, the system was simply not ready. In both countries, the rigidity

of the secondary school systems meant that a one-size-fits-all approach had to be adopted, which, given the circumstances, was far from ideal.
6. 'These ratings serve as a policy instrument that directly informs institutions' reputation and, more broadly, aims to validly and reliably capture students' satisfaction with their learning'. Thus, 'if items within the NSS are aligned to pedagogic constructs that are ill-defined, or if there are sharp inconsistencies in interpretation, this is problematic for the reliability of NSS as a measurement' (Prodgers et al. 2022).
7. For example, West and Williams' 'concept of a shared "Vision" (which incorporates shared goals and missions) and "Function" (which encompasses shared actions) spoke directly to [Prodgers et al.'s] third theme of mutuality and the shared experience (or "feeling together"), whereas the concepts of "Relationships" (which encompasses sense of belonging and trust) and "Access" (which incorporates shared space and time) converged in our themes of "feeling connected" and "feeling included"' (Prodgers et al. 2022).

References

Adnan, M., and K. Anwar. 2020. Online learning amid the COVID-19 pandemic: Students' perspectives. *Journal of Pedagogical Sociology and Psychology* 2 (1): 45–51. https://doi.org/10.33902/JPSP.%202020261309.

Akyol, Z., and D.R. Garrison. 2011. Understanding cognitive presence in an online and blended community of inquiry: Assessing outcomes and processes for deep approaches to learning. *British Journal of Educational Technology* 42 (2): 233–250. https://doi.org/10.1111/j.1467-8535.2009.01029.x.

Alsawaier, R.S. 2018. The effect of gamification on motivation and engagement. *International Journal of Information and Learning Technology* 35 (1): 56–79. https://doi.org/10.1108/IJILT-02-2017-0009.

Anderson, L.W., and D.R. Krathwohl. 2001. A Taxonomy for Learning, Teaching and Assessing: A Revision of Bloom's Taxonomy of Educational Objectives: Complete Edition. New York: Longman.

Arbaugh, et al. 2008. Developing a community of inquiry instrument: Testing a measure of the Community of Inquiry framework using a multi-institutional sample. *The Internet and Higher Education* 11 (3–4): 133–136. https://doi.org/10.1016/j.iheduc.2008.06.003.

Bailey, E., et al. 2021. Bridging the transition to a new expertise in the scholarship of teaching and learning through a faculty learning community. *International Journal for Academic Development* 1 (14): 265–278. https://doi.org/10.1080/1360144x.2021.1917415.

Barber, M., et al. 2012. Oceans of innovation: The Atlantic, the Pacific, global leadership and the future of education. https://www.ippr.org/publications/oceans-of-innovation-the-atlantic-the-pacific-global-leadership-and-the-future-of-education. Accessed 29 October 2022.

Betoncu, O., et al. 2021. Designing an effective learning environment for language learning during the COVID-19 pandemic. *Frontiers in Psychology* 12. https://doi.org/10.3389/fpsyg.2021.752083.

Bond, M., et al. 2021. Emergency remote teaching in higher education: Mapping the first global online semester. *International Journal of Educational Technology in Higher Education* 18: 50. https://doi.org/10.1186/S41239-021-00282-X.

Bozkurt, A., et al. 2020. A global outlook to the interruption of education due to COVID-19 pandemic: Navigating in a time of uncertainty and crisis. *Asian Journal of Distance Education* 15 (1): 1–126. https://doi.org/10.5281/zenodo.3878572.

Carlén, U., O. Jobring, M. Qvistgård, and M. Nilsen. 2004. Constituents of Online Learning Communities. In proceeding of IADIS International Conference of Web Based Communities (pp. 341–349). Lisbon, Portugal, 24–26 March, 2004, At: Lisbon, Portugal https://www.researchgate.net/publication/267550803_Constituents_of_online_learning_communities.

Carless, D. 2015. Exploring learning-oriented assessment processes. *Higher Education* 69: 963–976. https://doi.org/10.1007/S10734-014-9816-Z.

Carreres, Á. 2014. Translation as a Means and as an End: Reassessing the Divide. *The Interpreter and Translator Trainer* 8 (1): 123–135. https://doi.org/10.1080/1750399X.2014.908561.

Cocea, M. 2006. Assessment of Motivation in Online Learning Environments. In AH 2006. LNCS vol. 4018, eds. V. P. Wade et al., pp. 414–418. Heidelberg: Springer.

Cook, G. 2010. *Translation in Language Teaching*. Oxford: Oxford University Press.

Conrad, D., and J. Openo. 2018. Assessment Strategies for Online Learning: Engagement and Authenticity. Athabasca: Athabasca University Press.

Cutri, R.M., et al. 2020. Faculty readiness for online crisis teaching: Transitioning to online teaching during the COVID-19 pandemic. *European Journal of Teacher Education* 43 (4): 523–541. https://doi.org/10.1080/02619768.2020.1815702.

Davies, A., J. Ramsay, H. Lindfield, and J. Couperthwaite. 2005. Building learning communities: Foundations for good practice. *British Journal of Educational Technology* 36 (4): 615–628. https://doi.org/10.1111/j.1467-8535.2005.00539.x.

Denden, M., et al. 2021. Effects of gender and personality differences on students' perception of game design elements in educational gamification. *International Journal of Human-Computer Studies* 154: 102674. https://doi.org/10.1016/J.Ijhcs.2021.102674.

Dietrich, N., et al. 2020. Attempts, successes, and failures of distance learning in the time of COVID-19. *Journal of Chemical Education* 97 (9): 2448–2457. https://doi.org/10.1021/Acs.Jchemed.0c00717.

Florida, R. 2012. *The rise of the creative class: Revisited*. New York: Basic Books.

Hayes, A.S. 1963. Language Laboratory Facilities: Technical Guide for the Selection, Purchase, Use, and Maintenance. Washington, DC: U.S. Department of Health, Education and Welfare.

Heathcote, D. 1984. The Authentic Teacher: Signs and Portents. In *Collected Writings Of Drama And Education*, eds. D. Heathcote et al. London: Hutchinson.

Hodges, C., et al. 2020. The difference between emergency remote teaching and online learning. *EDUCAUSE Review*. https://er.educause.edu/articles/2020/3/the-difference-between-emergency-remote-teaching-and-online-learning

Hoffman, M., and J. Morrow. 2022. Investigating 'sense of belonging' in first-year college students. *Journal of College Retention Research Theory and Practice* 4 (3): 227–256.

Holmes, K. 2020. Sustaining learning communities through and beyond COVID-19. UNESCO Futures of Education Ideas LAB. https://en.unesco.org/futuresofeducation/holmes-sustaining-learning-communities-COVID-19. Accessed 02 November 2022.

Keyser, W., et al. 2022. Empathy in action: Developing a sense of belonging with the pedagogy of 'real talk'. *Journal of University Teaching & Learning Practice* 19 (4): 1–27. https://ro.uow.edu.au/jutlp/vol19/iss4/10.

Klimova, O. 2021. "From Blended Learning to Emergency Remote and Online Teaching: Successes, Challenges, and Prospects of a Russian Language Program before and during the Pandemic." *Russian Language Journal* 71 (2): Article 5. https://doi.org/10.26067/CX61-PC87.

Knowles, E., and K. Dennis. 2007. An Investigation of Students' Attitudes and Motivations Toward Online Learning. *InSight: A Journal of Scholarly Teaching* 2. https://doi.org/10.46504/02200708kn.

Kyriacou. 2006. *Essential Teaching Skills*. Blackwell.
Lai, C., et al. 2016. Enhancing learners' self-directed use of technology for language learning: The effectiveness of an online training platform. *Computer Assisted Language Learning* 29 (1): 40–60. https://doi.org/10.1080/09588221.2014.889714.
———. 2018. Understanding the nature of learners' out-of-class language learning experience with technology. *Computer Assisted Language Learning* 31 (1): 114–143. https://doi.org/10.1080/09588221.2017.1391293.
Laviosa, S. 2014. Translation and Language Education. Pedagogical Approaches Explained. New York and London: Routledge.
Leonardi, V. 2010. *The Role of Pedagogical Translation in Second Language Acquisition: From Theory to Practice*. Bern: Peter Lang.
Malmkjaer, K. 2010. Language Learning and Translation. In *Handbook of Translation Studies*, eds. Y. Gambier and L. V. Doorslaer, pp. 185–190. Amsterdam: John Benjamins.
Maestas, R., et al. 2007. Factors impacting sense of belonging at a Hispanic-serving institution. *Journal of Higher Education* 6 (3): 237–256.
Mclean, H. 2018. This is the way to teach: Insights from academics and students about assessment that supports learning. *Assessment and Evaluation in Higher Education* 43 (8): 1228–1240. https://doi.org/10.1080/02602938.2018.1446508.
Means, B., and J. Neisler. 2020. *Unmasking inequality: STEM course experience during the COVID-19 pandemic*. Digital Promise Global.
McMillan, D.W., and D.M. Chavis. 1986. Sense of community: A definition and theory. *Journal of Community Psychology* 14 (1): 6–23. https://doi.org/10.1002/1520-6629(198601)14:1<6::AID-JCOP2290140103>3.0.CO;2-I.
Milman, N. 2020. This is emergency remote teaching, not just online teaching. *EducationWeek*. https://www.edweek.org/leadership/opinion-this-is-emergency-remote-teaching-not-just-online-teaching/2020/03. Accessed 22 December 2022.
Ministero dell'Istruzione, dell'Università e della Ricerca. 2014. The Italian Education System. I Quaderni di Eurydice 30. Firenze: Indire.
Nieto-Escamez, F.A., and M.D. Roldán-Tapia. 2021. Gamification as online teaching strategy during COVID-19: A mini-review. *Frontiers in Psychology* 12. https://doi.org/10.3389/fpsyg.2021.648552.
North, B., and E. Piccardo. 2016. Developing illustrative descriptors of aspects of mediation for the CEFR. Education Policy Division, Council of Europe, Strasbourg. https://rm.coe.int/168073ff3. Accessed 29 October 2022.

Office for Students. 2019. Student satisfaction rises but universities should do more to improve feedback. https://www.officeforstudents.org.uk/news-blog-and-events/press-and-media/student-satisfaction-rises-but-universities-should-do-more-to-improve-feedback/. Accessed 29 October 2022.

Oli, G., and Olkaba, T. 2020. Practices and Challenges of Continuous Assessment in Colleges of Teachers Education in West Oromia Region of Ethiopia. *Journal of Education, Teaching and Learning* 5 (1): 8–20. STKIP Singkawang. Retrieved August 14, 2023.

Piazzoli, E. 2011. Didattica process drama: principi di base, estetica e coinvolgimento. *Italiano Linguadue* 3 (1): 439–462. https://doi.org/10.13130/2037-3597/1243

Pink, D.H. 2006. *A whole new mind: Why right-brainers will rule the future*. New York: Riverhead.

Poluekhtova, I.A., et al. 2020. Effectiveness of online education for the professional training of journalists: Students' distance learning during the COVID-19 pandemic. *Psychology in Russia: State of the Art* 13 (4): 26–37.

Popkova, E. 2018. Continuous Cumulative Assessment in Higher Education: Coming to Grips with Test Enhanced Learning. In Revisiting the Assessment of Second Language Abilities: From Theory to Practice, ed. Hidri Sahbi, pp. 331–349. Cham: Springer. https://doi.org/10.1007/978-3-319-62884-4_16.

Prodgers, L., et al. 2022. 'It's hard to feel a part of something when You've never met people': Defining 'learning community' in an online era. *Higher Education*. 85: 1219. https://doi.org/10.1007/s10734-022-00886-w.

Redondo Juárez, P. 2021. Innovación en el aula. Profundización en el elemento lúdico: Factores y aplicación didáctica. In *Internacionalización y Enseñanza del Español como Lengua Extranjera: Plurilingüismo y Comunicación Intercultural*, eds. M. Saracho-Arnáiz and H. Otero-Doval, pp. 1193–1211. Oporto: ASELE.

Sambell, K. 2016. Assessment and feedback in higher education: Considerable room for improvement? *Student Engagement in Higher Education* 1 (1): 1–14. http://insight.cumbria.ac.uk/id/eprint/2819/.

Tao, J., and A.G. Xuesong. 2022. *Language Teacher Agency*. Cambridge and New York: Cambridge University Press.

Tosey, P. 2006. Experiential methods of teaching and learning. In Jarvis, P. (Ed.). *The Theory and Practice of Teaching* (2nd ed.). Routledge. https://doi.org/10.4324/9780203016442.

Tulloch, R. 2014. Reconceptualising Gamification: Play and Pedagogy. *Digital Culture & Education* 6: 317–333.

UNESCO. 2020. From Subregional to a Continental Response Strategy in Support of More Resilient and Responsive Education Systems in Africa COVID–19 (C–19), April– June 2020. Regional office for Eastern Africa. https://en.unesco.org/sites/default/files/covid_19_emergeny_response_plan_–_all_sectors–final–05apr2020.pdf. Accessed 22 December 2022.

United Nations Children's Fund and International Telecommunication Union. 2020. *How many children and young people have internet access at home? Estimating digital connectivity during the COVID-19 pandemic.* New York: UNICEF.

Ushioda, E. 2011. Why autonomy? Insights from motivation theory and research. *Innovation in Language Learning and Teaching* 5 (2): 221–232.

Villarroel, V., et al. 2018. Authentic Assessment: Creating a Blueprint for Course Design. *Assessment and Evaluation in Higher Education* 43 (5): 840–854. https://doi.org/10.1080/02602938.2017.1412396.

Wagner, T. 2009. *The global achievement gap: Why even our best schools don't teach the new survival skills our children need—And what we can do about it.* New York: Basic Books.

Wagner, T., and T. Dintersmith. 2016. *Most likely to succeed: Preparing our kids for the innovation era.* New York: Scribner.

Way, B. 1967. *Development through Drama.* London: Longmans.

West, R.E., and G.S. Williams. 2017. "I don't think that word means what you think it means": A proposed framework for defining learning communities. *Education Tech Research Dev* 65: 1569–1582. https://doi.org/10.1007/s11423-017-9535-0.

Yuan, J., and C. Kim. 2014. Development of online learning communities. *Journal of Computer Assisted Learning* 30: 220–232. https://doi.org/10.1111/jcal.12042.

Zhang, D.Y., and P. Pérez-Paredes. 2021. Chinese postgraduate EFL learners' self-directed use of mobile English learning resources. *Computer Assisted Language Learning* 34: 1128–1153. https://doi.org/10.1080/09588221.2019.1662455.

Zhang, K., and H. Wu. 2022. Synchronous online learning during COVID-19: Chinese university EFL students' perspectives. *SAGE Open* 12: 215824402210948. https://doi.org/10.1177/21582440221094821.

Zhao, C.M., and G.D. Kuh. 2004. Adding Value: Learning Communities and Student Engagement. *Research in Higher Education* 45: 115–138. https://doi.org/10.1023/B:RIHE.0000015692.88534.de.

Zhao, Y., and J. Watterston. 2021. The changes we need: Education post COVID-19. *Journal of Educational Change* 22: 3–12. https://doi.org/10.1007/S10833-021-09417-3.

Zhao, Y., et al. 2019. Tackling the wicked problem of measuring what matters: Framing the questions. *ECNU Review Education* 2 (3): 262–278. https://doi.org/10.1177/2096531119878965.

Zhao, X., et al. 2022. A comparison of student and staff perceptions and feelings about assessment and feedback using cartoon annotation. *Journal of Further and Higher Education* 46 (5): 586–604. https://doi.org/10.1080/0309877X.2021.1986620.

Part I

English as a Foreign Language:
Italian Case Studies

2

Authentic and Continuous Assessment During the Pandemic: Teachers' and Students' Perspectives

Antonella Giacosa

1 Introduction

Since the spring semester of 2020, the education system has been experiencing an unprecedented revolution worldwide. Almost overnight, teachers and students had to adjust to the sudden transition from in-person classes to emergency remote teaching (ERT). This term refers to a newly emerging research field that, as a new branch of distance education, is considered a temporary and unplanned solution to the educational crisis due to COVID-19 (Bozkurt et al. 2020). ERT involves fully remote teaching for education that would otherwise be delivered face to face and that will return to a bricks-and-mortar environment once the crisis or emergency is over (Barbour et al. 2020).

After the first wave of the pandemic, two more academic years were affected by restrictions to curb the virus. The so-called New Normal

A. Giacosa (✉)
University of Turin, Turin, Italy
e-mail: antonellamaria.giacosa@unito.it

began in the context of changing circumstances affected by variable restrictions (World Economic Forum 2020). Accordingly, teachers and students experienced flexible learning settings where asynchronous, online synchronous, and blended synchronous classes alternated. In this unstable situation, assessing students was challenging in several respects—as also mentioned in Fiorucci's Introduction—including in terms of self-organisation and online cheating (Butler-Henderson and Crawford 2020; Nguyen et al. 2020). Moreover, evidence-based research showed that during the systemic disruptions from the pandemic emergency, remote assessment played a vital role in addressing the repeated concerns about widening equity and well-being gaps and unequal access to quality education during the emergency (Cooper et al. 2022).

Research highlights that cheating in online exams during the pandemic could also be linked to students' lack of motivation and purpose, which was another relevant concern for ERT. On the one hand, in both teachers' and students' perceptions, online settings offer more opportunities to engage in dishonest behaviours such as impersonation, forbidden aid, peeking, peer collaboration, and outside assistance (Adzima 2020; Chirumamilla et al. 2020). On the other hand, case studies highlight that academic cheating correlates with a perception of increased anonymity in the online environment, dissatisfaction with the perceived quality of the educational experience, and insufficient involvement of higher-order thinking in the tasks (Srikanth and Asmatulu 2014; Czerniewicz et al. 2020). Therefore, the time is ripe to address questions regarding possible changes to the syllabi in their grading components and to the common practice of summative final examinations (Butler-Henderson and Crawford 2020; Dadashzadeh 2021). As a possible countermeasure against cheating, alternative assessments should stem from better design principles applied to both modules and assessment (Rahim 2020). Assessment could, for instance, include a mixture of open-book online examinations (Eurboonyanun et al. 2021), tasks involving higher-level thinking (Villarroel et al. 2020), and continuous and formative assessment (García-Peñalvo et al. 2021; Moorhouse and Kohnke 2022). Moreover, evidence-based research suggests that teachers should develop specific pedagogical strategies to face the challenges of synchronous online teaching through videoconferencing software (VCS), which has become a common mode of instruction during COVID-19, either taken on its own or integrated into hybrid teaching. This increasingly digital professional competence encompasses assessing students in various types of digital environments while guaranteeing fair and reliable evaluation (Moorhouse and Kohnke 2022).

These reflections on the need to rethink assessment in the troubled times of the pandemic resonate with the call to action issued by scholars of different fields, such as the philosopher Morin (2000) and the psychologist Siemens (2005), already at the beginning of the new millennium. Teachers were called upon to help students to develop the skills they needed in order to adapt to the rapid obsolescence of knowledge and to critically discern between true and false information in an increasingly complex world (Morin 2000; Harari 2018). Yet, right before the pandemic, notions were still being taught that would be obsolete and useless by 2050 (Harari 2018). In Italy, for instance, and at different levels of education systems, curiosity and the desire to learn are buried under a mass of information repeated over the years, where what is tested is the memorisation of decontextualised subject knowledge (Recalcati 2014).

During the emergency, it was understood, first, that assessment needed attention with a view to managing ERT. Soon, though, it was also realised that assessment needed attention with a view to enhancing the teaching and learning experience more generally. The present study is informed by a preliminary investigation carried out at Italian universities in the spring of 2020, which identified assessment as an urgent concern. Teachers and lecturers found online assessment to be time-consuming and demanding in many respects. In turn, in addition to technological issues, students found it difficult to organise their schedules and obtain clear information about exams, which made them feel that they were not ready to be assessed.[1] Moving forward from these findings, this study focuses on the teachers' and students' experiences of combined authentic and continuous assessment (henceforth ACA) in university modules following the first outbreak of the pandemic during 2020–2021. This data-driven two-year study aims to address the following research questions:

RQ 1: What opportunities were provided by ACA in EFL university modules during the years affected by the pandemic?

RQ 2: What were the main challenges for ACA in EFL university modules during the years affected by the pandemic?
RQ 3: What suggestions can be identified to address the main challenges for ACA faced by teachers and students?

Through an evidence-based method (qualitative and quantitative analysis of answers to online questionnaires and semi-guided interviews), this investigation provides the basis of an argument for an alternative approach to evaluation. Albeit responding to the compellingly immediate challenges of the pandemic, our findings will be relevant to future developments of language provision in higher education.

The worldwide educational emergency caused by the pandemic (UNESCO 2020) has shown that the need for digital, fair, and relevant assessment is a global and crucial issue for teachers and students from different geographical contexts. Although this study is based on empirical data collected at Italian universities, teachers' and students' difficulties and needs during the pandemic resonate with what colleagues from different countries experienced. Therefore, the lessons learned in the Italian context will prove useful and pertinent to other educational settings, thus contributing to the body of knowledge on emergency remote assessment (Cooper et al. 2022) worldwide. Furthermore, this study focuses on examples of ACA in English as a foreign language (EFL) classes, a common and steadily growing setting (2019), which makes its outcomes relevant to a wide readership.

This contribution first introduces its conceptual framework while providing a brief literature review on authentic assessment (AA) and continuous assessment (CA), illustrating how these can be combined (ACA). Second, it briefly outlines the method of data collection and analysis. Finally, it presents and discusses the findings in terms of opportunities, challenges, and suggestions from the teacher and student perspective, based on their experience of emergency remote assessment and its pedagogical implications.

2 Background of the Study

The COVID-19 pandemic has transformed the need for a change in assessment into an urgent matter (Dadashzadeh 2021). Even though end-of-course summative examinations are the widely preferred and accredited form of validating knowledge, educators had noted the limitations associated with single-point summative examinations before the pandemic. Alternative assessment options were advocated well before spring 2020 (Butler-Henderson and Crawford 2020). Research before and during the pandemic focused on both authentic and continuous assessments as possible ways to make the learning experience more meaningful, hence eliciting both motivation and engagement from students. These concepts of 'authentic assessment' and 'continuous assessment' have been investigated separately and in different local contexts, even though common ground can be found, as demonstrated in this study.

2.1 Authentic Assessment

Authentic assessment (AA) is a contextualised approach to teaching and assessing involving higher-order thinking skills (Villarroel et al. 2018, 2020). It is deeply rooted in a constructivist conception of knowledge and focuses on curriculum goals, enhancement of individual competence, and integration of instruction and assessment (Tessaro 2014; Atmojio 2021). It aims to integrate what happens in the classroom with employment, replicating the tasks and performance standards faced by professionals in the world of work. Therefore, it is deemed an effective way to assess real competences and twenty-first-century skills, such as critical thinking, which are crucial for new generations of students (Timmis et al. 2016; Care and Kim 2018; Atmojio 2021). Critical thinking, for example, cannot be developed and assessed by focusing only on knowledge reproduction. The findings of empirical studies on second language acquisition (SLA) show encouraging results for authentic assessment's capacity to enhance the different skills in the second language (Inayah et al. 2019; Sumarno and Tatik 2019)—this approach has been fruitfully adopted to train communicative skills in EFL classes (Tessaro 2014).

Authentic assessment can prove a fruitful approach, capable of bridging social distance and keeping students motivated in different educational contexts (Corsini and Agrusti 2021; Sutadji et al. 2021). If students perceive assessment as a learning opportunity and are engaged in authentic tasks such as case-study analysis, plagiarism and cheating are limited (Cooper et al. 2022). Pre-pandemic research identified widespread teacher resistance as a barrier to authentic assessment, despite the known benefits. Teachers are reluctant to change because of the risks involved and the costs regarding the time, energy, and intellectual resources required (Villarroel et al. 2018). Research into education during the pandemic acknowledged the challenges of the shift towards new forms of assessment. At the same time, it suggests that this was the right moment to experiment, as the need for change could not be postponed (Atmojio 2021), which is also the stance of this contribution.

2.2   Continuous Assessment

Pre-pandemic research highlighted that continuous assessment (CA) could be an effective and relevant alternative to end-of-course final exams, contributing to a more meaningful experience (Tolosa 2019; Butler-Henderson and Crawford 2020). The umbrella term 'continuous assessment' refers to a form of educational examination evaluating student progress throughout a prescribed course. Modularised curricula in HE institutions (HEIs) encourage active learning through feedback, which presents this approach as formative and student-centred (Guadu and Boersma 2018; Dejene 2019). Even though scholars recommend CA, this is not a mainstream practice in worldwide HE. Pre-pandemic research shows that possible challenges are large class size, instructor workload, student attitude, and lack of specific criteria for checking subjective forms of assignments (Popkova 2018; Tolosa 2019; Oli and Olkaba 2020). Some concerns refer to students' difficulties in keeping pace with ongoing evaluation, the value of feedback accompanied by a grade, and test anxiety. Moreover, the literature lacks agreement on the associated concepts (Popkova 2018). This study will focus on continuous summative assessment stemming from the collection of information during the course, which may be stored for later reference when calculating the aggregate total at the end of the course (Cross and O'Loughlin 2013; Holmes 2018).

Research on ERT maintains that subjects should be continuously assessed to better distribute activities in a way that replaces single-point summative examination (García-Peñalvo et al. 2021; Cooper et al. 2022; Moorhouse and Kohnke 2022). This is in line with UNESCO's pre-pandemic suggestions, which recommended continuous assessment for all levels of education to create more inclusive and learner-friendly environments (UNESCO 2015; Farrell and Seery 2019). This can be achieved through observations, portfolios, checklists of skills, tests and quizzes, self-assessment, and reflective journals. Indeed, a variety of tasks are recommended as a valid and fair way to give every student the possibility to succeed, as different tasks can involve different types of learning styles, thus making assessment more inclusive (Villarroel et al. 2018; Ajjawi et al. 2020). Moreover, research on EFL argues that CA presents even more benefits to foreign language teachers than to those involved in teaching mainly knowledge-transmitting subjects (Popkova 2018).

That said, if teachers and instructors tend to agree on the benefits and challenges of CA, less is known about the students' perspectives on this in terms of attitudes, workload, and adequate time spacing between graded tests (Popkova 2018). Moreover, concerning the years affected by the pandemic, the literature on CA consists mainly of guidelines, whereas ERT requires further empirical investigations (Rahim 2020; García-Peñalvo et al. 2021).

2.3 A Case for Authentic and Continuous Assessment (ACA)

The literature on AA and CA shows relevant similarities. First, they are both considered to be beneficial for student involvement, understanding, and inclusion. Second, they encourage similar assessing practices, such as various tasks requiring higher-order thinking (such as portfolios and the analysis of case studies). Thirdly, they are not necessarily mainstream practices in HE, as both encounter the same barriers due to resistance to change, fear of an increased workload, or negative student reactions.

This research investigates alternatives to the traditional end-of-course examination, encompassing both authentic and continuous assessment (ACA). It thus aims to contribute to the body of knowledge on assessment in a number of respects. First, it addresses the need for empirical studies regarding alternatives to traditional assessment from an original angle (Brown 2019; Kaplan and Lewis 2013; Sumarno and Tatik 2019; Rahim 2020; Cooper et al. 2022). Second, it provides deep insight into ERT, addressing an issue of concern identified by previous studies (Butler-Henderson and Crawford 2020; Dadashzadeh 2021). Third, it focuses on assessment in EFL classes. Fourth, by comparing students' and teachers' experiences, it addresses a gap in the literature on assessment, which generally investigates the two perspectives separately. Whilst the case study is based in Italy, the research that underpins it has an international, even global, range, which makes this study relevant beyond the local context. This study draws on data from EFL classes at two different universities, and its outcomes will provide further insight into the practice of CA in years that were trying for EFL students and teachers all over the world.

3   Methodology

In line with other studies on ERT (Nguyen et al. 2020; Moorhouse and Kohnke 2022), this investigation adopted a mixed-method approach, collecting quantitative and qualitative data. It draws on two data collections carried out in the 2020–2021 and 2021–2022 academic years through one questionnaire, a semi-guided interview for teachers, and one online questionnaire for students. This data-driven study involved three English Linguistics teachers from two different universities and two different cohorts of students who attended their modules in 2020–2021 and 2021–2022. All the teacher participants taught BA and MA courses in the foreign language and literature department. The student respondents are BA and MA students from the same two universities as their teachers. To ensure the anonymity of the participants, their university affiliation is not a variable considered in this study.

The first round of data collection was carried out in the autumn term of 2020 when modules started in hybrid mode but moved online due to new waves of the pandemic. In contrast, the second round of data collection provides information about the 2021 autumn term and 2022 spring term, when the modules were delivered again in hybrid mode. First, in the late spring of 2021, the teachers were asked to complete an online questionnaire. In addition, they were sent the link to the student questionnaire, which was displayed on the course page (368 answers, 80% approximate response rate). For the second round of data collection, the teachers were involved in a semi-guided interview in the late spring of 2022 and concurrently asked their students to compile the student questionnaire (47 answers, 30% approximate response rate). Whereas the number of teacher informants did not vary in the two data collections, a consistent decrease in the students' response rate can be noticed. This can be partly explained by the changes in the size of one of the modules, as well as by survey fatigue, as their teachers involved their students in different studies. As this study does not aim to compare the two cohorts' experiences of ACA, the academic year is not considered a variable here, so the decrease in student answers will not affect the discussion of the findings. The percentages reported in the findings refer to the first data collection round, which collected a significant number of answers. In contrast, the qualitative data stem from both rounds of data collection, as their value does not rely on quantity.

The teacher questionnaire consisted of 21 questions (closed-ended, 5-point Likert scale, and open-ended questions). It investigated teachers' reasons and goals for adopting ACA, the organisation of evaluation, their satisfaction with the outcomes, and their suggestions for improvements. The semi-structured interviews were carried out online through the videoconferencing tool Webex. These lasted approximately 45 minutes and were recorded. They focused on the experience of ACA during the pandemic, the changes made in 2021–2022, and suggestions for improvements based on teachers' experience and their students' outcomes. Regarding the students, their questionnaire consisted of 21 questions (open-ended, 5-point Likert, and closed-ended questions). It focused on their experience of learning with ACA during the pandemic. It collected information about the challenges they faced and their attitudes towards this kind of evaluation, as well as their suggestions for improvements. The same student questionnaire was used in both rounds of data collection, as it addressed students of two different cohorts.

Regarding the data analysis, the quantitative data refer to the closed-ended questions in the questionnaires and were analysed using frequency and percentage. In contrast, the qualitative data were derived from the open-ended questions in the questionnaires, which were discussed in the semi-guided interviews. The instruments adopted in this study made the dataset valid and reliable and allowed the researcher to collect qualitative and quantitative data. Despite the limited number of informants, the mixed-method approach to data collection and analysis allowed the researcher to gain a deeper understanding of ACA from the teachers' and students' perspectives. As the participants' answers refer to both MA and BA contexts in two different universities, they provide a varied overview of the context and its challenges and opportunities. As far as ethical considerations are concerned, all participants were informed that the data would be used for research purposes and that their identities would be kept confidential.

4 Findings on Experimenting with ACA During the Pandemic

In order to answer the three research questions of this study, first the opportunities that ACA uncovered during the pandemic are highlighted, and then the challenges and the proposals to address them are presented side by side. Even though the aim of this study is to report on experiences concurrently encompassing both AA and CA, the peculiarities of the two components will be discussed separately to give a more in-depth view of the opportunities and challenges offered by these alternatives to traditional end-of-course evaluation, as they arose in the context of emergency remote assessment.

4.1 Teachers' and Students' Opinions Regarding Opportunities (RQ1)

Continuous assessment allows students to become aware of their weaknesses while learning.
[…] I strongly believe that continuous assessment promotes better teaching and more efficient and interactive learning.
A Lecturer (April 21)

I had never experienced a course with continuous tasks before.
Therefore, it was not easy to get into the picture.
However, I can say that it was a very good opportunity.
A Student (April 21)

In the online questionnaire and the semi-guided interview, the three teacher respondents referred to the same need for change in assessment as reported in the literature review (Tessaro 2014; Farrell and Seery 2019). In their opinion, it became urgent during the pandemic, even though they stressed that the need had been felt prior to it. They chose ACA for different reasons. On the one hand, they thought it could promote better teaching and more efficient and interactive learning. In their opinion, it could allow the lecturer to monitor the students' commitment and gain a deeper understanding of their progress. At the same time, it was a way during the pandemic to engage students and help teachers manage the summer exams more efficiently. This is in line with research reporting on necessary changes in common approaches to teaching and assessing due to the peculiar setting of ERT, which eventually made teachers more creative and effective in restructuring assessment to meet students' needs (Cooper et al. 2022). In turn, students commented positively on this alternative to the end-of-year exam. Their positive attitude demonstrates that the fears of possible negative reactions are arguably unfounded, thus addressing one of the barriers to continuous assessment mentioned in the literature (Villarroel et al. 2018).

Students appreciated the variety of assignments, as they met different needs (49%), respected the various learning styles (53%), allowed them to show their talents and skills (35%), and enabled them to express their creativity (46%). Thirty-three per cent of students stated that dealing with different tasks helped them, especially during the pandemic, by increasing their self-confidence as they learned about themselves, their strengths, and their weaknesses. This positive reaction showed that the decision to opt for a new form of assessment paid off, as the outcomes met the teachers' expectations regarding student engagement. During lockdown, the teachers had to reframe the tasks so that they could be accomplished via digital platforms, thus enhancing their digital skills. Even though universities could already rely on digital tools such as virtual learning environments (e.g. Blackboard and Moodle), the pandemic pushed teachers to increase collaborative writing on shared files, polling activities to help students revise and become involved, and experimentation with new design tools for presentations. In turn, students were encouraged to create their presentations using the same interactive tools, thus increasing their own digital skills. Eighty-two per cent of students appreciated the focus on digital tools and did not have difficulties using them. If they encountered problems while being isolated and confined to their homes, they asked the lecturer (57%) or their classmates (66%) for help. On the one hand, this increased the workload for the teachers, as they had to support their students in different ways, ranging from answering emails or forum posts to creating tutorials to support students while experiencing trying teaching conditions.[2] On the other hand, it increased collaboration among students and thus a sense of community.

Regarding the types of tasks, teachers opted for assignments more connected to professional skills and less focused on testing knowledge. On the one hand, they wanted to assess their students in various work-related tasks to better integrate assessment into a meaningful and involving learning experience. On the other hand, they needed to cope with the possibility of online cheating, a well-known risk in online exams, which became an urgent issue during the pandemic (Butler-Henderson and Crawford 2020; Nguyen et al. 2020). For example, to promote authenticity in its various meanings, they made more use of presentations, essay writing, translations, and glossary compiling than multiple-choice tests. As Tables 2.1, 2.2, and 2.3 show,[3] the teachers chose tasks involving a critical elaboration on theoretical concepts and the production of

Table 2.1 Assignments of Lecturer A's course

	2020–2021	2021–2022
Lecturer A (MA course)	2 MC tests (I) 1 Glossary (I) 2 PP presentations (G) 1 written report—analysis of a case study (G or I)	2 MC tests (I) 2 PP presentations (G) 2 written reports of a case study (G, I)

Table 2.2 Assignments of Lecturer B's course

	2020–2021	2021–2022
Lecturer B (BA course)	1 paper with commentary (I) 2 online tests (I) 1 PowerPoint presentation (G) 1 open question (I) or case study report (G) 1 translation (I) or case study report (G) 1 case study report (I or P)	1 paper with commentary (pair work) 1 PowerPoint presentation (group work) 1 open question (individual) 1 essay (individual, pair, or three-person activity)
Lecturer B (MA course)	Written report (P) (skippable) Translation (I) (synchronous) (skippable) Presentation (G) + creation of 5 entries for the #ReframeCovid database (G) (skippable) Test (I) (obligatory synchronous individual activity)	Written report (P) Post-editing of a machine translation output + commentary (I) synchronous individual work Presentation (G) +creation of 5 lemmas for a metaphor dictionary (asynchronous group work)

Table 2.3 Assignments of Lecturer C's course

	2020–2021	2021–2022
Lecturer C	1 translation (I) 1 written report involving critical appraisal of a translation (G) 1 collaborative reading and commenting (G)	1 translation (I) 1 written report involving critical appraisal of a translation (G) 1 collaborative reading and commenting (G)

materials by using a foreign language and applying analytical tools. They deemed it very helpful to encourage students to produce original work, which confirms the findings of research on ERT (Butler-Henderson and Crawford 2020; Nguyen et al. 2020).

Even though one of the three teachers kept in two multiple-choice tests among the assignments, they stated that other tasks, such as the creation of a glossary, provided a more comprehensive idea of student learning and understanding. The other two teacher informants dropped the quiz after one year or avoided it in the first place, as quizzes did not help save time and could be deemed unfair. Indeed, Lecturer B stated that clear tasks were difficult and time-consuming to prepare. When they had to test their students online for the first time after the sudden shift of classes onto digital platforms, Lecturer B had chosen quizzes as a quick way to monitor student learning. However, they soon realised that the benefits of this tool did not outweigh the drawbacks. Several students experienced technical issues and did not manage to take the test or obtain satisfying results. It was very difficult to tell whether a low mark was due to a lack of preparation or the technical difficulties and connection problems they encountered during the test. Overall, they considered quizzes unfair and decided to drop them after the first year of the pandemic, in line with suggestions from studies on ERT (Butler-Henderson and Crawford 2020; Cooper et al. 2022).

All the informants devoted specific attention to students' professional and digital skills and the reproduction of the pressure of a work environment. In line with studies on emergency remote assessment (Cooper et al. 2022), the teacher informants stated that the peculiar conditions determined by the pandemic encouraged, or even forced, them to go digital by experimenting with digital tools while also evaluating students. Therefore, they asked students to work on digitally shared documents and reshaped their tasks to fit the new digitally enhanced context by using the different options offered, in their cases, by Moodle (Wikis, surveys, etc.). The students' open-ended comments confirmed that they felt more involved in tasks that were not only content-based but also involved critical thinking (49%) and new skills (63%). Despite being satisfied with this form of assessment, MA students wished that the tasks were more practical and less theoretical: compared to their undergraduate counterparts, they showed an increased interest in professional (employability) skills.

Although teachers and students agreed on the benefits of authentic assessment, they had different opinions regarding group assessment. The three lecturer respondents alternated between group and individual assessments to manage their workload and help their students develop professional and soft skills related to teamwork. Moreover, during lockdown, working in groups helped students feel less isolated, and it strengthened a sense of learning community. However, students' comments are highly critical of the unfair amount of work they had to take on because of their teammates' lack of commitment and/or poor linguistic and digital skills. On the one hand, they appreciated their involvement in groups, since it could help build a sort of support net to lessen the sense of isolation—one of the major concerns for young people's mental health during the pandemic. On the other hand, they complained that some groupmates claimed to have poor connection or health issues that did not allow them to complete their part of the tasks, thus increasing the burden for other students. This issue was discussed in the semi-guided interviews with the teachers, who were aware of the problem. However, they still defended group assessment as both relevant training and a tool to help students connect with their peers more systematically, thereby aiding a sense of learning community.

Regarding continuous assessment, the three respondents adopted in-course evaluation to promote better teaching and more efficient and interactive learning. They believed that CA could be beneficial, as it helped maintain student involvement and improve their performance through feedback. Moreover, one out of three chose CA to make their workload more manageable, which was a key issue during the pandemic, as teachers reported working longer to manage the transition onto digital platforms. Their positive view aligned with the students' answers. In their open-ended comments, students described CA as a novelty they willingly embraced. Indeed, 77% thought it was a good idea, and 53% were curious. The teacher informants noticed that the need to experiment with technology and new forms of assessment during the pandemic encouraged students to be more open and curious about different methods of assessment—hence, more engaged. CA is particularly relevant in Italy and, in general, the Mediterranean area, including, for instance, Spain and Greece, where continuous assessment is not mainstream yet (Siarova et al. 2017), in contrast with countries in the North European area or overseas like the USA, New Zealand, Australia, and China (USNEI 2008; Zhan 2020).

Even though 31% of the students initially felt anxious when informed of the new forms of assessment, 99% decided to attend the course. Only a working student asked for a traditional exam, which shows that ACA could be more challenging for students with family or work commitments (see Sect. 4.2). Data showed that keeping up with the pace of the assessment was a relevant issue for students but that, eventually, they were able to manage it despite the difficulties they faced during the pandemic. Even though they were not used to these new forms of assessment, according to 62% of the students, it was *fairly easy* or *very easy* to meet the deadlines, which helped them to become better organised (70%), hence promoting autonomous learning. The teachers stated that ACA was a game changer during the pandemic because it helped with student retention even as students were suddenly confined at home and deprived of their usual schedules and learning environments. Indeed, their learning was deeply affected by ACA. Seventy-five per cent stated that it enabled them to attend classes regularly because they could watch the recorded lessons to compensate for classes missed due to clashes. Although all the teachers considered ACA an effective option even in ordinary circumstances, students' open-ended comments highlight that the regular attendance required by in-course assessment could have been easier during the lockdown. Indeed, only 50% of them thought that ACA could always be *useful*. Students noticed a positive impact on time management (49%), planning (54%), and the quality of learning in relation to self-confidence (70%), which were also seen as advantages by the teachers. For example, the latter considered ACA to be beneficial for both students and teachers. In their open-ended comments, students explained that it was easier for them to focus more attentively on the topics, as the assignments refer to smaller portions in comparison with an end-of-course summative exam. Moreover, the in-course assessment allows students to better understand the task as they could work under the teachers' supervision or at least ask for clarifications during classes.

That said, this study goes further than existing research on assessment (e.g. Tessaro 2014; Farrell and Seery 2019; Villarroel et al. 2018, 2020), confirming the benefits of ACA. Moreover, this study argues that the combination of the two (ACA) played a relevant role in student engagement during the pandemic. In line with research showing the positive impact of this kind of assessment on student understanding and learning, progressively assessing students during the course and involving them in authentic tasks proved successful. Teachers reported that these tasks substantially limited the online cheating elsewhere reported in the literature on online assessment (Butler-Henderson and Crawford 2020; Nguyen et al. 2020), as the tasks required a personal contribution, stimulating motivation and engagement. Students felt more involved in practical tasks (e.g. video-making tasks), which were integrated with other tasks, more theoretically focused. This combination in turn curbed plagiarism.[4] In summary, both teachers and students expressed an overall approval of and satisfaction with this form of assessment, despite the critical points discussed in Sect. 4.2.

4.2 Challenges of Authentic and Continuous Assessment (RQ2) and Evidence-Based Suggestions (RQ3)

Do it only if you are truly committed, or else it can be very heavy.
Make sure you have appropriate training and assistance.
Obtain a helper.
A Lecturer (April 21)

Having other lessons and a lot to study,
sometimes it is difficult to manage everything without being superficial.
A Student (April 21)

Teachers reported no major challenges regarding authentic assessment (AA), as shown in Table 2.4. In contrast, in their open-ended comments, students complained about the theoretical requests of some tasks and the perceived unfairness of group work. In the semi-guided interviews, the teachers stated that universities should provide students with theoretical pillars to direct their practical and work-related experience and achieve more comprehensive learning. They underlined that they tried to avoid

Table 2.4 Authentic assessment: challenges and suggestions

Challenges for teachers	Suggestions	Challenges for students	Suggestions
–	–	Tasks involving theoretical knowledge	Make the goals of the activity explicit
–	–	Group work	A combination of individual and group work

lowering the bar for their students during the pandemic, even though they acknowledged having made more concessions. In line with experience-based suggestions from research on emergency remote assessment (Cooper et al. 2022), teacher informants felt that AA helped them to provide students with quality education and meaningful learning experiences despite the difficulties of ERT. For example, lecturers suggested that teachers should make the goals of the activities very explicit to help students better understand the purposes of tasks such as 'compare and contrast' translations, invoking theoretical justifications. Regarding group work, teachers considered collaborative skills to be crucial for their students' future. Moreover, working in groups contributed to their well-being during the pandemic, when isolation and loneliness could affect their mental health. Teachers were aware that not all the students were satisfied with group evaluation, because they thought it did not always reflect every team member's commitment. To address this issue, they alternated between group and individual evaluation: teachers thought that the overall level of a single student's preparation and learning would eventually emerge across the different tasks.

The results showed that the main challenges for teachers and students arose in relation to continuous assessment (CA). As shown in the literature, time constraints and individual workload are the main difficulties they encounter (Villarroel et al. 2018). Teachers stated that continuous assessment could work very well with classes of 50–70 students, but it could be challenging for large-sized modules. They complained that continuous assessment was time-consuming and increased the workload because of the number of tasks that necessitated feedback in comparison with one end-of-year examination. Indeed, providing feedback on in-course examinations was demanding, and teachers had difficulties keeping up with the pace of the evaluation, which was stressful given the increased amount of work needed to update their teaching methods and support students in the new setting. Thus, on the one hand, they believed that workload had increased during the pandemic because—as mentioned in the Introduction to this volume—they suddenly had to take on different roles at once (pedagogical and intellectual, managerial and organisational, technical), making up for the loss of the social presence and support provided during face-to-face lessons. On the other hand, teachers believed that having to assess different tasks instead of one increased the workload regardless of the pandemic. At the same time, in line with findings on emergency remote assessment (Cooper et al. 2022), they felt that CA was worthwhile if students received immediate feedback.

The need for immediate feedback was also raised by students, who complained about receiving delayed feedback. They suggested that teachers could plan the tasks better and in advance to provide timely feedback (on the notion of formative feedback, incorporating considerations on purposely 'delayed' feedback, see Heinrich's chapter in this volume). Lecturer C suggested that general feedback and examples could be provided for students to clearly understand what they were supposed to do and submit improved work, which would require fewer modifications. Moreover, indicators and assessment criteria should be more transparent so that students can understand on their own the reasons for a specific mark without requiring further explanation via emails or during office hours.[5] In addition to group evaluation, the teacher respondents reduced the number of tasks after the first year they experimented with this ACA, as shown in Tables 2.1 and 2.2. Moreover, to better manage the increased workload due to ACA and the pandemic, the teacher informants tried to encourage student self- and peer-assessment to speed up feedback. By providing the keys to mock exams and general feedback or asking students to provide feedback on their classmates' work, the teachers were able to reduce the amount of time they spent reading and writing comments on students' works while increasing student self-awareness and learning.

In their open-ended comments, students complained about the short time between the tasks and the overlap with the commitments required

Table 2.5 Authentic assessment: challenges and suggestions

Challenges for teachers	Suggestions	Challenges for students	Suggestions
Time constraints Pressure The need for immediate feedback	Better planning Reduce the number of tasks Training	Time span Pressure Delayed feedback	Better planning (for students and teachers) Set and communicate the deadlines at the beginning of the course (for teachers)
Workload	Reduce the number of tasks Group evaluation Provide general feedback Provide clear rubrics and descriptors Training	Overlapping with other tasks Difficulties for working students	Shared calendar (rejected by the teachers) Asynchronous tasks
Size of the classes	Split the modules Teaching assistant Training	Disappointing results due to lack of time	Better planning (for students)

in other modules, as shown in Table 2.5. This led to anxiety and dissatisfaction with the effort they were able to put into the tasks. Teachers B and C confirmed that not all the outcomes were satisfying, but they conceded that the pandemic situation was challenging for everybody, even though they stressed that university students, especially at the MA level, were supposed to show time-management and self-organisation skills. Although 62% of the students found it easy to keep up with the pace of the course, 48% still struggled, which shows that there is room for improvement. Data showed that students who did not have difficulties managing the deadlines considered themselves well-organised. In contrast, students who found it *somewhat easy* (30%) and *not easy at all* (7%) to keep up with the pace of the evaluation suggested that teachers should better plan the course to distribute the tasks more carefully. Moreover, some of them were working students who reported the difficulties of juggling study, work, and family commitments and underlined the need for knowing the deadlines well in advance to better plan their schedules. In the semi-guided interviews, teachers agreed with this suggestion but rejected students' requests for better collaboration between teachers of different modules for a better distribution of the tasks through a shared calendar of the tests. Indeed, this would prove very hard, given the variety of modules in which students are enrolled.

According to teachers' and students' suggestions, careful planning and clarity of instructions from the very beginning of the module are crucial to help teachers to manage their workload and students to boost independent learning through self-management. After all, time management and organisation are among the learning goals of continuous assessment. Among the suggestions for addressing this issue, Lecturer B proposed the possibility of asynchronous evaluations: for example, students could be given a report to write or a text to translate in a set time, to submit by the end of the day (though this may be standard practice in the UK, for example, it certainly is not in Italy, where synchronous, in-person, examinations still prevail). This would allow working students to accomplish the task when it best suits them without disrupting their working day. As already pointed out (see Sect. 4.1), to avoid plagiarism, this would require the teachers to create original, specific tasks and activities matching the course content and requiring personal contribution and competence more than knowledge.

Finally, the size of university classes has a profound impact on choices regarding assessment. In Teachers A's and B's modules, the scores achieved for the accomplishment of the assignments were added together and resulted in a final mark. In contrast, the tasks given by Lecturer C were used to build a portfolio that partly contributed to the final mark (20%) and was used as a starting point for the oral discussion. As clarified in the semi-guided interviews, these differences can be explained by considering the different sizes of the modules. Lecturer C teaches in modules attended by fewer than 30 students, which allows them to make the students sit for an oral exam where they can show their learning and understanding by commenting on their portfolios. Given that Lecturer A's and B's modules involve more than 100 students, they wanted to avoid end-of-the-course exams, which consisted of open written questions to test students' knowledge. Lecturer B felt that CA was a game changer during the pandemic and improved student success rates compared to pre-pandemic years. However, having to assess 500 students a year, they stated that the next year, they would partly drop CA, despite its advantages for students' learning and understanding. Lecturer A and Lecturer C stated that they would continue using continuous assessment as the course size and the presence of a helper would make the amount of work manageable. Regarding the students' comments, class size was never mentioned as an issue of concern either in the first year of the pandemic or in the two following years.

To date, the challenges regarding AA and CA have been discussed separately to unearth specific difficulties and suggestions. Regarding the combination of AA and CA in the modules investigated, the findings showed that ACA was an efficient alternative to end-of-course examinations during the pandemic in teachers' and students' opinions. Moreover, in their open-ended comments, they conceded that ACA was convenient during the lockdown, but they stressed that it could be effective regardless of the learning environment. Therefore, they recommend it for online, hybrid, and in-person classes. However, students feared that in post-pandemic years, when in-person modules might be fully resumed, CA could be more challenging because of the overlapping of different commitments. It would require more effort to keep up the pace of the evaluation and achieve good results. Further research is needed to identify possible differences between the various teaching and learning environments in terms of the associated task types and schedules.

To conclude, a comparison between the strategies adopted by teachers and students to face challenges experienced during the pandemic showed that better planning is crucial for both groups. Indeed, better planning of tasks and commitments should be a priority of the teaching and learning process. As the teacher respondents underlined, it requires training and experience and should be part of every teacher's competence regardless of the teaching environment. However, this resonates with the need for specific training highlighted by recent research on the pandemic, which suggested that teachers should acquire the ability to adapt to changing and digitally enhanced teaching environments to meet their students' needs.

Furthermore, better-trained teachers could also help their students learn how to plan and organise their schedules more effectively. Students' open-ended comments express their need to better manage time, which is a call to action that deserves attention. In turn, studies on ERT (Barbour et al. 2020; Giacosa 2021) have shown that students also struggle with technology despite widespread assumptions about their digital competence. Not only did they face technical issues while attending from home, such as poor bandwidth or insufficient technological equipment, but some of them also had to become accustomed to the educational platforms they were using for the first time, as Lecturer B underlined, which increased their anxiety and adversely affected their learning experience and consequently their results. Even though enhanced digital skills are considered a positive side effect of the trying years under the shadow of the pandemic, student digital training should be on the HE agenda. This demands funding support for better resources to help learners fully benefit from the new and constantly upgraded teaching tools, as research on ERT has shown (Barbour et al. 2020; Bozkurt et al. 2020).

5 Conclusions

The sudden transition of the education system onto digital platforms was challenging for both teachers and students in many respects. However, every cloud has a silver lining. Along with the difficulties, new possibilities for learning, teaching, and assessment were revealed to learners and instructors. Although the data of this study refer to a small sample, it shows that the new needs and opportunities experienced in HE during the pandemic prompted change in contexts such as the Italian context, where teachers tend to be more traditional and prefer testing knowledge over skills (Appolloni et al. 2021).

Drawing on previous research into ERT, this study focused on assessment as a relevant and timely research topic both during the pandemic and under normal circumstances (e.g. Cooper et al. 2022). Indeed, the need for change towards more authentic and meaningful tasks was felt by teachers and students before the COVID-19 education emergency. Nevertheless, the mainstream assessment in tertiary education consists of end-of-year written exams, as shown in research on different HE contexts around the world (e.g. Indire 2014 for the Italian context, Popkova 2018 for Russian universities, Villarroel et al. 2018 regarding Chile, and Oli and Olkaba 2020 with reference to the Ethiopian context). When teachers had to teach and assess remotely in 2020, they had to question the traditional end-of-year examination and then change it to fit the new setting. The present study investigated experiences encompassing both authentic and continuous assessment (here called ACA) in EFL university modules. It collected data during the pandemic when the need for more relevant and effective assessment became urgent. In addition to contributing to the body of knowledge on assessment in ERT, its findings could also prove useful under different circumstances, as they show an alternative way of assessing students suited to different contexts and therefore sustainable.

The investigation of the first research question on opportunities offered by ACA shows that the teachers' choice of an alternative to end-of-course examinations was appropriate and their expectations were fulfilled. First, ACA was favourably accepted by their students, which proved that fears of student resistance to change might be unfounded. Second, the student respondents benefitted from in-course tasks involving higher-order thinking from different points of view. Despite the challenges of ERT, they were motivated and engaged and improved their soft and digital skills, as well as critical thinking. The students' overall satisfaction with this form of the assessment showed that ACA helped navigate the troubled waters of the pandemic. Based on this positive experience, this study argues that ACA could help better integrate evaluation into the study experience and offer opportunities for further learning in future teaching scenarios. This investigation did not involve a control group assessed with the traditional end-of-course exams during the pandemic. However, both students and teachers were asked to compare their experience of ACA with their previous experiences of end-of-course assessment, which made their reflections meaningful and reliable. This study was limited to three teacher respondents working in the same field who could be biased in favour of this form of assessment since they adopted it. Nonetheless, they were open about the difficulties they encountered, which confirmed the findings of previous research. Further studies could investigate larger samples of respondents to provide statistically relevant data to measure the impact of ACA in different fields of study.

Despite its many advantages, ACA presented challenges, as investigated by the second research question. Both teachers and students identified time management and increased workload as the main difficulties in comparison with traditional end-of-the-course exams. The findings agreed with the issues raised by previous research and show that despite the benefits, alternatives to one end-of-the-course evaluation are time-consuming and demanding. Consequently, teachers may feel overwhelmed and abandon this beneficial and student-centred form of assessment. However, teachers and students provided suggestions based on their experience, as explored by the third research question. Both groups identified better planning as a game changer for teachers and students. On the one hand, teachers should carefully and effectively plan tasks and choose meaningful assignments. Better teacher planning could have the additional benefit of helping students organise themselves better. On the other hand, authentic and relevant assignments could motivate students and boost their learning and work-related skills. Further research on the challenges of ACA could provide teachers with a set of tools and specific training to ease the workload, thus helping them maintain this approach. This study did not measure the impact of the two components of ACA either separately or combined, because this would have gone beyond its scope. Further research is needed to unearth how continuous and authentic assessment could be fruitfully combined to prove a workable option in future teaching scenarios. Possible research questions for future investigations could explore the impact of different types of meaningful and appropriate assignments in the various learning environments to identify how to tailor ACA effectively to the setting. Finally, in-depth studies on EFL classes would help identify the impact of ACA on different language skills.

Despite its limitations, the present study provided evidence-based insights into an effective alternative to traditional end-of-course examinations from the teacher and student perspectives. The findings of empirical studies such as the present one could be used in teacher training to provide instructors with powerful tools for future teaching scenarios and new generations of students. As teachers' and students' positive comments show, further research on and training in ACA is worthwhile to achieve better teaching and learning in a smart new world.

Acknowledgements I would like to thank all the lecturers and students who participated in this study and allowed me to conduct my research. I would also like to thank the reviewers for their insightful comments, which helped me dig deeper and gain a more comprehensive understanding of my data.

Notes

1. This preliminary study is part of a broader investigation for a PhD thesis to be discussed in Spring 2023. It involved 29 EFL teachers from 13 different Italian universities and over 800 students, and it collected information about challenges and opportunities offered by ERT from teacher and student perspectives.
2. This necessarily raises the question of what this meant for teachers who were not on a salary and who were, for example, paid by the hour. Although this is too complex a topic to tackle within the limited scope of this chapter, it should be noted that, broadly speaking, the pandemic caused insecurity across a range of categories. This instability, inside and outside of academia, was exacerbated for women, especially those in insecure employment (Churchill 2020; Wenham et al. 2020).
3. (I) refers to individual evaluation, (P) refers to a task accomplished by two or three students, (G) refers to group work (four to five students), and (PE) refers to peer-evaluation.
4. The latter was also avoided by using specific anti-plagiarism software and proctoring tools (e.g. Turnitin and Respondus), yet this goes beyond the scope of the present paper, and it presented its own challenges.
5. In large-size courses, teachers could be helped with the marking by teaching assistants, which would of course require investment in additional staff.

References

Adzima, K. 2020. Examining online cheating in higher education using traditional classroom cheating as a guide. *The Electronic Journal of E-Learning* 18 (6): 476–493. https://doi.org/10.34190/JEL.18.6.002.

Ajjawi, R., et al. 2020. Aligning assessment with the needs of work-integrated learning: The challenges of authentic assessment in a complex context. *Assessment and Evaluation in Higher Education* 45 (2): 304–316. https://doi.org/10.1080/02602938.2019.1639613.

Appolloni, A., et al. 2021. Distance learning as a resilience strategy during COVID-19: An analysis of the Italian context. *Sustainability* 13 (1388). https://doi.org/10.3390/su13031388.

Atmojio, A. 2021. Facilitating positive washback through authentic assessment in EFL assessment. *Acitya: Journal of Teaching and Education* 3 (2): 226–233.

Barbour, M., et al. 2020. Understanding pandemic pedagogy: Differences between emergency remote, remote, and online teaching. *Project: CANeLearn: K-12 Remote Learning in Canada.* https://doi.org/10.13140/RG.2.2.31848.70401.

Bozkurt, A., et al. 2020. A global outlook to the interruption of education due to COVID-19 pandemic: Navigating in a time of uncertainty and crisis. *Asian Journal of Distance Education* 15 (1): 1–126. https://doi.org/10.5281/zenodo.3778083.

British Council. 2019. Annual report 2018–2019. https://www.britishcouncil.org/sites/default/files/annual-report-2018-19-web.pdf. Accessed 31 October 2022.

Brown, S. 2019. Developing authentic assessment for English language teaching. *The International Journal of Language and Cultural (TIJOLAC)* 1 (1): 12–24.

Butler-Henderson, K., and J. Crawford. 2020. A systematic review of online examinations: A pedagogical innovation for scalable authentication and integrity. *Computers and Education* 159: 104024. https://doi.org/10.1016/j.compedu.2020.104024.

Care, E., and H. Kim. 2018. Assessment of twenty-first century skills: The issue of authenticity. In *Assessment and teaching of 21st century skills. Educational assessment in an information age*, ed. E. Care et al., 21–39. Cham: Springer. https://doi.org/10.1007/978-3-319-65368-6_2.

Chirumamilla, A., et al. 2020. Cheating in E-exams and paper exams: The perceptions of engineering students and teachers in Norway. *Assessment and*

Evaluation in Higher Education 45: 940–957. https://doi.org/10.1080/02602938.2020.1719975.

Churchill, B. 2020. COVID-19 and the immediate impact on young people and employment in Australia: A gendered analysis. *Gender, Work and Organization* 28: 783. https://doi.org/10.1111/gwao.12563.

Cooper, A., et al. 2022. Emergency assessment: Rethinking classroom practices and priorities amid remote teaching. *Assessment in Education: Principles, Policy and Practice* 29 (5): 534–554. https://doi.org/10.1080/0969594X.2022.2069084.

Corsini, C., and F. Agrusti. 2021. Indagine esplorativa sugli esami universitari a distanza. *Cadmo: giornale italiano di pedagogia sperimentale* 1: 63–80.

Cross, R., and K. O'Loughlin. 2013. Continuous assessment frameworks within university English pathway programs: Realizing formative assessment within high-stakes contexts. *Studies in Higher Education* 38 (4): 584–594. https://doi.org/10.1080/03075079.2011.588694.

Czerniewicz, L., et al. 2020. A wake-up call: Equity, inequality and COVID-19 emergency remote teaching and learning. *Postdigital Science and Education* 2 (3): 946–967. https://doi.org/10.1007/s42438-020-00187-4.

Dadashzadeh, M. 2021. The online examination dilemma: To proctor or not to proctor? *Journal of Instructional Pedagogies* 25: 1–11.

Dejene, W. 2019. The practice of modularized curriculum in higher education institution: Active learning and continuous assessment in focus. *Cogent Education* 6 (1): 1–16. https://doi.org/10.1080/2331186X.2019.1611052.

Eurboonyanun, C., et al. 2021. Adaptation to open-book online examination during the COVID-19 pandemic. *Journal of Surgical Education* 78 (3): 737–739. https://doi.org/10.1016/j.jsurg.2020.08.046.

Farrell, O., and A. Seery. 2019. 'I am not simply learning and regurgitating information, I am also learning about myself': Learning portfolio practice and online distance students. *Distance Education* 40 (1): 76–97. https://doi.org/10.1080/01587919.2018.1553565.

García-Peñalvo, F.J., et al. 2021. Recommendations for mandatory online assessment in higher education during the COVID-19 pandemic. In *Radical solutions for education in a crisis context. Lecture notes in educational technology*, ed. Daniel Burgos et al., 85–98. Singapore: Springer. https://doi.org/10.1007/978-981-15-7869-4_6.

Giacosa, A. 2021. From classroom to screen: Lessons learned in teachers' and students' experience. *Proceedings of the Mooc2Move conference on 'Moocs, language learning and mobility: Design, integration, reuse'*, 9–10 April 2021, Turin.

Guadu, Z.B., and E.J. Boersma. 2018. EFL instructors' beliefs and practices of formative assessment in teaching writing. *Journal of Language Teaching and Research* 9 (1): 42–50. https://doi.org/10.17507/jltr.0901.06.

Harari, Y.N. 2018. *21 lessons for the 21st century.* London: Random House UK.

Holmes, N. 2018. Engaging with assessment: Increasing student engagement through continuous assessment. *Active Learning in Higher Education* 19 (1): 23–34. https://doi.org/10.1177/1469787417723230.

Inayah, N., et al. 2019. The practice of authentic assessment in an EFL speaking classroom. *Studies in English Language and Education* 6 (1): 152–162.

Kaplan, I., and I. Lewis. 2013. *Promoting inclusive teacher education: Curriculum.* Paris: United Nations Educational, Scientific and Cultural Organization and UNESCO Bangkok.

Ministero dell'Istruzione, dell'Università e della Ricerca. 2014. The Italian education system. In *I Quaderni di Eurydice*, vol. 30. Firenze: Indire.

Moorhouse, B., and L. Kohnke. 2022. Conducting formative assessment during synchronous online lessons: University teachers' challenges and pedagogical strategies. *Pedagogies: An International Journal* 30 (3): 1–19. https://doi.org/10.1080/1554480X.2022.2065993.

Morin, E. 2000. *La testa ben fatta.* Milano: Cortina editore.

Nguyen, J.G., et al. 2020. Minimize online cheating for online assessments during COVID-19 pandemic. *Journal of Chemical Education* 97 (9): 3429–3435. https://doi.org/10.1021/acs.jchemed.0c00790.

Oli, G., and T. Olkaba. 2020. Practices and challenges of continuous assessment in colleges of teachers education in West Oromia region of Ethiopia. *Journal of Education, Teaching and Learning* 5 (1): 8–20.

Popkova, E. 2018. Continuous cumulative assessment in higher education: Coming to grips with test enhanced learning. In *Revisiting the assessment of second language abilities: From theory to practice*, ed. Hidri Sahbi, 331–349. Cham: Springer. https://doi.org/10.1007/978-3-319-62884-4_16.

Rahim, A. 2020. Guidelines for online assessment in emergency remote teaching during the COVID-19 pandemic. *Education in Medical Journal* 12 (2): 59–68. https://doi.org/10.21315/eimj2020.12.2.6.

Recalcati, M. 2014. *L'ora di lezione.* Torino: Einaudi.

Siarova, H., et al. 2017. *Assessment practices for 21st century learning: Review of evidence, NESET II report.* Luxembourg: Publications Office of the European Union. https://doi.org/10.2766/71491.

Siemens, G. 2005. Connectivism: A learning theory for the digital age. *International Journal of Instructional Technology and Distance Learning* 2 (1): 1–6.

Srikanth, M., and R. Asmatulu. 2014. Modern cheating techniques, their adverse effects on engineering education and preventions. *International Journal of Mechanical Engineering Education* 42 (2): 129–140. https://doi.org/10.7227/IJMEE.0005.

Sumarno, W.K., and Mrs Tatik. 2019. Using Edmodo-supported E-portfolio as authentic assessment in EFL writing course. In *UNNES International Conference on English Language Teaching, Literature, and Translation (ELTLT 2018)*, 102–105. Zhengzhou: Atlantis Press. https://doi.org/10.2991/eltlt-18.2019.21.

Sutadji, E., et al. 2021. Adaptation strategy of authentic assessment in online learning during the COVID-19 pandemic. *Journal of Physics: Conference Series*. https://doi.org/10.1088/1742-6596/1810/1/012059.

Tessaro, F. 2014. Compiti autentici o prove di realtà? Authentic tasks or reality tests? *Formazione e Inegnamento* 12 (3): 77–88. https://doi.org/10.7346/-fei-XII-03-14_07.

Timmis, S., et al. 2016. Rethinking assessment in a digital age: Opportunities, challenges and risks. *British Educational Research Journal* 42 (3): 454–476. https://doi.org/10.1002/berj.3215.

Tolosa, M. 2019. Action research on exploring the effectiveness of continuous assessment on English common course in a case of plant science year I students. *International Journal Online of Humanities (IJOHMN)* 5 (4): 77–89. https://doi.org/10.24113/ijohmn.v5i5.112.

UNESCO. 2015. *Managing inclusive learning-friendly classrooms*. Paris: United Nations Educational, Scientific and Cultural Organization and UNESCO Bangkok.

———. 2020. *From subregional to a continental response strategy in support of more resilient and responsive education systems in Africa COVID-19 (C-19), April–June 2020*. Regional office for Eastern Africa. https://en.unesco.org/sites/default/files/covid_19_emergeny_response_plan_-_all_sectors-final-05apr2020.pdf. Accessed 22 December 2022.

USNEI. 2008. Structure of the U.S. education system: Educational Assessment. https://www2.ed.gov/about/offices/list/ous/international/usnei/us/edlite-evaluation.html. Accessed 22 December 2022.

Villarroel, V., et al. 2018. Authentic assessment: Creating a blueprint for course design. *Assessment and Evaluation in Higher Education* 43 (5): 840–854. https://doi.org/10.1080/02602938.2017.1412396.

———. 2020. Using principles of authentic assessment to redesign written examinations and tests. *Innovations in Education and Teaching International* 57 (1): 38–49. https://doi.org/10.1080/14703297.2018.1564882.

Wenham, C., et al. 2020. Women are most affected by pandemics – lessons from past outbreaks. *Nature* 583 (7815): 194–198. https://doi.org/10.1038/d41586-020-02006-z.

World Economic Forum. 2020. There's nothing new about the 'new normal' – And here's why. https://www.weforum.org/agenda/2020/06/theres-nothing-new-about-this-new-normal-heres-why. Accessed 26 April 2022.

Zhan, Y. 2020. Motivated or informed? Chinese undergraduates' beliefs about the functions of continuous assessment in their college English course. *Higher Education Research & Development* 39 (5): 1055–1069. https://doi.org/10.1080/07294360.2019.1699029.

3

Computer-Based Self-Assessment as a Customised Tool for the Strategic Implementation of an Updated Circular Teaching Model

Roxanne Barbara Doerr and Annalisa Zanola

1 Introduction: Academic Customised Assessment and Evaluation in the Post-pandemic Era

COVID-19 has had a major impact on foreign language teaching and learning all over the world, especially in terms of learners' self-assessment and teachers' assessment of linguistic competence. Social distancing and online learning have affected how people approach and study a foreign language: students worked within virtual communities that provided materials and activities that were spread over time and/or space, and they were also guided by a-synchronically available instructors. This resulted in evident gaps between questions and answers and a significant difficulty

---

Section 1 was written by Annalisa Zanola, Sects. 2, 3, 4, and 5 were written by Roxanne Barbara Doerr, and the conclusion (Sect. 6) was jointly written by both authors.

R. B. Doerr • A. Zanola (✉)
University of Brescia, Brescia, Italy
e-mail: roxanne.doerr@unibs.it; annalisa.zanola@unibs.it

in monitoring progress, in terms of both learners' levels and the course's effectiveness. This was also worsened by an increased distance between the content of the course and that of the final assessment, whose form and methods were instantly adapted to the change in teaching delivery. This situation was perhaps even more evident in Italy, where distance and online learning have often been associated with substandard levels of performance. This cultural attitude was mainly due to prejudices stemming from distance learning having, until then, been offered almost exclusively by private institutions, which are not regarded as favourably as the public ones. Therefore, when the pandemic suddenly hit, Italian teachers and instructors—with few exceptions—found themselves without prior training and without materials that could be effectively used for online teaching and learning.

In the specific case of the Northern Italian university hereby discussed,[1] which is currently in a phase of great expansion at both national and international levels, the main priority in facing the emergency was not only to ensure the quality of education whilst delivery moved online. The university was also concerned with maintaining a sense of belonging and, thus, community (as defined in the Introduction to this volume). The latter, as Fiorucci commented in the Introduction, was not necessarily the focus of institutions elsewhere. This university immediately directed its to the community by providing intensive training for all teachers and instructors (East 2022). Thanks also to the support of technicians and constant feedback on students' perceptions of the online courses and final assessments, teachers were provided with the tools to both adapt their course materials and accompany the courses now taking place online with activities that would enable students and teachers to closely monitor progress—thus, stimulating engagement.

The situation described above highlighted the need for rapid changes in conceiving courses and assessments within the learning cycle as a whole to ensure an effective move to online channels. In general, assessment procedures tend to control and direct the teaching and learning process, assuming that statistical data collection is an empirical resource that can be used to draw conclusions at the end of such a process. Although seemingly logical, this approach might prove inefficient unless we understand this process as a starting point for a new teaching activity, thus subverting the order of—but also joining up—the 'reflection-on action' and 'reflection-for-action' phases of teachers' reflective practice (East 2022, pp. 17–18). The need to update the circular model of the so-called teaching unit that forged generations of language teachers (Lado 1961, 1964; Titone 1974; Freddi 1985; Porcelli 1992) became, during the pandemic, more urgent than ever. On the one hand, error analysis (Corder 1971, 1981; Richards 1970, 1984; Nickel and Nehls 1982; James 1998) has increasingly become a way of guiding teachers' subsequent choices. On the other, the planning of strategically relevant content within new foreign language courses, which are increasingly characterised by a focus on eliciting motivation, is more and more centred on learners, as subjects who make mistakes. Serious insight into the specific role of assessment in academic contexts is thus necessary.

Because of the focus on summative 'fed-out' assessments (Marshall 2011), in Italy (and elsewhere, as Giacosa also notes in Chap. 2), language learners often perceive their courses or modules as standardised and mandatory, which they must attend and be graded on to progress in their studies. They do not necessarily perceive the usefulness of what they are being taught or asked to do,[2] especially during the assessment phase. In universities, the final assessment is considered a fundamental objective to obtain course credits and a final grade that will feed into the graduation mark and/or the possibility for students to study abroad with university programmes (e.g. Erasmus programmes, summer schools, and international internships).

Assessing and evaluating are both an essential part of the academic teaching routine and a fundamental step of the learning process. We are very indebted, in this respect, to the literature produced on foreign language assessment in recent decades (Ringbom 2010), which has brought great improvements in both learning and teaching methodologies. Far from seeing the teacher as the controller of language learning, we are now all familiar with a more learner-centred approach, which emphasises the learner's potential in moving towards authentic bilingual competence. Such an approach is especially useful in considering the inherent diversity and needs of each class, which becomes a means of engendering a sense of meaningfulness and belonging, within a student community that is, frequently, a multicultural one—increasingly so.

One major result of this shift of attention consists of increasing concern in monitoring and analysing learners' progress. From the standpoint of practice, we have become more aware of the long-term value of *error analysis* as a chief means of assessing both students' learning in general and the degree of matching between their learning and our own teaching: data from the classroom can both serve as an input to theoretical discussion and, after evaluation, feedback to the design of remedial curricula. More specifically, it assesses the 'accuracy' dimension of language learning, which is necessary before proceeding towards specialised language (Zanola 2023):

> Learner language can be described in terms of 3 dimensions: accuracy, complexity, and fluency. Learner language is accurate when it conforms to target language norms; it is complex when it contains a range of vocabulary and grammatical structures; and it is fluent when it is produced quickly and with few pauses. These three dimensions affect each other; for example, too much focus on accuracy can reduce fluency or complexity. Too much focus on complexity can reduce accuracy or fluency. (Centre for Advanced Research on Language Acquisition 2022)

In Candlin's words, the three objectives of error analysis consist in sustaining contrasting linguistics in predicting error, confirming the presence of areas to be learned through the formulation of learners' interlingual systems, and providing transfer theory and data that may be critically observed and contribute to discovering target language rules (in Richards 1984, p. x). Error predictability—with its subsequent useful formulation of rules—and its psycholinguistic consequences on learners are still among the most relevant aspects of the process of assessing foreign languages in academia.

Far from being an investigation, inspection, or scrutiny procedure, assessing English competence at the university level is the complex act of placing some value on the quality of oral or written textual production. It is time for language assessment at the university level to evolve from simplistic and reductive close tests, which are often aimed at collecting quantitative data without considering any following remedial or improvement phases. The two levels (testing and evaluating) are often confused because the final judgement cannot exist without testing, but not vice versa. Evaluating means studying the evidence of the collected data produced by students at the end of the learning process and comparing the teacher's initial objectives with the learner's final results. Moreover, assessment may provide a window for observing what goes on in the learner's journey: in our research, the term 'error' has no negative impact, nor does it imply anything undesirable in the learner's language. In contrast, errors are normal and inevitable features of the process of language learning. The study of learners' errors is primarily considered here as evidence not of failure to conform to L2 usage but rather of success and achievement during the learning process. Accordingly, error analysis research considers errors not as something to be dogmatically 'corrected' but rather as a divergence from standard language to be 'treated' with awareness and understanding of its potential consequences in communicative and professional contexts. In other words, the study of errors, their causes and their development, can provide valuable information on the underlying learning processes.

Although the terms 'mistakes' and 'errors' are still used interchangeably too often, they are totally distinct concepts. Mistakes entail failing to apply the rules consistently: students do not always follow the rules despite knowing them, which normally stems from a lack of proper application. On the other hand, an 'error' consists of

> the use of a linguistic item (e.g., a word, a grammatical item, a speech act, etc.) in a way which a fluent or native speaker of the language regards as showing faulty or incomplete learning. A distinction is sometimes made between an error, which results from incomplete knowledge, and a mistake made by a learner when writing or speaking, which is caused by lack of attention, fatigue, carelessness, or some other aspect of performance. […] In the study of second and foreign language learning, errors have been studied to discover the processes learners make use of in learning and using a language. (Richards and Schmidt 2010, p. 201)

Common mistakes in Italian native speakers' usage of English are often related to verb tense, vocabulary, subject/verb agreement, word and clause order, and level of formality, as research reveals (Doerr 2023). Nevertheless, our overview shows that the same learners more frequently fail to communicate successfully because of recurring errors (not mistakes), such as inaccurate or incomplete sentences, simplification, overgeneralisation, and hypercorrection. Because these are interlingual errors, that is, they are due to linguistic interference and crosslinguistic influence, understanding each cohort's specific cultural and linguistic constitution and its connection to the most frequent errors is of the utmost importance.

In the following sections, we will describe a complex system of assessment created *ad hoc* for students starting their academic career in the department of Economics and Management at a mid-sized Italian university. This system of assessment will be presented as a tool for analysing the language competences of incoming learners and as a foundation for the objectives and contents of the English course dedicated to them.

2 The Context of the Study

The computer-based self-assessment test under analysis was conceived, administered, and improved over the course of two academic years (2020–2021 and 2020–2021) as a substitute for the previously implemented OFA exam during the first year[3] and a means to strategically design and structure the course's online supplementary grammar lessons. This was especially important in enabling teachers to achieve a student-tailored approach, given the high number of students attending the course (approximately 700–800 each year) and the limited number of hours available for extra lessons. The students were divided into three groups of 150–200 each academic year; two groups were composed of first-year students attending the Business Administration degree course (hereinafter referred to as 'Business Administration A–G' and 'Business Administration H–Z'), and one composed of both first-year students of the Banking and Finance course and second-year students of the Economics and Digital Firm course (hereinafter referred to as 'Bank and Finance and Digital Firm'). The self-assessment test allowed students whose secondary school-level preparation of English had been impacted by the COVID-19 emergency to gain awareness of their overall level and, if relevant, of critical areas of weakness in language competence. In this sense, the test aligns with Fenwick and Parsons' definition of self-assessment as 'the act of identifying standards or criteria and applying them to one's own work, and then making a judgment as to whether—or how well—you have met them' (2009, p. 111).

The self-assessment test was made available to students to complete autonomously on the course's platform, which put them at ease, as online self-assessment is not very different from other online tasks (Conrad and Openo 2018), with which students would have already been familiar since the move online in the spring of 2020. The test was divided into two parts, one consisting of open questions requesting personal, biographical, and educational information, and the other consisting of multiple-choice questions on various areas of the English language. The aim was to gain insight into students' previous experience with languages and language learning (Cocea 2006; Conrad and Openo 2018) and identify areas of English grammar that needed special attention. The current study will focus on the second part of the test to better investigate the process of customising course planning through the initial computer-based self-assessment test. It will do so by focusing on both teachers' and students' responses. Interestingly, regarding the teachers' experience, the results of the second part of the test diverged from the authors' expectations and enabled them to challenge the traditional notion of progression in grammar teaching and lesson planning. It therefore proved that self-assessment has the potential to be more than a mere final evaluation or evaluation of progress: rather, it can be an initial measure for improvement, encouraging flexibility and a different strategy in course design and implementation. From the students' perspectives, the test was also meant to make them understand that their learning experience would be gauged, then customised and properly mapped out for them from the very beginning, thus maintaining intrinsic motivation (Knowles and Kerkman 2007) throughout the course. The test was created bearing in mind that 'students want to feel sense of community with their peers and instructors; institutional bonds are in turn associated with enhanced learning' (Prati et al. 2018, p. 917). The authors and instructors wanted to foster 'feelings of community' (Gautam and Rosson 2021, p. 1): the students knew that they were being considered as part of a unique and developing community and not simply as just another group that would enrol in a standardised course conceived for an abstract audience.

The self-assessment test was devised with the following research questions in mind:

RQ1: What is the overall level of the class (including both attending and non-attending students)?
RQ2: Which common topics of English grammar are most difficult for the students and to what extent?

2.1 Variables

The independent variable consisted of the grade the students attained on the 'self-assessment test' that had been prepared, in 2020–2021, on the basis of the entry-level requirements of the previously implemented admission exam and OFA test and, in 2021–2022, with improvements to the self-assessment test of the previous year, which will be detailed in the following section. To avoid impacting the students' motivation or inducing them to tie their results to a grade, the feedback from the results (ranging from 0 to 100) was divided into three categories: in 2020–2021, they were 'nice try' (0–30, with admission of the student into the basic level English lessons as well as the supplementary lessons); 'good' (31–80 and encouragement to attend the supplementary lessons); and 'very good' (81–100 with the suggestion to only attend the supplementary lessons on topics where they had made multiple mistakes). In light of the results of the self-assessment test and related exams, in 2021–2022 the categories were adjusted to 'nice try' (0–30 and admission to the basic level English lessons); 'good' (31–85 and encouragement to review areas with mistakes and attend the English conversation course); and 'very good' (86–100 with the suggestion to only attend the English conversation course). The dependent variable consisted of a series of questions on the student's biographical information and background on educational/foreign language competence and learning, with the intention of gaining awareness of the level of diversity in the student community on the one hand, and gathering information about their previous experience with native and non-native English teachers and speakers on the other.

Having considered the context in which the self-assessment test was conceived and the factors that impacted its conceptual stage, the next section will describe the instrument itself in further detail by outlining its composition and the reasons for these choices.

3 Instrument: The Computer-based Self-Assessment Test

The self-assessment test was made available for students on the Moodle platform that was used to upload the main course material, video lessons of the asynchronous parts of the course, and extra resources provided to encourage the autonomous practice of listening and reading comprehension skills throughout the course by using authentic material (articles, websites, podcasts, TED talk channels, etc.), related to their field of study.

In both academic years, the self-assessment test lasted 60 minutes and was divided into two parts: one consisted of 10 open questions requesting personal, biographical, and educational information for both years, and the other consisted of 50 multiple-choice questions on various areas of English grammar (3 options worth 2 points) in 2020–2021 and 53 questions total (43 multiple choice and 10 closed short answer questions on mixed verb tenses) in 2021–2022. This change was introduced to make the test more challenging and verify students' ability to elaborate and insert, and not simply select, the correct answer. This was decided considering students' ability to recognise the correct answer when provided, but their difficulties in correctly spelling and conjugating verbs when required to do so during the final written exam. The questions were based on the areas of grammar that were commonly included in the programme of the supplementary lessons (between a B1 and B2 level, which is the target level for the end of the course).

The students were allowed to try the self-assessment test twice in case of technical difficulties or hesitations with the use of the quiz format on the first try, and the best of the two results were considered for the present analysis. This limit was imposed to ensure that students would not attempt to get a higher mark and, therefore, feel exonerated from attending the number of lessons they needed, by retaking the test multiple times until they attained a satisfactory 'best result'.

3.1 Creation and Adjustment of the Questions in 2020–2021 and 2021–2022

To better understand the composition of the student community, and therefore detect any possible discrepancies in educational and personal needs and requirements, the first 10 questions of the test in both academic years requested the following:

1. Name (for verification in cases of technical difficulties)
2. Age
3. Nationality
4. Type of high school
5. Average grade in English at high school
6. Other languages studied at school
7. Mother tongue/bilingual (to understand the reason for possible linguistic interference)
8. Native language and/or conversation teachers
9. Degree course and year (enrolled or pending enrolment)

In 2020–2021, the multiple-choice questions of the second part of the self-assessment test were randomly chosen from a previously prepared database of B1–B2 level questions, which were then divided into separate categories with three to five questions each. The number of questions for each area was based on the authors' expectations of the difficulty the students would have with each category and the degree of variety in content for each area. Therefore, there were fewer questions for categories that were assumed to be easier for students and hence less likely to be covered during the supplementary lessons and more questions for areas that were often perceived as difficult by students or revealed, in previous years, to lead to many mistakes.

3 Computer-Based Self-Assessment as a Customised Tool...

Table 3.1 Division of 50 multiple-choice questions for the 2020–2021 self-assessment test

Category	No. of questions per category
Conditionals	4
Definitions and examples of word categories	3
Future verb tenses	3
Conversational interactions/responses	3
Modal verbs	5
Passive verb tenses	5
Past verb tenses	3
Prepositions	5
Present verb tenses	3
Pronouns	3
Questions	3
Statements	5
Vocabulary	5

Source: Authors' elaboration

The areas that were assessed in the second part of the test are indicated in Table 3.1:

The self-assessment test enabled the supplementary and main course lessons to be better focused on areas where the students realised that they needed more support. Nevertheless, the final exams of 2020–2021 demonstrated that the students had a slightly distorted perception of their level, compared to that shown in the exam, and that they were strong in comprehension but less so in tasks requiring creative production and critical elaboration. As a result, the self-assessment test was adjusted for 2021–2022 to dedicate fewer questions to more 'familiar' areas and more space to questions on areas of potential difficulty. It also introduced students' short answer questions on mixed verbs, to be conjugated within a text to assess production skills within a determined context, rather than isolated questions.

As a result, while the first part of the test remained the same to verify whether there were any relevant differences in the student community composition, the second part was restructured as illustrated in Table 3.2 (the adjusted and new areas are in bold):

In both academic years, the self-assessment test was presented two weeks after the beginning of the authors' main courses to allow students

Table 3.2 Division of 53 multiple-choice and short answer questions for the 2020–2021 self-assessment test

Category	No. of questions per category	Type of question
Conditionals	4	Multiple choice
Definitions and examples of word categories	3	Multiple choice
Future verb tenses	**4**	**Multiple choice**
Conversational interactions/responses	3	Multiple choice
Modal verbs	**3**	**Multiple choice**
Passive verb tenses	**3**	**Multiple choice**
Past verb tenses	3	Multiple choice
Prepositions	**4**	**Multiple choice**
Present verb tenses	3	Multiple choice
Pronouns	3	Multiple choice
Questions	3	Multiple choice
Statements	**4**	**Multiple choice**
Vocabulary	**3**	**Multiple choice**
Mixed verbs text 1	**5**	**Short answer**
Mixed verbs text 2	**5**	**Short answer**

Source: Authors' elaboration

to become familiar with the lesson schedule and the Moodle platform, as well as to provide instructions. Students were instructed to try the self-assessment test in their free time to encourage autonomy in their preparation outside of class and enforce the idea that the self-assessment test would be completely detached from the final exam. Students were encouraged to complete the self-assessment test (which was a prerequisite to accessing the material starting from Unit 2 of the official course) within two weeks to allow the authors to gather the results before the beginning of the basic and supplementary courses. This allowed the authors and their instructors to understand which areas needed more and urgent attention and prioritise those in programming the supplementary and main lessons, instead of proceeding from the simplest to the most difficult areas as had been done in the past, and as is common practice in traditional English language courses in Italian HE.

4   Dataset and Results of 2020–2021 and 2021–2022

After describing the instrument, as well as the reasoning underlying its creation and modification, the following section outlines the results of the self-assessment test in the two years in which it has been implemented thus far (2020–2021 and 2021–2022). The two academic years are considered separately and in chronological order to better describe not only the results but also the reflections on language teaching that they yielded for the authors, as well as the consequent improvements that have been integrated and potential areas that could still greatly benefit from further adjustment. It will be followed by final considerations on the computer-based self-assessment test's remaining limits and its present and potential relevance for the authors' courses and university language teaching in general.

4.1   Results and Considerations in 2020–2021

The data of the three groups (Bank and Finance and Digital Firm, Business Administration A–G, and Business Administration H–Z) were gathered separately from their respective Moodle pages between 21 and 29 September 2020. They were then compared to plan the lessons of both the authors' main courses and the instructors' supplementary and basic courses, starting from the areas in most need of attention. To find these critical areas, the best of the two attempts of all the students who had taken the test during the indicated time period were isolated, and the total points scored in each area were divided by the number of questions for that specific area to calculate the average result of each question within that category.

A ranking, ranging from the area with the fewest points to that in which the students scored the most points, was then created. The results of the tests are presented in Table 3.3, and the five most relevant areas (those where the students scored the least), based on the scored points per question, are in bold:

The results enabled the authors to verify that the areas in need of attention were almost identical among all three groups, regardless of the number and average grade of the attempts, and therefore testified to the student community's needs and levels of competence being substantially consistent. This led to the detection of areas of need that were commonly not focused on in favour of others that were commonly considered more necessary because they are emphasised in textbooks and traditional courses. Moreover, the content of the final exams was partially reviewed to insert specific tasks to assess whether these students had become aware of and worked on the areas in which they experienced the most difficulties when completing the self-assessment test.

At the end of the course, the authors determined it would be possible to further improve and adjust the self-assessment test, although it had already proven to be a valid pilot study, and—as gathered in end-of-year feedback—students appreciated being able to gain awareness of and focus on areas of grammar that they did not suspect could create any difficulties.

4.2   Results and Considerations in 2020–2021

In 2021–2022, the number of hours available for supplementary and basic courses and the increasingly urgent need for students to work on their in-person conversation skills rather than grammar—determined by the social isolation imposed by the COVID pandemic—had resulted in an even more reduced number of hours for grammar lessons outside of the main course. This resulted in the need to use such hours even more carefully and not necessarily associate the 'good' (score of 31–85) and 'very good' (score of 86–100) feedback categories with the obligation to

3 Computer-Based Self-Assessment as a Customised Tool… 75

Table 3.3 Results of the 2020–2021 self-assessment tests (21–29 September 2020)

Bank and Finance and Digital Firm (131 tests, average grade 68.14/100)			Business Administration A–G (90 tests, average grade: 69.32/100)			Business Administration H–Z (210 tests, average grade 67.22/100)		
Points per area	Points per question	Area	Points per area	Points per question	Area	Points per area	Points per question	Area
784	156.8	Prepositions	314	104.67	Future tenses	700	233.33	Future tenses
474	158	Future tenses	552	110.4	Statements	760	253.33	Prepositions
476	158.67	Definitions	332	110.67	Definitions	1226	245.2	Definitions
816	163.2	Statements	358	119.33	Past tenses	1318	263.6	Statements
680	170	Conditionals	598	119.6	Prepositions	818	272.67	Past tenses
510	170	Passives	498	124	Conditionals	1392	278.4	Modal verbs
892	178.4	Modal verbs	636	127.2	Vocabulary	1152	288	Conditionals
930	186	Past tenses	650	130	Modal verbs	1452	290.4	Vocabulary
476	186.67	Present tenses	652	130.4	Passives	1460	292	Passives
934	186.8	Vocabulary	412	137.33	Present tenses	908	302.67	Present tenses
618	206	Questions	418	139.33	Questions	962	320.67	Questions
690	230	Pronouns	434	144.67	Interactions	996	332	Interactions
630	315	Interactions	454	151.33	Pronouns	1040	346.67	Pronouns

Source: Authors' elaboration

attend an extra course, except upon specific request. In light of the results of the previous self-assessment test and of the 2020–2021 exam sessions, the self-assessment test was adjusted in accordance with the changes mentioned in Sect. 3.1, when illustrating the structure and distribution of the questions (fewer questions in less problematic areas and more in those presenting greater difficulty, introduction of two texts requiring short answers to be inserted by correctly conjugating the provided verb). The authors initially also tried to attribute 1 point instead of 2 to two areas (past verb tenses and present verb tenses), but this, in combination with the fact that both categories only presented three questions each, penalised these areas of competence—which the students had generally acquired—excessively. Therefore, the scores were recalculated by attributing 2 points for each question and yielded the results that may be seen in Table 3.4, where the five most relevant areas (those where the students scored lowest), based on the scored points per question, are in bold:

The final results of the 2021–2022 self-assessment test led to significant feedback: with the exception of the Bank and Finance and Digital Firm group, the number of attempts doubled within the same amount of time compared to the previous year, and there were numerous attempts to take the test again, even when the students had achieved a high score that would exonerate them from any extra lessons. This suggests that the students had realised that there were still areas in which they were making mistakes that they had not anticipated and that they wanted to revise before trying the self-assessment test again (with different questions from the Moodle platform's question bank) on their own. Moreover, although the second version of the self-assessment test was more challenging due to the greater number of questions and increased difficulty, the average score of the tests for each group increased, except in the case of the Business Administration H–G group, which was the most numerous and varied in terms of linguistic and cultural background.

The insertion of the two short answer mixed verb texts, which prevented correct answers based on simple guessing or passive recognition, made the test more difficult and resulted in them being present (in one or both versions) in the top five difficult areas of all groups. This highlighted an important need: that of not focusing on verbs within isolated sentences, as often happens in class, but rather of taking any revision on verb

Table 3.4 Results of the 2021–2022 self-assessment tests (20–29 September 2021)

Bank and Finance and Digital Firm (84 tests, average grade 68.96/100)			Business Administration A–G (299 tests, average grade: 69.42/100)			Business Administration H–Z (401 tests, average grade 66.95/100)		
Points per area	Points per question	Area	Points per area	Points per question	Area	Points per area	Points per question	Area
322	80.50	Future tenses	1278	319.50	Future tenses	1872	374.40	SA mixed verbs 1
348	87	Conditionals	1424	356	Statements	1692	423	Future tenses
454	90.80	SA mixed verbs 1	1800	360	SA mixed verbs 2	1896	474	Prepositions
378	94.50	Prepositions	1458	364.50	Prepositions	2410	482	SA mixed verbs 2
418	104.50	Statements	1102	367.33	Definitions	1458	486	Definitions
526	105.20	SA mixed verbs 2	1480	370	Conditionals	1988	497	Statements
320	106.67	Definitions	1118	372.67	Past tenses	1492	497.33	Past tenses
332	110.67	Past tenses	1974	394.80	SA mixed verbs 1	2004	501	Conditionals
338	112.67	Present tenses	1206	402	Passives	1606	535.33	Passives
354	118	Modal verbs	1244	408	Modal verbs	1634	544.67	Vocabulary
354	118	Vocabulary	1234	411.33	Present tenses	1636	545.33	Modal verbs
356	118.67	Passives	1250	416.67	Vocabulary	1684	561.33	Present tenses
392	130.67	Questions	1364	454.67	Questions	1742	580.67	Questions
410	136.67	Interactions	1422	474	Interactions	1862	620.67	Interactions
444	148	Pronouns	1492	497.33	Pronouns	1938	646	Pronouns

Source: Authors' elaboration

tenses a step further by providing a realistic context in which the students pick up clues from the surrounding clauses and sentences and must hence ensure that the conjugations are homogenous. Moreover, the fact that in both years the most mistakes were made in questions on future tenses, conditionals, statements, and prepositions further confirms students' difficulty in elaborating acquired structures within a context that does not clearly indicate which tense is to be used, but which requires such information be gleaned from the surrounding text instead. Further proof of such a finding lies in the fact that the average score of the self-assessment test for all tests in both years is 68.33, which is more than sufficient but leaves much room for improvement, which seems to be based on the ability to pick up subtleties and clues from the information that is given within the text. This is even more significant considering that this linguistic ability is especially necessary in a course based on business communication, where skills such as mediation, negotiation, feedback, and intercultural competence are fundamental.

5   Relevance and Remaining Limitations of the Computer-based Self-Assessment Test

In both academic years, the self-assessment test revealed itself to be of the utmost importance, as it allowed supplementary courses and lessons to be focused on real needs of which the students could become aware through testing themselves without the pressure of feeling 'under exam'. This is especially relevant at a transitional stage of a student's academic career because it gives them feedback on their actual level within a new academic field and a new student community, at a crucial time in which 'it's difficult for individuals to know who they are and difficult to present themselves to others' (Conrad and Openo 2018, p. 157). From an educational perspective, the computer-based self-assessment test entailed a twofold advantage: on the one hand, it enabled the authors and instructors to know and consider each class as a unique student community with its own prior knowledge and needs and not just a standard group, or a recipient of standardised content. On the other hand, to compensate for the limited number of available hours and resources, the self-assessment test indicated in which areas it was necessary to find and provide additional material for students' self-study and review of critical areas. In this manner, the students could work at their own pace and ask the authors for help if they still encountered problems. Moreover, it permitted the official course to determine in which units it was important to focus more on business content, and to what extent such business communication skills needed to be integrated into lesson revisions and applications of grammar rules.

Like the students, the self-assessment test did well but can still improve: one limit consisted of the analysed data being limited to a very brief period before the beginning of the courses. A comparison with another administration of the test after the course and before the final exams could help understand if and how much the courses—as redesigned after the self-assessment results—have helped in improving on those areas in a short-term period. Another limit consists of the absence of other potential critical areas that are briefly covered in the official course but should be included in the computer-based test (e.g. reported speech, direct/indirect questions, and relative clauses). The next version of the self-assessment test could therefore substitute high-scoring areas, such as pronouns, past tenses, and present tenses (especially since verb tenses are already part of the mixed verbs short answer texts) with these. This could bring the number of questions to 55, which is still feasible in an hour, given that most of the test is made up of multiple-choice questions. More short answer questions in substitution of multiple-choice questions for areas such as passives and modal verbs could also be useful to further verify conjugation and spelling skills.

6 Conclusions

The theoretical considerations and implementation of the self-assessment test have demonstrated that computer-based self-assessment can be a starting point for teachers in course design and not just a final evaluation tool. By providing reliable data on students' preparation, it also enables more conscious and focused training, self-study, and the correct choice of extra material for students who prefer to improve their English autonomously. It could also allow students to verify their level at the end of the course and their self-study period. Such preparation encourages collaboration with teachers, and thus makes students accountable for their own learning while not feeling isolated from the community, especially in the case of foreign and/or non-attending students.

The self-assessment test represents a promising pilot study that could and will be improved based on upcoming exam sessions. In its current form, it has already proven to be productive in deconstructing and reconceiving *ad hoc* course modules and represents a starting point and parameter to compare students of subsequent years to test whether their initial level of preparation was solely due to the COVID-19 emergency or whether it also stemmed from limitations in traditional face-to-face courses and the 'teaching unit' model. On a broader level, the input deriving from these self-assessment tests could also be used to prepare and improve other language courses provided by institutions that are affiliated with course degrees, such as university language and cultural centres. Moreover, in view of the growing number of collaborations between universities and secondary schools, the data could be used to inform teachers in secondary schools of areas where high school students still struggle after years of learning English, thus enabling them to favour these areas over redundant revisions of well-known—and therefore less-stimulating—rules and tenses. This will be especially important in the current context, where students are still recovering from and adapting to the instability and forced changes that have been implemented due to the COVID pandemic in language teaching and learning (King et al. 2021).

Notes

1. The university in question is located in a north-western Italian region. It is middle-sized (eight departments, four areas—Medicine, Engineering, Laws, and Economics—and 15,000 students), with a strong focus on internationalisation. Five out of 17 MScs are taught in English, courses in

EFL, ESP, and EAP are provided in 24 bachelor degree programmes, 17 master degree programmes, 43 schools of specialisation, and 9 PhD programmes, and it currently has 270 agreements with European and non-European universities for Erasmus programmes, dual degrees, research projects, and other international initiatives.
2. In the corporate world, the tendency is to programme short, job-specific language courses with an emphasis on certain skills; in the academic world, on the contrary, short courses are only designed as intensive, pre-sessional, or even in-sessional seminars, the emphasis being on helping students to cope with their future studies or professions. As a result, the two contexts approach final assessment procedures differently. In many business situations, for example, tests may be inappropriate and only take place on demand, whereas, as above-mentioned, in HE they must take place to provide graded outcomes.
3. OFA (*Obblighi Formativi Aggiuntivi*) is an Italian acronym that stands for 'Additional Learning Requirements'. Before enrolling in many universities, students must sit an exam that verifies whether they have already achieved a basic level of knowledge and competence in a number of subject areas. Those who do not show to have already reached this level are assigned an 'OFA deficit', meaning that they must study for a later make-up exam to fulfil the OFA before being able to take the corresponding official exam. The OFA in English was abolished in the Department of Economics and Management in 2021–2022.

References

Center for Advanced Research on Language Acquisition (CARLA). 2022. Overview of error analysis. https://carla.umn.edu/learnerlanguage/intro.html#:~:text=Learner%20language%20can%20be%20described,quickly%20and%20with%20few%20pauses. Accessed 10 June 2022.
Cocea, M. 2006. Assessment of motivation in online learning environments. In *AH 2006. LNCS*, ed. V.P. Wade et al., vol. 4018, 414–418. Heidelberg: Springer.
Conrad, D., and J. Openo. 2018. *Assessment strategies for online learning: Engagement and authenticity*. Athabasca: Athabasca University Press.
Corder, Pit S. 1971. Describing the learner's language. *Interdisciplinary Approaches to Language, CILT Reports and Papers* 6: 57–64.

———. 1981. *Introducing applied linguistics*. London: Penguin.

Doerr, R.B. 2023. *Academic style proofreading: An introduction*. Oxford: Peter Lang Group AG.

East, M. 2022. *Mediating innovation through language teacher education*. Cambridge: Cambridge University Press.

Fenwick, T.J., and J. Parsons. 2009. *The art of evaluation: A resource for educators and trainers*. 2nd ed. Toronto, ON: Thompson Educational Publishing.

Freddi, G. 1985. Insegnare per unità didattiche. *Lingue e Civiltà* 13: 7–14.

Gautam, S., and M.B. Rosson. 2021. Exploring feelings of student community across a geographically distributed university. *Proceedings of the ACM on human–computer interaction* 5(CSCW1), 93: 1–16. https://doi.org/10.1145/3449167.

James, C. 1998. *Errors in language learning and use: Exploring error analysis*. London and New York: Routledge.

King, R.C., et al. 2021. *Online world language instruction training and assessment: An ecological approach*. Washington, DC: Georgetown University Press.

Knowles, E., and D. Kerkman. 2007. An investigation of students' attitude and motivation toward online learning. *Student Motivation* 2: 70–80.

Lado, R. 1961. *Language testing*. London: Longman.

———. 1964. *Language testing: A scientific approach*. New York: McGraw-Hill.

Marshall, B. 2011. *Testing English: Formative and summative approaches to English assessment*. New York and London: Continuum International Publishing Group.

Nickel, G., and D. Nehls, eds. 1982. *Error analysis, contrastive linguistics and second language learning*. Heidelberg: J. Groos Verlag.

Porcelli, G. 1992. *Educazione linguistica e valutazione*. Padova: Liviana.

Prati, G., et al. 2018. The influence of school sense of community on students' well-being: A multilevel analysis. *Journal of Community Psychology* 46 (7): 917–924. https://doi.org/10.1002/jcop.21982.

Richards, J. C. 1970. *A non-contrastive approach to error analysis*. TESOL Convention (San Francisco). https://files.eric.ed.gov/fulltext/ED037721.pdf. Accessed 12 June 2022.

Richards, J.C. 1984. *Error analysis: Perspectives on second language acquisition*. London: Routledge.

Richards, J.C., and R. Schmidt. 2010. *Longman dictionary of language teaching and applied linguistics*. 4th ed. Harlow: Pearson Longman.

Ringbom, H. 2010. Error analysis. In *Pragmatics in practice (handbook of pragmatics highlights 9)*, ed. J.O. Östman and J. Verschueren, 149–152. Amsterdam: John Benjamins.

Titone, R. 1974. *Methodology of research in language teaching. An elementary introduction*. Bergamo: Minerva Italica.

Zanola, A. 2023. *La lingua inglese per la comunicazione scientifica e professionale*. Rome: Carocci Editore.

Part II

Practices in the Virtual Classroom

4

Revisiting the Language Lab in the Age of Online Learning: Videoconferencing, Teacher Feedback, and Learner Self-Correction

Tobias Heinrich

1 Introduction

The conventional foreign language laboratory has been out of fashion for some time now. Yet, from the 1950s until the widespread introduction of the personal computer in the 1980s, language labs were considered state-of-the-art technology in both schools and universities. In many ways, the emergence of the language lab in post-war education reminds us of current trends in online language education. Similar to contemporary approaches to online (and/or emergency remote) learning discussed in this volume, the language lab's success was both the result of a global crisis and of technological innovation.

The sharp increase in the demand for proficient foreign language speakers during and after World War II (WWII) led the US armed forces to introduce specialised programmes for staff training (Roby 2004, pp. 524–525). In contrast to the traditional grammar-translation method

---

T. Heinrich (✉)
University of Kent, Canterbury, UK
e-mail: T.Heinrich@kent.ac.uk

and its emphasis on written texts (Richards and Rodgers 2014, p. 58), the Army focused on its staff's ability to understand and speak foreign languages. The other decisive factor that revolutionised language learning after WWII was the invention of the magnetic tape, as well as resulting improvements in the quality of sound recordings, and the ways in which they could be edited (Roby 2004, p. 525). Therefore, listening and speaking not only gained importance from a pedagogical perspective, but technology also provided the tools for those skills to take centre stage in the language classroom.

The typical layout of a 1960s language lab would see the learners placed in individual booths or cubicles equipped with a tape recorder, a microphone, and a headset. The learners' cubicles were mostly arranged in rows, with a teacher's console facing them (Hayes 1963, pp. 2–4). Prerecorded material could be played centrally from the teacher's console or individually by each learner. This arrangement allowed learners to listen to the recordings repeatedly and in their own time, but also to record themselves in response to the presented material. Teachers could use their consoles to listen in while learners speak, to give feedback, and to interact with them individually. In contrast to the traditional classroom set-up, the language lab was geared towards individuality and simultaneity. According to the advocates of the language lab, the fact that learners interacted with technology rather than with each other would allow them to practise more intensely and progress faster (Hayes 1963, p. 16).

Later methodologies rejected the language lab's pedagogical individualism and opted for settings that encouraged cooperation and group work. With the dawn of more communicative approaches from the 1970s onwards, the popularity of technology in language teaching and, in particular, the use of language labs dropped significantly. These were now perceived to be more of a hindrance than a facilitator of linguistic interaction. However, initially due to the COVID-19 emergency, technology has yet again taken centre stage in pedagogical debates on foreign language teaching. Both public and private providers of language tuition were forced to develop remote alternatives during the COVID-19 pandemic, and even after the return to face-to-face teaching, many institutions chose to continue to teach some classes online through videoconferencing software like Skype, Zoom or Microsoft Teams alongside their more conventional offer.

Before proceeding, a clarification of the terminology employed in this chapter is needed. As Fiorucci explains in the Introduction, terms like 'online' and 'distance learning' are not used interchangeably in this volume, and they should not be confused. There are, in fact, substantial differences between the two—plus, because of pandemic-induced social restrictions, the definition of Emergency Remote Teaching (ERT; previously clarified by Fiorucci and Giacosa) was coined, throwing another expression into the mix. In the present chapter, I will not make reference to 'distance learning', in that with this term we normally refer to a course that traditionally involves self-study and education 'by correspondence'. In distance learning, materials and resources are provided to students via online sharing platforms (or, in the past, also via mail); there is no face-to-face component and little to no interaction between learners and teachers. Students will complete the given tasks and assessments remotely, as per the course schedule. In ERT, we have seen in previous chapters of this volume, the pivot to online delivery of content previously delivered face to face is understood as unplanned, and it is not necessarily underpinned by pedagogical notions of online learning. In this chapter, our focus is on online rather than distance or emergency remote education. The described practices are the result of theory-informed planning and setting up of online resources and teaching strategies, which occurred in the summer of 2020, before the 2020–2021 academic year started. The distinction between emergency remote and online education was certainly blurry in 2020–2021 due to the suddenness of the pivot to online. Yet, what this chapter will describe is a series of activities that were delivered in 2020–2021, whose underpinning principles were drawn from theories on the use of the language lab and comparable modern technologies as tools for language learning—more specifically, for formative assessment and feedback in the development of speaking and listening skills. In particular, the chapter will explore how videoconferencing software allows learners to interact with each other in a virtual classroom setting while also enabling them at a later stage to analyse and correct their language production, just as the language lab did. It will then demonstrate how some of the features of online language teaching can broaden teachers' pedagogical toolbox within the sphere of formative feedback that, though created as a result of social distancing rules, can easily be transported into any teaching set-up.

The scope of the present study is limited. The three scenarios presented are only meant to furnish practical examples of the theoretical formulations provided in the first part of the chapter. They were not designed, and were not intended, to be used as a case study involving an analysis of ensuing data collection. Further research is thus needed to consolidate the theoretical points made in this chapter and take its underpinning principles further. The present work is meant to elicit discussion on, and introduce the potential of, utilising videoconferencing as a tool for formative feedback, and more effective community building, within the context of online language training activities.

2 The Language Lab

The technologies of the language lab were theoretically underpinned by the emerging audiolingual method, prioritising spoken over written language, perceiving language learning primarily as habit formation, and, therefore, emphasising drill exercises and pattern formation as the main classroom activities (Richards and Rodgers 2014, pp. 58–77). Audiolingual teaching relied heavily on the behaviourist assumption that learners' language production should take place in response to a linguistic stimulus and that the subsequent teacher feedback would serve to reinforce correct utterances or suppress the production of incorrect responses (pp. 63–64). Many of the learning activities consisted of repetition and memorisation of prefabricated dialogues (Roby 2004, p. 525). Therefore, the language lab provided the ideal means to put the audiolingual method into practice, as it allowed for the presentation of a wide variety of recorded stimuli with simultaneous and individual learner response. The teacher's role was primarily to monitor the learners' language production and to provide correcting assessment and feedback.

As behaviourist positions were brought into question by novel developments in linguistics and foreign language pedagogics, the popularity of the audiolingual method and the technologies of the language lab began to fade during the 1970s (Roby 2004, p. 72). In many schools and universities, language labs became little more than 'electronic graveyards' (Turner 1969, p. 1) until some of them were turned into multimedia self-study environments. This was made possible by the introduction of audio cassettes, VHS recorders, and, finally, the personal computer (Roby 2004, p. 528). Yet still, the language lab carries a prevailing negative legacy:

> Despite [...] their undoubted contribution to the development of language teaching and learning, the term 'lab' nowadays also triggers memories about a place where students disappear behind technology, separated from each other, delving head first into the electronic environment and fighting a lone battle with linguistic requests from mysterious authorities. (Bräuer 2001, p. 185)

The perception that technology-enhanced language learning can be counterproductive due to the risk of isolating the individual learner and denying the benefits of group-based learning environments has been shared by recent studies on the use of technologies for remote learning during the pandemic (e.g. Dewaele et al. 2022, p. 8). Besides the broader range of technologies employed in language laboratories, or 'multimedia learning centers' (Roby 2004, p. 528), as many of them were referred to later on, practitioners have attempted to break away from the isolated position that the conventional set-up placed learners. In light of the communicative approach and its functional theory of language (Richards and Rodgers 2014, p. 87), which has largely replaced the audiolingual method and, to a certain extent, still dominates language teaching today, suggestions have been made by which technological equipment of the language laboratory could be used to allow for more meaningful interaction between learners—for instance, within the context of formative assessment. MacDonald (2011), for example, proposes a range of activities for what she calls the 'Virtual Language Lab', from group translations via document sharing (see Pérez-Nieto's chapter on interactive discussion boards in this volume) to the use of podcasts and social media for language learning. Here, the concept of the language lab serves as an umbrella term for the incorporation of digital communication technology into the language classroom. While the suggested activities are only loosely connected to the repetitive pattern drills of the olden days, similar to the concept of the conventional language laboratory, MacDonald envisages an environment where teachers step back and students take control of their own learning process: 'As opposed to the days when we put a textbook in an instructor's hands and said, "Go teach this," now the onus will be on the instructor to navigate their students through the myriad possibilities for the achievement of methodological goals and student learning objectives' (p. 155). Another way in which MacDonald's ideas mirror the argument of earlier advocates of the language lab is that technology allows individual learners to progress at their own pace and in their individual learning styles (p. 154). It enables a more tailor-made experience in contrast to the homogenising tendencies of a conventional classroom setting.

In contrast to MacDonald's focus on digital technology, Guttridge (2002) proposes a variety of activities that make use of the traditional language lab's equipment (i.e. individual cubicles and a teacher console). Guttridge suggests, for instance, that learners could listen to each other's recordings in order to extract specific information or they could reconstruct together a larger text that is chopped up into pieces and provided to them in their individual cubicles. Guttridge, therefore, turns the language lab's apparent weak point, that is the relative isolation of the learners in their workstations, into an opportunity for communication between them during activities and formative assessment. While the linguistic stimuli are presented individually in the first place, collaboration is then required to solve the tasks.

3 Videoconferencing and Corrective Feedback

Even though approaches like MacDonald's and Guttridge's were conceived before the COVID-19 pandemic, they surface potential for online learning scenarios, in particular when taking into account the opportunities that videoconferencing software provide for monitoring progress in education. The history of videotelephony goes back to the 1920s as a series of more and less successful attempts to establish the technology for the mass consumer market (Schnaars and Wymbs 2004).

While the internet and smartphones had already made videoconferencing widely available in recent decades, it was the global pandemic of 2020 that made videoconferences part of everyday life for many people in the Western world and beyond. During periods of lockdown, a large amount of private and professional socialising was carried out via online communication (Li et al. 2022). Empirical studies have shown that even after the lifting of restrictions, a lot of social interaction, in particular for work and education, has remained online (p. 8). In terms of communication technology, we are thus finding ourselves in a situation not too dissimilar from the post-war era, the heyday of the language lab. Technological innovations have opened up new possibilities for studying and learning, and a global crisis has accelerated their adoption in educational institutions.

Since digital videoconferencing has proven to be more than just a short-lived replacement for face-to-face social interaction, plenty of studies have been conducted to explore its benefits for language learning. Lenkaitis (2020), for instance, in her study of synchronous computer-mediated communication in Spanish L2 education at a US university, highlights how platforms like Zoom can be a valuable tool to boost learner autonomy. Lay and Giblett (2020), reporting on practices in the context of teaching German as L2 within ERT at the University of Sydney, praise the ability to facilitate group work through breakout rooms. They also focus on the opportunity for learners and instructors to synchronously interact with each other through spoken and written language (text chat)—these functionalities, as Fiorucci et al. illustrate in their chapter in this volume, contribute to developing a learning community by aiding communications and making students and teachers quickly accessible to each other. Schneider (2020) summarises the changes made to provision of learning materials at the University of Leeds' Language Centre following the COVID-19 emergency. In so doing, he demonstrates how videoconferencing makes it possible to mix formal and informal, teacher- and student-led learning environments. In this respect, videoconferencing can facilitate innovation in language teaching, aiding in the establishment of a language-learning community in higher education, be it within online or blended learning formats.

Similar to the tape-recording technology that enabled the development of the post-war language lab, videoconferencing has already had a significant impact on computer-assisted ways of teaching and learning languages. Just like the language lab, most videoconferencing technology allows users to record their interactions. During the pandemic, recording events or larger meetings became common practice, for example, when these were subsequently made available for asynchronous viewing by the public or a selected audience. However, there is only scarce research on the use of recording videoconferences as a device for learning and teaching languages. Rather than on recording of conversations or whole classroom sequences, which can be easily done using platforms like Zoom, Microsoft Teams, or Google Meet, most scholarship has so far focused on recorded video or audio presentations. The use of technology by learners to record themselves while speaking in a foreign language is often regarded as a legitimate compensation for the lack of individual speaking time in class or the lack of opportunities to engage with native speakers in the target language. Rojas and Arteaga (2019) explore English as a foreign language (EFL) students' perceptions on the use of self-recording videos (SRV) to develop speaking skills at two Ecuadorian universities. According to them, learners feel that recording videos in the target language can help them to both improve their pronunciation and, generally, become more confident in speaking (p. 65). Manzini, in her chapter in this volume, demonstrates a link between improved pronunciation through the use of recording platforms and improved self-confidence in speaking. Similarly, Hsu (2016) has shown that regular voice blogging by students of English as a foreign language (the study was conducted in Taiwan) can improve the complexity of their spoken output. Tecedor and Campos-Dintrans (2019) compared teaching methods in Spanish as L2 at a US university, involving voice recording and videoconferencing on the one hand and conventional face-to-face classroom settings on the other. They found that the use of voice recording tasks produces similar learning results to face-to-face interaction and can therefore be regarded as a suitable alternative, while the use of videoconferencing produced learning results that were sometimes even superior to the conventional setting.

However, the study did not explore the potential of combining recording and videoconferencing technologies.

In post-war language labs, teachers monitoring learners' spoken production and the option for learners to record themselves and, therefore, later listen to these recordings and correct what they had said was an integral part of the learning set-up. When it comes to corrective feedback in formative assessments, most research has focused on immediate rather than delayed feedback (Bygate 2009, p. 425). Studies that compare the two come to differing results but generally conclude that both forms of feedback are effective (Quinn 2014; Arroyo and Yilmaz 2018; Fu and Li 2020). Champions of delayed feedback argue that immediate corrections by the teacher interrupt the learners' communicative flow and, therefore, run counter to the goals of communicative language teaching (Hunter 2012). At the same time, communicative approaches have struggled to develop strategies that achieve the same levels of accuracy and complexity as more grammar-focused methods (Hunter 2012). Delayed feedback can help to solve this dilemma, as it allows learners the opportunity to first speak freely and uninterruptedly in a communicative setting and then to look at questions of lexical, grammatical, and pragmatical correctness separately.

The linguist and EFL teacher James Hunter has recently developed a free web-based platform (comsem.net) that language teachers can use to record and correct mistakes that occur during spoken classroom activities and subsequently provide learners with appropriate feedback or exercises (Hunter 2021). In a conventional face-to-face set-up, the challenge remains for teachers to notice and document errors while, at the same time, continuing to follow what learners are saying. This becomes even more difficult if speaking activities are conducted as group work and, therefore, several conversations are taking place simultaneously. This is where the recording functionality of videoconferencing can be a game changer, as it allows both teachers and learners to record what is being said and rewatch the conversations at a later stage. As most platforms also allow breakout rooms or similar subdivisions of a videoconferencing session to be recorded, even simultaneous conversations can now be analysed appropriately and in depth. Recording spoken classroom interaction, rather than simply basing corrective feedback on teachers' notes, might also help to tackle some of the issues that have been highlighted with regard to delayed feedback. Fu and Li (2020), for example, argue that if corrections are provided too long after the learner's utterance and the instruction on which it was based, flawed structures might become internalised and feedback might be perceived as less relevant (p. 22). While this is valid to some extent, the use of video recordings allows learners to easily and directly recall the mistake itself and its communicative context by watching their performance, which would also remind them of any specific instructions that were given. Especially in conjunction with computer-mediated tools to track and repair mistakes, the option to record individual conversations or whole lessons when delivered online might be able to combine the benefits of both immediate and delayed corrective feedback.

4 Self-Correction

While teacher monitoring was an important part of the conventional language lab's set-up, it also provided the opportunity for learner self-correction. With the limited technological resource of the tape recorder, this usually meant comparing their own spoken utterances with those of the recorded native speakers. In contrast, videoconferencing allows for a much broader range of teaching and learning strategies that aim to motivate learners to engage with their own mistakes (one such example is provided in this volume by Manzini, who in her chapter analyses the use of Vocaroo for improving pronunciation). From a cognitive perspective, learners need to be able to differentiate between their own language production and the target language's norms. In other words, they need to be able to recognise both errors and mistakes in order to grow their competence in the second language. This ability is commonly referred to as 'noticing' (see Schmidt 1990; Robinson 1995; Schmidt 2001). Studies have shown that most learners are able to improve their spoken output in the target language if they are given enough time to notice and correct (self-repair) their mistakes (Shehadeh 2001). Unfortunately, this is rarely the case in conventional classroom settings, where the aim is usually to give as many learners as possible the opportunity to speak, frequently to the detriment of formative feedback. Therefore, relatively little time is given for the individual learner to reflect and, where necessary, to correct themselves. Scholars have used recording technology for learners to analyse (and, often, also to transcribe) their spoken language production and to correct themselves (e.g. Stillwell et al. 2010; McCormick and Vercellotti 2013). While there appears to be a lack of studies that have analysed the recording function of videoconferencing software for these purposes, the option to record dialogues and conversations has at least theoretically been mentioned (Stillwell et al. 2010, p. 453). The default set-up for research into self-correction and self-repair on the basis of recorded oral production is usually a spontaneous or semi-spontaneous (based on notes) presentation that learners give on a certain topic. The speech is recorded, and subsequently learners are asked either to transcribe what they have said, correct themselves, and then repeat the speech or to do the speech again right after listening to their recording, without time set aside for formalised self-correction. Videoconferencing software makes it easier than ever to record a wide variety of spoken language production involving one or multiple learners. In addition, there is a wide variety of easy-to-use online platforms that can create automated transcriptions, often in various languages, or even subtitles for video recordings (e.g. otter.ai, descript.com, veed.io). Basic use is often free, but it is frequently limited to shorter recordings of about 10 minutes. Depending on the teacher's preference and the time available, learners can be asked to produce their own transcriptions of the recording as a whole or of specific passages (e.g. only those where they suspect an error). Alternatively, they can base their self-correction on automated transcripts created by platforms like the ones mentioned above. When used by teachers, automated transcripts can also be helpful for the implementation of tools like comsem.net, which can support formative feedback through tracking and subsequent repairing of mistakes.

5 Working with Recorded Videoconferences: Three Sample Scenarios

In this part of the chapter, I will outline three scenarios that put some of the technologies previously discussed into practice. The options described are by no means exhaustive. Rather, they are intended to illustrate some of the possibilities that recording videoconferences offers as a learning and teaching device. These scenarios were tried out for the first time during Emergency Remote Teaching and subsequently embedded in regular teaching practices after the return to face-to-face teaching, following positive students' feedback and outcomes.

The videoconferencing sessions themselves can be part of a regular online language class within a module delivered in blended form, or they can also be set as homework and/or independent study after a face-to-face learning experience. As mentioned in the Introduction, these activities were devised in the summer of 2020 to be delivered online in 2020–2021. The goal was manifold. First, I intended to tackle issues with motivation and engagement, which had become apparent worldwide with the move to ERT. As Giacosa explains in her chapter, one way of addressing the issue is through continuous assessment, which research before and during the pandemic has identified as a possibility to make the student's learning experience more meaningful, hence stimulating both motivation and engagement. In my planning, I accordingly focused on activities for formative assessment, with a strong emphasis on formative feedback. Secondly, I planned the delivery of feedback with a view of stimulating a sense of a learning community to tackle the apparent issues that were being caused worldwide by social isolation. To achieve this, I have not only planned group work as the core element of the formative activities, but I have also devised feedback delivery in a way that would involve the whole class in the spotting and correcting of mistakes, both individually and as a group-based activity.

Scenario 1: Student-Led Self-Correction
In this scenario, students speak to each other while their conversation is recorded. They then watch the recording and analyse their mistakes if

they find any. Optionally, they can then repeat the conversation in order to implement their learning. This exercise can be done at virtually any level and with a wide range of conversation tasks: from basic communicative dialogues between two learners (e.g. ordering in a restaurant or asking for directions) to more complex and group-based conversations on challenging topics. The length of the conversation can range from only a couple of minutes to more than an hour. Keep in mind, however, that learners will have to rewatch their recordings, perhaps even several times. For practical purposes, it can therefore be helpful to limit the length of conversations to 20 minutes, which is what I opted for based on previous experience with end-of-year summative oral exams.

In preparation for this chapter, this scenario was tried with two groups of German language students during their second and fourth years of study, at levels B2 and C1 of the Common European Framework of Reference for Languages (CEFR), respectively. The students were made aware of being part of a trial. For one of the conversations, students in the C1 group were asked, first, to introduce their favourite piece of art. Then, they were instructed to have a conversation with their peers about what it is that they liked specifically about them. Students at a B2 level were asked to engage in a dialogue about one or more of the following topics: inquiring about a room in a shared flat, talking about summer plans, and cultural stereotypes (they could cover all the topics or just one, depending on the time they would dedicate to each).

These topics were introduced during online teaching sessions via Zoom. Students were then randomly assigned to breakout rooms of two to four students each, and they were given between 10 and 20 minutes for their conversations. After the conversations had finished, there was a chance to ask questions or clarify vocabulary. As homework, students were instructed to watch their recordings and to take notes of any issues they spotted in their own speech, regardless of whether these concerned the use of vocabulary, grammar, or pronunciation. Students were also asked to transcribe at least three and a maximum of ten instances where they believed they recognised a mistake and to offer a corrected version. During the next online class, students repeated their conversations in the same groups and with the same tasks.

Students in this scenario showed remarkable results in the ability to notice mistakes, and the majority of their self-corrections amounted to significantly improved versions. The repeated conversations were not systematically compared with the original ones, but students were invited to do so in their own time. Then, through teacher-led formative feedback, students invariably reported an increase in self-confidence and perceived fluency after the second attempt.

Scenario 2: Teacher Feedback
As discussed earlier in this chapter, the recording function of most videoconferencing platforms can not only give learners the opportunity to analyse and correct their own mistakes. It also gives teachers opportunities to significantly improve the feedback they provide, be it formative or summative. This option is informed by the 'try again' method, also known as 'repeat-until-correct' feedback, where formative feedback advises learners of their incorrect responses, and more attempts are allowed to discover the correct answer (Shute 2008). In the following scenario, the teacher takes a more central role. The tasks can be similar to the ones in the first scenario, or slightly shorter, and they need to be more oriented towards a specific communicative goal in order to allow for a greater focus, and better feedback, when analysing the recordings.

This scenario was tried with a group of second-year German language students in preparation for their year abroad. Tasks therefore included bank appointments, job interviews, and various conversations around studying at a foreign university. In this scenario, the teacher is the first to view and listen to the recorded videos. They will then use comsem.net to record students' mistakes (and errors) and give the learners the opportunity to correct themselves. As recording all inaccuracies would often prove too time-consuming, the focus can be on specific areas of vocabulary, grammar, or pronunciation. Mistakes can be recorded on comsem.net with the option to provide a correction right away or to let students find the correct forms themselves following the 'try again' method. The context/vocab field in the comsem worksheet can be used to record the time stamp in the original video, thereby allowing students easy access to the passage of the recorded conversation during which the mistake occurred. Comsem provides the option for students to re-record the faulty expression and for teachers to approve or reject the corrected version. Depending on teachers' and learners' preferences, self-correction can stop at this point or, similar to the first scenario, the whole conversation can be re-recorded once all—or the most salient—individual mistakes have been identified by the students.

As emerged from the formative feedback to this scenario (one-to-one with the teacher), students particularly appreciated the attention given to the details of their language production. When having to find the correct forms themselves and re-record the respective passages, some students have noted that a lot of time and effort is needed for this activity. Therefore, it is important that topics chosen are sufficiently relevant and practice-related in order to sustain their motivation and, therefore, their engagement: the lesson content, that is, needs to be meaningful (Betoncu et al. 2021, p. 1).

Scenario 3: Group Feedback
The third and final scenarios adopt the group setting of the videoconference whilst also catering for learners' self-correction. Let us take a brief detour to consider the theoretical arguments that have determined this choice of feedback. Although there is extensive literature on feedback for individual performance (London 2003), the role played by feedback in groups to the group as a whole, or to individual members, has not been studied in enough depth (Barr and Conlon 1994; Kozlowski and Klein 2000; Bunderson and Sutcliffe 2003; London and Sessa 2006). Yet, according to London and Sessa, 'groups that set goals and receive feedback on their goals are more likely to improve their performance than groups that do not' (2006, p. 306). Considering the wide use of group work in the modern language classroom, this is an area of formative assessment and feedback practices that deserves more attention.

All previously mentioned tasks can be used here, but it is preferable if the speaking time of the individual learners is roughly equal. This scenario has been tried with fourth-year German students, where group debates on various topics were recorded. Learners would then watch their recordings together. This can be done face to face or online, via screen share or utilising a platform such as SpatialChat—this is a collaborative online workspace which, among other functions, allows users to play videos within the virtual environment, but directly from their computers (hence, with the obvious advantages for users of being able to adjust the volume, play the video at a better quality than via screenshare, etc.). While students watch the recording, their task is to prepare themselves to repeat the conversation, but the second time around learners are swapping roles. Each one will take the role of another member of the group, repeating and improving their speech. It is therefore particularly important for learners to actively try and remember what is being said, but without blindly imitating their predecessors' words and, therefore, risking the repetition of mistakes. While watching the video, learners are encouraged to talk about flaws in the speech that they notice via chat and to consequently help the group as a whole to improve. In this final scenario, learners have to be particularly aware of everyone else who is involved in the conversation, the appropriateness of what is being said, and also the dynamic of the group. While the previous two scenarios focused mainly on the individual learner and their ability to self-correct, here the process of noticing and repairing is genuinely a collective one. Then, as London and Sessa claim, group learning is interwoven with individual learning. Individual group members, and the group of which they are members, are learning simultaneously and continuously. Hence, individual members will influence the groups to which they belong in the learning process. At the same time, the groups—responding to outside influence as applied, for instance, by the teacher—will have an effect on the individual learners' motivation and engagement (2006, pp. 316–317). When planning activities that will be concluded by group feedback of this kind, therefore, it is important to consider the dynamics at play.

Case in point, although students appreciated the opportunity to work together throughout the process and to use their collective knowledge, they revealed other issues with the group feedback set-up that will determine a change in the layout in future applications of this scenario. When watching and discussing the recording together, some students found it challenging to work with peers whose ability in the target language they perceived as stronger than their own. Therefore, and depending on the specific group of learners, teachers might want to consider this part of the activity optional, or—as has been my choice in subsequent use of this scenario—they can implement strategies to minimise its potential for competitiveness and comparison. Drawing on the notion that 'felt equity is important to feedback in a group context' (London and Sessa 2006, p. 315), it is crucial to set up group feedback in a way that students do not feel the continuous target of corrections, whilst others perceive that, in comparison, not much effort is needed on their part as they are already performing above the group average. To attain feedback equity, for instance, the teacher could ask students to spot only a fixed number of mistakes in their classmate's speech, which would provide balanced feedback across the cohort. In order to stimulate more positive responses to the feedback and ensuing reflections, it would also be very important to spot an equivalent, or in any case, fixed, number of instances where their classmates deserve praise: 'Individuals are more likely to perceive accurately and accept positive than negative feedback' (London and Sessa 2006, p. 14). To achieve balance and elicit a positive response from students, the teacher needs to be aware of what areas of strength and weakness their students tend to present when speaking. For instance, an online test such as the one described by Doerr and Zanola in Chap. 3, but geared towards speaking skills, could proceed with the videoconferencing exercise. The teacher would then ask students to assess their performance by focusing on certain areas only, which they will have identified through correction of the online test.

6 Conclusions

Taking inspiration from the post-war language laboratory and its focus on listening and speaking on error-analysis and self-correction, this chapter has explored the potential of videoconferencing platforms within contemporary language learning. It has done so by focusing specifically on the recording option for self-directed, teacher-led, and group feedback.

At the level of improving language skills and preparing for summative assessments, video recordings allow learners to improve their ability to notice discrepancies between their own and the standards of the target language. Although I provided a specific example based on my own virtual classroom experience, many more layouts can be adopted (within or outside of classroom activities), which would allow students to record their speaking performance. For instance, Dzakiah et al.'s study (2020) demonstrated that students' performance, with specific regard to fluency and comprehension, was improved by the use of smartphone video recording. Students had been tasked to record videos by themselves, speaking about a number of given topics. The emphasis here is on the learner's agency, as students control the device they use and they also know it very well, in line with MacDonald's earlier suggestions (2011). Lestari (2019) claims that video blogging is also an effective way to foster speaking skills: according to the study, this type of activity allows students to advance their language skills in terms of vocabulary, accent, pronunciation, and culture knowledge.

Whatever the chosen layout, if implemented within a predominantly face-to-face or blended setting, then activities can be either individual or in group or both. If the learning context is predominantly online, however, group work remains the preferred method. The risk is, otherwise, to incur in what was the weakness of the language lab as traditionally conceived, namely, student's isolation and subsequent lack of a sense of learning community. Although the present work has obvious limitations in terms of the size and scope of the involved participants and activities, relevant research, mentioned throughout the present volume, does point to the necessity to incorporate activities in educational settings, which favour and stimulate communication among learners both online and face to face. This is necessary to engender a sense of a consistent—or 'reliable', to put it in Fiorucci et al.'s words—learning community. This is in turn crucial to both motivation and engagement.

For teachers, the recording and analysing of videoconferences provide a chance to engage with learners' oral language production more deeply and to support them with better and more comprehensive formative feedback. Following Shute (2008), these activities—or variations of them—enable teachers to focus their feedback on the task and not on the learner: an analysis and evaluation of specific aspects is, in fact, conducted either by the learners themselves or by the group, or—when the feedback is teacher-led—it focuses on pre-established language aspects (e.g. pronunciation and grammar) by identifying specific flaws. A more student-focused rather than task-focused feedback can, however, also be provided. This can occur, for instance, face to face and in delayed form, but more to maintain a rapport between learner and teacher (hence, for the fostering of a learning community) than to deliver additional feedback. The predominance of a task-focused approach to feedback is, in any case, fundamental for making sure that feedback does what it is supposed to, namely, supporting learning by informing students of where their performance stands compared to a specific goal (hence, focusing on both weaknesses and strengths), and what they should do to achieve that goal (Daniels and Daniels 2006). As previously mentioned, research on the effects of group work feedback on individual learners is so far rather scarce. Although it has been argued that the impact of individual feedback may result in more positive relationships among the group members and a more positive attitude towards the L2 (Archer-Kath et al. 1994), the prevalence of group activities in language learning calls for more established practices in the area of group work formative feedback. A systematic combination of individual with group feedback would hence provide students not only with the necessary tools to self-correct, thus improving motivation through increased confidence. It would also improve engagement in class activities through goal-oriented feedback and subsequent reflection on the group's performance. The systematic application of group feedback (always combined with individual feedback) could lead cohorts to 'develop a feedback culture and individuals develop a feedback orientation as a result of their experiences with feedback [...]. In a positive feedback culture, individuals, and by extension groups, [...] are more likely to seek and be receptive to feedback for learning' (London and Sessa 2006, p. 16).

To conclude, when working with video recordings, not only is the act of speaking a group effort, but it can also turn the analysis and the correction of spoken language, and therefore the improvement of a key skill, into a collective endeavour, turning technologies of social distancing into a means of collaborative learning.

References

Archer-Kath, J., et al. 1994. Individual versus group feedback in cooperative groups. *Journal of Social Psychology* 134: 681–694. https://doi.org/10.1080/00224545.1994.9922999.

Arroyo, D.C., and Y. Yilmaz. 2018. An open for replication study: The role of feedback timing in synchronous computer-mediated communication. *Language Learning* 68 (4): 942–972. https://doi.org/10.1111/lang.12300.

Barr, S.H., and E.J. Conlon. 1994. Effects of distribution of feedback in workgroups. *Academy of Management Journal* 37: 641–655.

Betoncu, O., et al. 2021. Designing an effective learning environment for language learning during the COVID-19 pandemic. *Frontiers in Psychology*. https://doi.org/10.3389/fpsyg.2021.752083.

Bräuer, G. 2001. Language learning centres: Bridging the gap between high school and college. In *Pedagogy of language learning in higher education: An introduction*, ed. G. Bräuer, 185–192. Westport, CT; London: Ablex.

Bunderson, J.S., and K.M. Sutcliffe. 2003. Management team learning orientation and business unit performance. *Journal of Applied Psychology* 88 (3): 552–560.

Bygate, M. 2009. Teaching and testing speaking. In *The handbook of language teaching*, ed. M.H. Long and C.J. Doughty, 412–444. Chichester: Wiley-Blackwell.

Daniels, C.D., and J.E. Daniels. 2006. *Performance management*. Atlanta: Performance Management Publications.

Dewaele, J.M., et al. 2022. Is flow possible in the emergency remote teaching foreign language classroom? *Education Sciences* 12 (7): 444. https://doi.org/10.3390/educsci12070444.

Dzakiah, D., et al. 2020. Smartphone video recording as a learning tool to improve Indonesian EFL students speaking performance. *Indonesian EFL Journal* 6 (2): 10.25134/ieflj.v6i2.3384.

Fu, M., and S. Li. 2020. The effects of immediate and delayed corrective feedback on L2 development. *Studies in Second Language Acquisition* 44 (1): 2–34. https://doi.org/10.1017/S0272263120000388.

Guttridge, J. 2002. The language laboratory is useful and fun. *Modern English Teacher* 11 (4): 37–40.

Hayes, A.S. 1963. *Language laboratory facilities: Technical guide for the selection, purchase, use, and maintenance*. Washington, DC: U.S. Department of Health, Education and Welfare.

Hsu, H.-C. 2016. Voice blogging and L2 speaking performance. *Computer Assisted Language Learning* 29 (5): 968–983. https://doi.org/10.1080/09588221.2015.1113185.

Hunter, J. 2012. 'Small talk': Developing fluency, accuracy, and complexity in speaking. *ELT Journal* 66 (1): 30–41. https://doi.org/10.1093/elt/ccq093.

———. 2021. Comsem.net: An online platform for providing and tracking delayed corrective feedback. *WAESOL Educator* 46 (2): 29–32. https://waesol.org/wp-content/uploads/2022/01/11. Accessed 11 August 2022.

Kozlowski, S.W.J., and K.J. Klein. 2000. A multilevel approach to theory and research in organizations: Contextual, temporal, and emergent processes. In *Multilevel theory, research, and methods in organizations: Foundations, extensions, and new directions*, ed. K.J. Klein and S.W.J. Kozlowski, 3–90. San Francisco: Jossey-Bass.

Lay, T., and K. Giblett. 2020. Zoom, Padlet, Screencast + Co.—Fremdsprachen lehren und lernen in Zeiten der Corona-Krise. *MehrSprachen Lernen und Lehren* 25 (2): 553–565.

Lenkaitis, C.A. 2020. Technology as a mediating tool: Videoconferencing, L2 learning, and learner autonomy. *Computer Assisted Language Learning* 33 (5–6): 483–509. https://doi.org/10.1080/09588221.2019.1572018.

Lestari, N. 2019. Improving the speaking skill by vlog (video blog) as learning media: The EFL students perspective. *International Journal of Academic Research in Business and Social Sciences* 9 (1): 915–925.

Li, L., et al. 2022. To zoom or not to zoom: A longitudinal study of UK Population's activities during the COVID-19 pandemic. *PLoS One* 17 (7). https://doi.org/10.1371/journal.pone.0270207.

London, M. 2003. *Job feedback: Giving, seeking, and using feedback for performance improvement*. 2nd ed. Mahwah, NJ: Lawrence Erlbaum.

London, M., and V. Sessa. 2006. Group feedback for continuous learning. *Human Resource Development Review* 5: 303–329. https://doi.org/10.1177/1534484306290226.

MacDonald, L. 2011. The 'virtual language lab': Virtually painless, simply real. *IALLT Journal of Language Learning Technologies* 41: 137–160.

McCormick, D.E., and M.L. Vercellotti. 2013. Examining the impact of self-correction notes on grammatical accuracy in speaking. *TESOL Quarterly* 47 (2): 410–420. https://doi.org/10.1002/tesq.92.

Quinn, P. 2014. *Delayed versus immediate corrective feedback on orally produced passive errors in English*. Doctoral Dissertation, University of Toronto. https://central.bac-lac.gc.ca/.item?id=TC-OTU-65728&op=pdf&app=Library&is_thesis=1&oclc_number=1032908200. Accessed 10 August 2022.

Richards, J.C., and T.S. Rodgers. 2014. *Approaches and methods in language teaching*. 3rd ed. Cambridge: CUP.

Robinson, P. 1995. Attention, memory, and the "noticing" hypothesis. *Language Learning* 45 (2): 283–331. https://doi.org/10.1111/j.1467-1770.1995.tb00441.x.

Roby, W.B. 2004. Technology in the service of foreign language learning: The case of the language laboratory. In *Handbook of research on educational communications and technology*, ed. D.H. Jonassen, 2nd ed., 523–541. Mahwah, NJ: Lawrence Erlbaum.

Rojas, M.A., and S.M. Arteaga. 2019. Perceptions about self-recording videos to develop EFL speaking skills in two Ecuadorian universities. *Journal of Language Teaching and Research* 10 (1): 60–67. https://doi.org/10.17507/jltr.1001.07.

Schmidt, R.W. 1990. The role of consciousness in second language learning. *Applied Linguistics* 11 (2): 129–158.

———. 2001. Attention. In *Cognition and second language instruction*, ed. P. Robinson, 3–32. Cambridge: CUP.

Schnaars, S., and C. Wymbs. 2004. On the persistence of lacklustre demand—The history of the video telephone. *Technological Forecasting and Social Change* 73 (3): 197–216. https://doi.org/10.1016/S0040-1625(02)00410-9.

Schneider, C. 2020. Setting up a language learning environment in Microsoft Teams. *Studies in Self-Access Learning Journal* 11 (3): 263–270. https://doi.org/10.37237/110312.

Shehadeh, A. 2001. Self- and other-initiated modified output during task-based interaction. *TESOL Quarterly* 35 (3): 433–457. https://doi.org/10.2307/3588030.

Shute, V.J. 2008. Focus on formative feedback. *Review of Educational Research* 78: 153–189. https://doi.org/10.3102/0034654307313795.

Stillwell, C., et al. 2010. Students transcribing tasks: Noticing fluency, accuracy, and complexity. *ELT Journal* 64 (4): 445–455. https://doi.org/10.1093/elt/ccp081.

Tecedor, M., and G. Campos-Dintrans. 2019. Developing oral communication in Spanish lower-level courses: The case of voice recordings and videoconferencing activities. *ReCALL* 31 (2): 116–134. https://doi.org/10.1017/S0958344018000083.

Turner, E.D. 1969. *Correlation of language class and language laboratory. ERIC focus reports on the teaching of foreign languages*. https://files.eric.ed.gov/fulltext/ED034451.pdf. Accessed 23 December 2022.

5

Teaching Translation into Spanish Asynchronously: Assessment and Engagement in the Times of COVID

Nazaret Pérez-Nieto

1 Introduction

Translation has always played a pivotal role in language learning, but its use as a pedagogical tool has not been exempt from controversy. The implementation of the grammar-translation method for language learning across Europe in the nineteenth and twentieth centuries, where the focus was on linguistic structure and written language, with no attempt to inscribe translation within a communicative framework (Carreres 2006, p. 5), was soon opposed by the advocates of the communicative approach in language teaching. The development of communicative approaches moved the focus away from mastery of structures to communicative proficiency, giving students the opportunity to work with authentic language in use and produce 'real' language for a specific purpose. Consequently, this approach rejected the grammar-translation method, opposing by default the use of translation in language learning

N. Pérez-Nieto (✉)
Cardiff University, Cardiff, UK
e-mail: perez-nieton@cardiff.ac.uk

and thus also closing the door to potential opportunities for dialogue and reconciliation.

Since then, many scholars have questioned the dismissal of translation in language learning (Cook 2010; Leonardi 2010; Malmkjaer 2010; Laviosa 2014; Carreres 2014), arguing that translation was in fact the 'victim' of the grammar-translation method rather than the 'villain'. In this sense, the issue was not directly linked to the use of translation in itself but, rather, to a teaching methodology that hindered its communicative purpose. Not surprisingly, then, since the 2000s there has been an increase in the number of studies which have challenged the negative perception of translation in language learning and called for re-examination (and rehabilitation) of its role. These studies have been driven by the questioning of the monolingual principle in language pedagogy (see Cook 2010; Hall and Cook 2012) and the innovations in the field of professional translation didactics and audiovisual translation (see Talaván 2013; 2019)—and even more recently by the success of translation-based digital platforms such as Duolingo and the introduction of the notion of mediation in the Common European Framework of Reference for Languages (CEFR; Carreres and Noriega-Sánchez 2021, p. 83).

As this thriving new world of opportunities opened up for the use of translation in foreign language learning, the arrival of the COVID-19 pandemic and the restrictions imposed across the globe had an unprecedented impact on Higher Education Institutions (HEIs) and on their delivery of language-learning activities. The sudden swift shift to a blended or, in some cases, wholly remote teaching setting (ERT) challenged universities to provide a more flexible, immediately applicable approach to their learning and teaching strategy, minimising face-to-face, introducing synchronous and asynchronous online activities into the curriculum, and providing new ways to enhance students' engagement with assessment. Learning outcomes for language modules, however, remained the same and the commitment to enabling students to fulfil these objectives was unchanged.

The new possibilities offered by the recent re-evaluations of the use of translation into the foreign language, alongside the exploration of innovative ways of delivering online teaching and assessment during the pandemic, emphasise the need to undertake studies that evaluate these practices to inform our language-teaching policies moving forward. This case study, undertaken during the 2020–2021 academic year, aims to respond to this need. It does so by examining students' perceptions of translation activities within a Year 2 Spanish Advanced language module at the undergraduate, B2 level (CEFR 2020). The focus is on the analysis of how translation-into-Spanish activities designed to meet the learning outcomes and delivered asynchronously using online discussion boards are received. This analysis contributes to the study of translation into Spanish and, more broadly, of foreign languages. The analysis explores the role that discussion boards play in delivery, monitorisation, assessment of tasks, and community building.

In order to address the aims outlined above, this chapter presents a theoretical framework that serves as the basis for our proposal. In Sects. 2 and 3 we will explore the recent re-evaluations of the role of translation into the foreign language in language learning. Section 4 offers an overview of changes to the academic landscape due to the COVID-19 pandemic, with an emphasis on teaching translation into the foreign language asynchronously and the use of discussion boards. This analysis is followed by the description of the methodology used to achieve our objectives: the creation of a survey to measure the impact of the activities proposed, distributed to Year 2 advanced students of Spanish (Sect. 5). Section 6 provides a thorough description of and insight into the activities presented to students, looking specifically at activities targeting assessment, while Sect. 7 presents the outcomes of the survey and analyses how these results will assist in shaping our teaching delivery post-pandemic. Finally, Sect. 8 outlines the conclusions, limitations, and potential further research opportunities.

2 Research Context

2.1 Recent Re-evaluations of the Role of Translation in Language Learning

Over the last two decades, there has been an increase in the number of studies reassessing the role of translation and discussing the benefits but also the limitations of its use in Foreign Language (FL) pedagogy. The long-standing association of translation with the grammar-translation method resulted in the perpetuation of perceptions of translation as an 'unnatural' activity with no communicative purpose, to be therefore excluded from playing any part in communicative methodologies. Nonetheless, as pointed out by Pintado (2020, p. 173), many of the flaws that translation in FL teaching presented over the years have now been tackled through the development of new theoretical and empirical studies.

In an attempt to explore and resolve the controversies around the use of translation and translation into the FL in particular, Carreres (2006, pp. 5–7) lists and contests five of the main arguments found in the literature. Firstly, she states that over the years translation has been cast as an artificial, stilted exercise that confines language practice to reading and writing only, arguing that translation was not the problem as such but, rather, the methodology used, which hindered the communicative function of translation. Secondly, she addresses the claim that translation into the target language (L2) causes interferences and a dependence on the mother tongue (L1) that inhibits free expression in L2. In contrast, she points towards the concept of 'silent translation', as literature has proven that learners of a foreign language refer to their mother tongue to aid the process of acquisition of the L2 more generally. Thirdly, detractors claim that inverse translation is a pointless exercise that has no relation to the real world as professional translators will always translate into their mother tongue. Carreres answers that this is the definition of an ideal situation rather than a description of actual practice, since in the world of commercial and technical translation, where most translators work, other factors such as the knowledge of the field and the specific terminology are determining when employing a translator, who may thus not necessarily be a native speaker. With the aim of dismantling the myth of the native speaker as the absolute authority in terms of correctness and style, in a more recent publication, Carreres et al. (2017, p. 103) note that the historical and demographic factors of a community play an important role in directionality of translation practices. Translating into the second or further language(s) is accepted and common practice in some postcolonial societies in which the language of the colonising nation continues to be widely used. Likewise, speakers of minority or poorly represented languages in a society often find it necessary to translate from their native language into the majority language due to the difficulty of finding native speakers of the target language with sufficient knowledge of the minority language. Fourthly, it is said that students are not able to attain the level of accuracy of their teacher's version in exercises in translation into FL, making the activity frustrating, demotivating, and designed to underline mistakes. In answer to this point, Carreres highlights that it is essential to set realistic objectives and judge the tasks on the basis of different criteria from those that would be used to review translation into the L1. She acknowledges that there is less room for creativity when not translating into the mother tongue, but, on the other hand, she emphasises that it is an exercise that promotes discussion and encourages students to share and defend their own translation proposals. Fifthly, Carreres deals with the assumption that translation is an exercise that may be best suited for students with a literary interest who are grammar- and lexis-oriented. While she agrees that translation taught in a traditional manner was unsuitable for those students without literary orientations, she emphasises that translation must not be restricted to literary passages and can be taught in more engaging ways. She also reports in her study that 100% of her students in the second and third years of their modern languages degree in Spanish at the University of Cambridge agree that translation should be taught as part of a modern languages undergraduate degree, with students rating 4.6 (out of 5) in favour of translation from English into the FL as a useful means of learning the foreign language.

In 2013, the Directorate-General for Translation and the European Commission undertook a large-scale study aimed at researching the role of translation in language teaching in different academic settings (primary, secondary, and higher education). The study concluded (Pym et al. 2013, p. 135) that translation is, in its own right, a communicative activity that can enhance the learning of an L2 and that in most countries, although not specifically mentioned in the official curricula, translation is used in the language classroom. The report points out that translation can be used as scaffolding in initial L2 learning and as a complex multi-skill communicative activity at higher levels, which would explain why translation has a stronger presence in higher education. According to the report (Pym et al. 2013, p. 125), the value of translation in language learning is tacitly recognised by the fact that almost all university first-degree programmes in foreign languages offer at least one course in it. The study also reports that translating, either professionally or para-professionally, is one of the activities foreign language graduates may opt for after graduating. When looking at the literature on the use of inverse translation in Higher Education (HE) specifically, Carreres (2006, p. 4) notes that it is surprising to see how translation into the L2 is regarded as an 'undesirable but persistent feature' in modern languages degrees. As she points out, the answer may be that language practitioners can see the benefits of using translation in certain learning contexts despite the negative perception of translation in general. This would explain why the teaching community within the Directorate-General for Translation and the European Commission report widely perceives translation as the 'fifth' skill (Pym et al. 2013, p. 139), stating it is a skill in its own right in addition to speaking, listening, writing, and reading. In relation to the denomination of translation as the 'fifth skill', Carreres and Noriega-Sánchez (2021, p. 84) explain that the fundamental feature of recent approaches in language learning is the emphasis placed on translation as a 'real-world communicative activity', conceived as a skill, not just as a tool to gain linguistic knowledge. This skill is now being seen as essential for all language learners and not only for those students being trained as professional translators. This brings together professional translation practice and language learning and reframes the standard perception of translation towards acknowledging it as an end in itself, not just as a means (Cook 2010; Carreres 2014); this shift could therefore be seen as advocating a 'translation turn' in language pedagogy.

3   The Introduction of 'Mediation' into the CEFR

In 2001, the Council of Europe launched the *Common European Framework of Reference for Languages* with the aim of bringing standardisation and unity to foreign language learning, teaching, and assessment across all member states in Europe. This initial framework states that the language learner's communicative competences are triggered by performing a set of 'language activities' involving reception, production, interaction, and mediation (CEFR 2001, p. 14). The CEFR defines 'mediation' as written and/or oral tasks that make communication possible between individuals who for 'whatever reason' are unable to communicate with each other, including, but not limited to, translation and/or interpretation activities, highlighting the concept of the language learner as a social agent and communication facilitator.

Although promising, the CEFR 2001 framework did not quite meet expectations as the notion of 'mediation' was not explored to its full potential, and it failed to incorporate and provide detailed calibrated descriptors for mediating skills at all different levels of competence (from A1 to C2). Requests were made for these descriptors to be further developed, and in 2018 the *Companion Volume with New Descriptors* was published, including descriptors for mediation with an increased focus on the development of plurilingual competence. This reinforced the position of translation within the CEFR (Carreres and Noriega-Sánchez 2021, p. 84), as well as shaping the instructional practices of national organisations responsible for promoting the study and the teaching of languages. In the context of Spanish as a foreign language in particular, the 'Curricular Plan' of the Cervantes Institute included translation within its principles and guidelines as one of the activities for language learning (Carreres et al. 2017, p. 101).

The release of the most updated CEFR *Companion Volume* in 2020 enhanced the framework by adding examples of use in different domains for descriptors of online interaction, conversation, and discussion, together with mediation activities which are crucial for the purposes of our study. From the perspective of online interaction, this descriptor acknowledges the need for the CEFR framework to reflect the development of technology in language learning as well as the relevance of goal-oriented online synchronous/asynchronous transactions and collaboration in the educational setting, in contrast to face-to-face interaction.

As per the descriptors for mediation, the differentiation between 'mediation activities' and 'mediation strategies' still prevails. It is among the former that we can find a specific category for 'mediating a text' and a subcategory for 'translating a written text'. (For a classification of the notion of mediation, mediating a text, and translating a written text, please see CEFR 2020, p. 90.) It is important to note that, as stated in the guidelines, the descriptors for translating a written text in writing are not intended to relate to the activities of professional translators or their training, but rather acknowledges that plurilingual learners may be asked to provide written translations of texts in their professional or personal context (CEFR 2020, p. 44). In terms of directionality of the translation, the guidelines also indicate that 'Language A' and 'Language B' may well be different languages (cross-linguistic), varieties or modalities of the same language, different registers of the same variety, or a combination of these. This situates translation into the foreign language as a real activity taking place in a communicative context and as a skill that language learners need to acquire for their personal and academic development. For the purpose of this study, we look specifically at the B2 descriptors of 'translating written text in writing' with translation of documents ranging from letters, articles in magazines or newspapers, and colloquial writings to public documents describing general regulations, reports, academic papers, books, novels, short stories, and plays. (For a full picture of descriptors for translating a written text in writing B2 level with examples, please see CEFR 2020, p. 218.)

Despite its call to disassociate itself from professional translation practice, the emphasis on plurilingual competence in the most updated version of the CEFR *Companion Volume* has effectively welcomed and contributed to the return of translation to language learning. The introduction of the notion of 'mediation' gives the use of translation into the foreign language the 'thumbs-up' by providing a less negatively connoted label than 'translation,' still unavoidably associated with the grammar-translation method (Carreres et al. 2021, p. 7). Although we agree with

Carreres (2006, p. 6) that we are not aiming to provide qualified translator training to language students in HE, we have to acknowledge the professional opportunities that may turn up for them in the future.

What is also interesting to highlight from the perspective of community building, as noted by Huertas Barros (2011, p. 46), is that undertaking translation tasks collaboratively brings with it many advantages, including the creation of a class community that facilitates teamwork, peer review, interaction to construct meaningful learning, and the exchange of experiences to deal with and solve translation problems. Therefore, translation as a collaborative exercise can serve as a tool to enhance community building within language modules, delivered online or in person.

Regarding assessment, although the descriptors outlined in the CEFR are useful, assessing plurilingual competence presents a challenge in itself, particularly in situations where formal assessment is needed (Carreres et al. 2021, p. 14). For translation specifically, these authors advocate for the development of new assessment frameworks that embody translation as a skill, using translation not only as a tool to assess lexical and grammatical knowledge but also as an exercise to develop a wider range of transferable skills such as problem-solving, critical thinking, team working, and intercultural competence. In this context, and considering the constraints imposed by the pandemic, it is timely that new ways of assessing students' translation skills into the L2 are created, putting the focus on the communicative and reflective element of translation by not only creating activities that incite reflection but also creating comprehensive rubrics to assess this work.

Thus, this vision and all the arguments presented above guide and provide the cues for our exploration of the use of translation activities into L2 (Spanish, in our case) and their assessment in HE. We discuss these activities in relation to their asynchronous delivery through the use of discussion boards and the effects of this on community building in a Year 2 Spanish Advanced module.

4 Changes to the Academic Landscape: Blended Learning and Learning Outcomes

The arrival of the COVID-19 pandemic turned the world upside down, affecting all aspects of our lives, including education. Universities in the UK as in other parts of the world had to come up with new teaching strategies in a very short period of time while adhering to unprecedented social restrictions. This was also the case for Welsh universities, which moved rapidly to ERT after March 2020, with only a few months to plan for what was a very uncertain academic year ahead. Following Welsh government regulations and university-wide guidance, the School of Modern Languages at Cardiff University committed to adopting a blended learning model for the start of the 2020–2021 academic year. Anny King (2016, p. 13) defines blended learning as an approach to learning that incorporates different learning styles, environments, and activities (both face-to-face and online) in a flexible, integrated manner to enhance the students' needs and experience. Although this is not a new approach to language learning where the use of different media, different modes of delivery, and instructional strategies happen as a matter of principle, King's definition emphasises the role technology plays in making the blended approach 'both easier and more meaningful for learners' (2016, p. 13).

With this definition in mind, the blended learning model adopted was designed to meet the learning outcomes, with language modules having some online content in both synchronous (online sessions) and asynchronous formats (online materials that students could access in their own time following a guided structure) as well as some on campus, face-to-face provision. This blended learning framework was informed by five key underpinning principles (Cardiff University 2021):

1. To consider how to make the most effective use of online technology and time on campus, following the principle that the most effective and engaging online synchronous activities are interactive and student-centred. In contrast, asynchronous learning environments, such as

discussion boards, provide time and space for reflection and discussion of more complex topics.
2. To avoid using multiple platforms and creating too many multimedia resources—concentrating instead on engaging actively with students in online synchronous and asynchronous settings.
3. To enhance clarity and structure through the implementation of weekly module maps which explain the rationale behind online asynchronous, online synchronous, and face-to-face activities. These module maps also include information about assessment as well as its relationship to the learning outcomes.
4. To focus on quality by providing regular proactive and reactive engagement through on-campus activities and online platforms.
5. To ensure module design and resources are inclusive, acknowledging the different personal contexts and circumstances surrounding the students. This is done by offering a balance of accessible, well-designed, and scaffolded learning activities.

In relation to the specific learning outcomes of the course, it is important to highlight that the Year 2 Spanish Language Ex-Advanced module is designed to build upon the linguistic knowledge acquired during the first year of the students' degree in Spanish and prepare them for their compulsory period of study and/or working abroad in their third year. In the course there is an emphasis on the development of key language skills, these being receptive (reading and listening), productive (speaking and writing), mediation (translation between two languages), and intercultural awareness, corresponding to a B2 level of the CEFR.

Within the module description, clear importance is attached to enabling students to develop the transferable skills of translating from and into the Spanish language efficiently and of interpreting formal and informal texts between Spanish and English; this constitutes one of the five key learning outcomes as illustrated in Table 5.1.

In terms of skills to be developed throughout the course, the references to translation are explicit (see point 10 in Table 5.2). Nonetheless, it could be argued that the use of translation activities into Spanish can enhance the development of all the 12 points displayed in the module description. It can certainly increase the awareness of how the mother

Table 5.1 Module learning outcomes

On successful completion of the module, a student should be able to:
1. Read, understand, and speak Spanish to a level comparable with B2 of the Common European Framework of Reference for Languages (CEFR)
2. Engage confidently and with appropriate grammatical correctness and spontaneity in everyday conversation in Spanish. This includes explaining a viewpoint and discussing the advantages and disadvantages of topical issues relating to Spanish culture and society
3. Write coherent texts in Spanish in a range of registers on a wide range of topics relating to Spanish culture and society with appropriate grammatical and lexical accuracy
4. Extract and synthesise data and ideas from a range of authentic written and/or audio/audiovisual texts
5. Translate passages of text from and into English, evidencing an enhanced capacity for dealing with linguistic problems encountered in translation.

Table 5.2 Skills that students will practise and develop within the module

Students will develop:
1. An understanding of the principles of learning a foreign language intensively and organise their learning with guidance from the tutor
2. A greater awareness of how languages (including the mother tongue) function
3. The skills to be effective, independent and self-aware learners, including active reflection on learning processes and preferences so as to independently develop appropriate strategies and linguistic skills to ensure progression
4. The ability to work creatively and flexibly with others as part of a team
5. Cultural and linguistic awareness in preparation for the year abroad
6. Intercultural awareness, understanding, and competence, including a critical understanding of other cultures and practice other than one's own
7. Enhanced skills in effective communication, presentation, and interaction—both in an online environment and face to face
8. An awareness of registers (both written and conversational), accents, and pronunciation
9. Enhanced analytical skills
10. An understanding and appreciation of key translation problems and techniques for overcoming these
11. Enhanced digital literacy skills, including the ability to engage with appropriate language learning technologies
12. The ability to identify, assess, and make good use of appropriate reference materials (e.g. dictionaries, online resources, and self-study tools)

tongue and the target language work by comparing structures, lexical devices, and idiomatic expressions. It also fosters active individual/group reflection and strategy development to overcome linguistic issues by providing students with opportunities to research and justify their translation proposals. Furthermore, creativity can be boosted by encouraging learners to think outside the box in coming up with imaginative translation suggestions taking both the (inter)cultural and linguistic contexts and purpose into account. Last but not least, it aids them in identifying and making appropriate use of paper, digital, and online resources available to them.

4.1 Module Delivery: Teaching and Assessing Translation Asynchronously

The Year 2 Spanish Advanced module is structured around four different components, which are inextricably intertwined and delivered throughout the year: grammar, translation into Spanish, translation into English, and conversation. The distribution and ratio of online to face-to-face activities were informed by the key principles of the blended learning framework provided by the university, the applicability of which is analysed below.

The starting point was to decide which elements of the module would be best suited for face-to-face provision, synchronous online teaching, or asynchronous instruction. Initially, due to the interactive nature of this activity, it was suggested that conversation classes take place in a face-to-face format. However, the need to maintain two-metre social distancing among students and teachers and the compulsory use of masks in the face-to-face setting made this solution simply not feasible. Therefore, in order to make conversation classes accessible and inclusive for all students, it was agreed that the oral component would be taught online synchronously. As per the blended learning guidelines, grammar was taught as a hybrid component by providing asynchronous materials (video recordings of grammar aspects together with activities for consolidation) before the face-to-face sessions to maximise the time available for student-centred activities and on-campus experience. Finally, due to our commitment to presenting translation as a reflective process and to creating a space for insightful and meaningful conversations among students in the course, translation was delivered as guided asynchronous activities via online discussion boards. This move was supported by the surge of online environments and platforms providing students with a wider array of opportunities to discuss and reflect in the course of language learning. As mentioned earlier, in the CEFR's most updated version (2020), we can find descriptors for online interaction, conversation, and discussion and examples of these in different personal, professional, and academic settings. Among the B2 descriptors, we can see explicit references to: engagement through 'online exchanges', linking ideas to previous contributions in a given thread; understanding cultural implications; and—what is equally interesting—the figure of the moderator as mediator. (Descriptors for online interaction, conversation, and discussion B2 level with examples can be found in the CEFR 2020, pp. 192–193.)

In this respect, in a review of the history and current state of distance, blended, and online learning, Joksimović et al. (2015, p. 114) explain that the instructor's moderating role in guided discussions is of key importance in online cooperative and collaborative exchanges, noting the significance of providing timely, formative feedback on learning progress to students. Likewise, studies on asynchronous discussion forums and communication in language learning have shown that creating an open, interactive space where learners can reflect, exchange experiences, and interact with each other can enhance students' engagement with course content, enabling them to develop critical thinking in the target language and take responsibility for their own learning, which in turn increases satisfaction (Wilkins 2018; Chakowa 2019; Blake and Guillen 2020; Pais Marden and Herrington 2022). Furthermore, these studies report that the use of discussion boards for non-native language students fosters the development of the foreign language skills, aiding them in overcoming their linguistic deficiencies and increasing their participation in comparison to the face-to-face class environment. Equally important is that asynchronous facilitated conversations, according to these studies, allow students to gain socio-affective skills and serve as a platform to allow all the voices in the class to have a presence, regardless of geographical location—including the voices of those introverted learners who would not be as keen to contribute to face-to-face class discussions.

Once the distribution of face-to-face and online activities was decided and adopted, a channel was needed to deliver the asynchronous structured translation activities. Following the principle of 'keeping things simple' and avoiding the use of multiple platforms, we decided to use our web-based course management system, Learning Central (Blackboard), which is familiar to students and include a discussion forum function that is already completely integrated within each module. A generic overview of the module activities split by semesters and weeks is provided on a module schedule, while detailed information about the activities is presented in weekly module maps. The latter indicated the content and activities for the week in question, as well as where to locate them on Learning Central, together with indicative time commitment and an explanation of their relationship to the assessment and learning outcomes. In terms of engagement, the translation discussion boards were split into subgroups to facilitate teachers' and students' regular interaction and community building, seen as key to a successful asynchronous mode of delivery. Activities were also provided in an inclusive way by allowing students to learn at their own pace, in their own time, within the scaffolded learning approach provided.

Due to the reflective element being at the heart of the translation process and the need for the assessment to be authentic while fulfilling the requirements of the online environment (see Giacosa's chapter in this volume), the summative evaluation for this part of the module consisted of a 400-word journalistic text written in English, to be translated into Spanish. This was to be submitted individually and accompanied by a translation brief. The translation brief, taking from professional translators' training, helps situate the task in the real world, containing instructions and information to give students a purpose to serve and an audience to address. Traditional invigilated examinations undertaken in large groups under timed limited conditions were impossible during the pandemic, and so this assessed translation is presented to students as an open book assessment, for which they can access and assess resources, which is more in line with real-life situations. The translation is assigned together with a list of reflective questions to prompt discussion and aid students in developing their critical thinking, creativity, and problem-solving skills; this also prevents the activity from coming across as a mere linguistic operational exercise. The objective of the introduction of these questions is, furthermore, to raise awareness of the overreliance on automated translation devices and to encourage students to make their own informed translation decisions, as students suspected of using any multilingual machine translation service for producing a translation in its entirety are subjected to academic misconduct procedures. To that end, the marking criteria were developed for this assessment putting the reflective element at the core while integrating translation as a skill, assessing six blocks: (a) approach to reflective questions; (b) understanding and communication of meaning and style; (c) command of syntax and grammar/target language use; (d) knowledge and use of vocabulary in target language; (e) ability to use appropriate register and style and understand cultural context, and (f) spelling and punctuation.

Another aspect that should be mentioned regarding assessment is the greater possibilities for flexible arrangements in the blended learning context that the pandemic brought to light. Flexibility offers learners the opportunity to take control and ownership over the assessment process. While moving away from the rigid invigilated exam format, flexible assessment involves some elements of choice on the part of the student, taking their needs and personal preference into consideration. On this front, studies undertaken on the flexibility of assessment seem to favour this approach to empowering students on their learning journey (Cook 2001; Irwin and Hepplestone 2011; Wanner et al. 2021). In this module, we require students to submit at the end of the academic year an essay in Spanish; a translation into English; and a translation into Spanish, with all three tasks carrying the same weighting. Although the submission points are established from the beginning of the course, the students decide which piece of work they wish to submit for each submission point, giving students choices and enabling them to exercise autonomy over their learning as a result—an approach which has been very well-received by students in the module.

5 Methodology

In this chapter we explore the possibilities that translation into foreign languages (using Spanish as an example), taught asynchronously, can bring to HE language modules in terms of engagement with assessment and community building. To that end, we first introduce the platform and structure of the asynchronous exercises created and provide a thorough analysis of a sample of activities set for students in three different blocks: influential women in Spanish and Latin American society and culture; Spanish and Latin American cultural stereotypes; and the use of film and TV series in translation. Secondly, to capture the students' views on translation into Spanish, the activities designed, assessment and community building, a qualitative survey was developed and distributed via Google Forms. This classroom-based study involved 27 Welsh and English 19- to 21-year-old Spanish Language undergraduate students from Cardiff University, Wales. In order to protect participants' anonymity and privacy, no questions were asked that could lead to any degree of identification.

The 26-item questionnaire is partly based on a survey distributed by Wagstaffe (2018), including some questions used and reported by Carreres (2006) and Laviosa (2014), and supplemented with a selection of questions from the European Commission report. The questions comprised a mixture of 17 closed-ended questions and 5 open-ended questions to allow participants to expand and elaborate their responses. Questions 1–7 aimed to explore whether translation into Spanish should be taught as part of a modern languages degree—in particular, if it can be considered a skill in itself; a useful means to learn the language; and an enjoyable, intellectually stimulating activity; as well as valuable from an employability perspective. Questions 8–15 focused on reviewing the translation-into-Spanish activities designed for the module from the angle of whether these were felt to be helpful in developing their language skills; motivating; enjoyable; intellectually challenging; and beneficial from an employability point of view. Questions 16–22 addressed the suitability of the translation activities in terms of alignment with the assessment of this component; the extent to which these activities had an impact on the students' understanding of the marking criteria; their expectations for the assessment; and their preparation; as well as ranking the tasks that were most useful from the perspective of assessment. Finally, questions 23–26 focused on whether online translation boards enhanced the delivery of the translation activities; changed their approach to learning; and aided in developing a sense of community within the translation groups when these were dealing with the translation-into-Spanish tasks. The results of the survey are presented from the students' perspective, data analysis section.

6 Presentation of the Activities

As discussed previously in this chapter, the asynchronous translation-into-Spanish activities were presented to students through our web-based course management system, Learning Central (Blackboard), which has an integrated function for online discussion boards. An advantage of using this function is that external resources can be embedded to enrich the content by adding videos (via YouTube or Panopto), interactive exercises (EdPuzzle and Genially activities), external links, and images, among other options. The labelled 'online translation discussion boards' were split into different groups with a maximum number of 15 students per group, each group being then allocated to a dedicated member of staff for moderation and engagement purposes. The translation-into-Spanish activities were released to students in a fortnightly cycle with a completion deadline of a week, clearly structured in threads to recreate the stages of the translation process, with each activity feeding forward to the following exercise.

All the activities began with an introductory video which set the outline of the tasks and displayed the guidelines and explanations required to complete the exercises. There were three tasks in total per week with different submission points to allow tutors to access the activities and give feedback, but also to encourage students to regularly engage with the exercises. In a given week, tasks 1 and 2 (in preparation for the final translation) were to be completed by mid-week, while task 3 (translation and reflective questions) was due at the end of the week. Feedback for the last task was to be provided by the Wednesday the following week, closing the circle. Below we expound on some of the activities undertaken throughout the course following the above-mentioned three thematic blocks.

Block 1: Influential Women in Spanish and Latin America in Contemporary Society and Culture
This sequence of activities was designed around the Spanish singer Rosalía and her role in reinventing the music industry in Spain and Latin America, creating powerful new messages in her lyrics and dealing with pressing issues in today's society. It was presented as the first set of activities students had to complete asynchronously within the course, and so, in the introductory video, the dynamics of the translation discussion boards and activities were explained (how to access the activities and when to complete them, how to post comments on the threads and reply to these, etc.). A thorough description of the aspects to be dealt with in the activities and their outcomes was provided, divided into three categories (to which we will refer systematically in the explanation and analysis of all other activities analysed below):

1. Functional and cultural elements: including knowledge of the Spanish and Latin American music industry and styles; Spanish-speaking artists who have a global impact; music revolutions, new musical styles, and changes in Spanish and Latin American societies. Rosalía's background, biography, and music are also featured here.
2. Grammatical and syntactical content displaying common issues for learners of Spanish at this level: strategies to deal with the use of passive voice and the gerunds when translating into Spanish; gender agreements; past tenses; uses of 'ser and estar'; modal and phrasal verbs.
3. Lexical structures: vocabulary related to the music industry and different music styles; music lyrics; the role of women in the music industry; 'false friends' in Spanish and English, and vocabulary to describe interpersonal relationships.

Task 1 required students to introduce themselves on the translation board, indicating their name and the languages they were learning; whether they enjoyed translating into Spanish and why; what their expectations for the translation into Spanish part of the course were; and what specific points they wanted to improve, or they would like to see covered throughout the year. Lastly, they were asked to reflect on three main challenges they had faced when translating into Spanish in the past. With this activity, students were able to get to know each other and share their initial impressions of translating into the L2.

In task 2, students were tasked to watch a video entitled 'Entrevista a Rosalía' (Interviewing Rosalía, by Radio Latino) and answer a set of questions: firstly, if they agreed or disagreed with Rosalía's statements in the video on the lack of visibility of women in the music industry and why; to discuss the music styles mentioned by the artist, their roots, and state what type of music or styles they preferred and why.

The last task (task 3) was introduced by a translation brief in which the students were told that they were working for a newspaper in the UK which was looking to create a multilingual translation of the article into different languages, including Spanish for a Spanish-speaking audience. The text is accompanied by the following questions:

1. What strategies have you used to avoid the passive voice and the gerund in the Spanish version? What past tenses have you used and why?
2. What sort of clauses can we find within the text (e.g. temporary, relative, and reason)?
3. How would you translate idiomatic expressions such as 'blew my mind'/'super crazy jealous' for a Spanish-speaking audience?
4. And finally, what parts or sections have you found more difficult to translate and what steps and resources have you followed to resolve these issues?

While task 1 is an introductory activity, the connection between tasks 2 and 3 becomes more evident as students familiarise themselves with the topic, the vocabulary, and the grammatical structures related to the theme (task 2), in order to be able to then make appropriate use of these in the final translation task, following the instructions of the brief.

Block 2: Spanish and Latin American Cultural Stereotypes

In this section we explain how two activities, one targeting Spanish stereotypes and another one dealing with Latin American ones, helped to raise awareness of commonly held, simplistic beliefs about specific groups in these societies in preparation for the students' experiences abroad the following year.

Activity 1 was centred on the now-infamous article published by *The Times* entitled 'How to Be Spanish', written by its chief travel writer Chris Haslam (Haslam, 2018), who gave tips on how to behave as a 'true' Spaniard by listing a wide range of the most common Spanish stereotypes. The introductory video explained that:

1. Regarding functional and cultural content, the main points to be dealt with were sarcasm in the description of Spanish traditions; Spanish and British stereotypes; intercultural awareness; perception and reception of stereotypes; and humoristic translation of Spanish cultural references.
2. In terms of grammar content and register, special emphasis was given to the uses of the negative and affirmative forms of the imperative (to reflect how to give tips and recommendations in English vs Spanish), as well as the use of the subjunctive and the difference in the use of the forms 'tú' and 'usted' in Castilian Spanish.
3. Finally, in terms of vocabulary, the special focus was on expressions related to Spanish gastronomy, traditions, and social behaviours.

To start with, in task 1, students were asked to read the article published by *The Times* and then to work with a video released by the Spanish newspaper *El País* in which Simon Hunter, editor at *El País English Edition*, reviews the article and explains why it is so controversial from the perspective of his experience of being an English expat for over 18 years in Spain. This activity was designed using the platform 'EdPuzzle' with its multiple-choice function that tracks progress. Questions were asked in relation to the content and the vocabulary used by Simon in Spanish, allowing students to familiarise themselves with the topic, the context, the lexis, and the grammatical/syntactical structures needed for the final translation exercise. In addition, three opinion questions were posed to students on the discussion board that had to be answered in Spanish: (1) why they believed the piece of news had created such a stir and whether the reaction from the readers was disproportionate; (2) if they agreed or disagreed with Simon's views that the humoristic element that the author wanted to transmit was lost in the article; and (3) what their thoughts were on Simon's advice about how to be Spanish from his perspective, and whether they could add two more pieces of advice to his list.

Task 2 required students to read and respond to a tweet from a user showing her disappointment with the unfortunate article. Prior to this, in task 1, the students had read Simon's account of how the author of the piece had to change the privacy settings of his Twitter account due to the high volume of tweets received from numerous individuals complaining about it. Hence this exercise was designed for students to respond to this tweet in the discussion board, being able to express their views freely, adopting the more informal approach needed to communicate in the target language in the context of social media.

Task 3, the final translation exercise, was yet again introduced with a translation brief asking students to translate the article into Spanish for a Spanish newspaper, *ABC*, that was preparing a response in Spanish to the text published by *The Times* and needed their services to understand the content of the English article fully. This added authenticity to the task, as *ABC* did indeed respond to the article by publishing 'How to Be British'. Students were given access to it once the translation exercise was completed. The reflective questions on the translation exercise asked students to consider how to translate idiomatic expressions (e.g. 'swear like a trooper'), familiarise themselves with different concepts such as *pintxos* and *tapas* (introducing other languages being spoken in the Spanish peninsula), and reflect on the use of colloquialisms in Spanish (where the expression *guiri* comes from, if they think it has a negative connotation and why). They were also asked to name and explain the three main difficulties they had encountered in the text and how they had overcome them.

Activity 2 was comprised of a video recording explaining the learning outcomes of the exercise: from a functional and cultural perspective, we gave the students opportunities to familiarise themselves with common myths and stereotypes surrounding Latin America, and particularly how Latin American figures are represented in TV series and films in Hollywood—for example, the tendency to foreground drug dealing and cartels. We took the life of drug dealer Pablo Escobar and the representation of his life in the Netflix show *Narcos* as our leading example. With regard to grammatical and syntactical content, students worked mainly with verbal periphrasis and conditional sentences, as well as reflecting on syntactical structures and how these differ from English to Spanish. Students were exposed to vocabulary related to stereotypes, cultural misconceptions, and slang used in the world of drug trafficking.

Task 1 required students to name stereotypes they would link to any of the Spanish-speaking countries in Latin America, analysing why and how they came across these associations. Likewise, they were encouraged to comment on other students' contributions, expanding any of their ideas further.

In task 2, students were asked to watch a video about Latin stereotypes in Hollywood and answer a set of questions: firstly, which of the stereotypes identified in the video had drawn their attention the most and why; if they found any of them surprising and in what way; followed by whether they could find any more examples of Latin stereotypes being represented in the same way in other films or TV series, or if they could find examples of Latinos being represented differently.

Task 3 was the final translation exercise in which students were asked to translate a text about the TV show *Narcos*, Pablo Escobar, and life in Colombia at the time for an article that a Latin American newspaper is preparing on the presence of Latin stereotypes, as these emerge in films and TV series consumed by UK audiences. The reflective questions targeted syntax, asking students to select and explain three syntactical structures that they had found difficult to translate and why and to select two cultural references they had found challenging in the text and explain how they had resolved them.

Block 3: The Use of Film and TV Series in Translation Exercises

One of the most important aims of this course is to prepare students for their period of study abroad. Therefore, we selected the following activity precisely to illustrate that the film and the activities are designed ultimately to contribute towards the achievement of this goal. The film used to create this sequence was *Perdiendo el norte* (*Off Course* 2015) which tells the story of two well-educated young Spanish men who move to Germany looking for a job, but they soon discover that finding a better living abroad is not as easy as they initially thought. This activity aims to reflect upon what moving and living abroad entails, as well as the challenges and rewards that this period of one's life can bring.

Taking the cultural and the functional contents into account, students were presented with activities meant to enhance their knowledge of the Spanish 'brain drain'—the reasons that make people move to a different country and the difficulties they experience when trying to find jobs. Other topics included immigration, establishing personal relationships with people from other cultures, interculturality, cultural shock, and perception/reception of differences between cultures. They are also encouraged to discuss the use of online translation software and explore the advantages and disadvantages of over-relying on these resources. Finally, they were also exposed to different types of translation—audiovisual translation and accessible translation in particular. From a grammatical and syntactical perspective, we asked students to reflect specifically on the uses of past tenses (in both indicative and subjunctive), impersonal structures, temporal sentences, and collocations. From a register point of view, students reflected on the use of slang and vulgar language in context and considered how these references can be translated into Spanish. With regard to lexical structures, the activities placed a focus on idioms, misunderstandings when overusing literal translation, and the use of informal language more broadly.

In task 1, students had to follow a translation brief in which they were asked to imagine that they worked for a translation agency, which requested them to check that the English subtitles for the film trailer of *Off Course* corresponded accurately to the audio in Spanish. To achieve this, they were handed a transcript in English and encouraged to translate some of the parts highlighted in red into Spanish; this translation was then compared to the audio in Spanish. Students were given opportunities to reflect on how they would translate the passages in red, and on their difference from the audio in Spanish, while also comparing the structures in Spanish and English.

For task 2, students were given an article entitled *Los peores errores de Google Translate en español* ('The worst errors made by Google Translate in Spanish') and were asked to translate sayings, idioms, and collocations literally while also providing an idiomatic translation. In groups, they had to come up with different examples of other structures (be it idioms, sayings, or collocations) in English that which translated literally into Spanish would not work or would lead to misunderstandings.

In task 3, an exercise was introduced that made use of audio description in Spanish. Firstly, the students were encouraged to read a document in which the different types of accessible translation were explained, including specific examples of audio-described videos in Spanish. The requirements of the (Spanish) National Standard UNE 153020 set by the standard agency AENOR on audio description and production of audio guides for the visually impaired are set out, so that students could apply these principles to the task. A clip from the film *Off Course* was attached to the task and in groups students had to create the audio description for the video, making use of the vocabulary, grammatical, syntactical, and lexical structures learnt in previous tasks. Students had to vote for the best audio-described video by posting a comment on the relevant thread, justifying their choice by taking the requirements of the UNE 153020 into consideration.

6.1 Activities and Assessment

All the exercises included in this module, as formative assessments, were also devised in order to prepare students for their final assessment. However, this is particularly true of the following two activities, as students were directly involved in the assessment process and had the opportunity to reflect on the application of the marking criteria against translation examples and their own work.

In Activity 1, the sometimes-counterintuitive way of translating film titles from English into Spanish was used as a starting point for debate and discussion. In the introductory video, the most relevant skills to be developed and content to be covered were explained, following the same pattern as the rest of the activities. From a functional and cultural perspective, students were exposed to the difficulties of translating film titles from English into Spanish, including being shown some examples of weak or inappropriate translations. Marking criteria analysis and applicability were also covered. For grammatical and syntactical content, we tackled points already studied in the course—such as the use of passive voice, gerunds, gender agreement, past tenses, subjunctive, and phrasal and modal verbs. From a register perspective, students reflected on expressions that are used orally in Spanish but may not be appropriate to a formal register, for instance, in written press articles. For lexical structures, students worked mainly with vocabulary related to cinema, films, and music, as well as 'false friends' between Spanish and English and anglicisms in Spanish.

In task 1, a video titled *Crazy Translations of Movie Titles* was used to generate discussions about the topic. The video was accompanied by some questions to check students' understanding. We had also highlighted some relevant expressions used throughout the video, asking students to translate them and state whether or not they would use them in formal contexts, such as in press articles. They also reflected on the use of anglicisms and how the Spanish Royal Academy for language (RAE) does prefer a more purist approach to the usage of Spanish words and expressions, even if they are not as commonly used as their equivalent in English, due to the influence of English on other languages.

In task 2, students were asked to translate a text titled 'Why Do Film Titles in Spain End Up with Such Strange Translations?' The translation brief explained that they were working for a communications and marketing agency in Spain, which had tasked them with the translation of the text so that the agency could write their own article on how the English-speaking world perceives translation of film titles into different languages and on the importance of providing accurate and professional translation services in the filming industry.

For task 3, students were given a copy of the marking criteria to mark translations into the foreign language and were asked to read and analyse the wording and the different sections. Students were encouraged to ask questions and discuss in groups the contents of the criteria. In the same way, they had opportunities to post whether they would add any other elements to the criteria or if they would word any of the sections differently. Once the criteria had been discussed, students were given an anonymised translation from a previous student with mistakes, the same that they had to complete in task 2. In groups, they had to check the mistakes, list them in the given categories, and reach a final mark justifying it. A table was provided to students to identify and classify both strengths and areas for improvement. This table was posted in the corresponding thread in the translation discussion forum, which made for interesting discussion too: the students could see what other groups had posted and the reasoning underpinning their decision for a chosen mark. Once everyone had contributed to the forum, the translation as it was marked by one of the staff members was uploaded to the forum, and students had to comment on whether they agreed with the mark awarded and why they thought they were close (or not) to the given grade. It is interesting to note that students in this exercise tended to be harder markers than their lecturers, giving the translation a generally lower grade.

Activity 2 was centred on the Mexican painter and artist Frida Kahlo as one of the influential women in Spanish and Latin American contemporary society and culture. The aim of the exercise was, from a functional and cultural perspective, to get to know Frida Kahlo, her work and biography—to show students her role in the creation and the rising of the feminist movement; challenging patriarchy; and her involvement in and support for the LGTBQ+ community. In terms of grammatical and syntactical content, they tackle points that tend to be problematic for students at this level, such as the uses of the subjunctive (present, imperfect, pluperfect), comparatives, and definite and indefinite articles. For lexical structures, students work mainly with vocabulary related to the world of art, feminism, and the concepts of autoexposure and introspection in Frida Kahlo's work.

For this exercise, students were asked to work in groups and complete the translation collaboratively. For that purpose, the students were split into groups, and the lists of the names of the translators (students in the translation group) were added to the discussion forums. The translation was accompanied by the following translation brief: students were asked to translate a text into Spanish that was going to be published on the occasion of a Frida Kahlo exhibition taking place in London, for those Spanish speakers attending the event. The students also had to answer three reflective questions:

1. What grammatical and syntactical structures studied in class have you applied to this text? Which ones have been the most helpful to complete the translation and why?
2. What part or aspects of the text have been more challenging? How have you solved them? Justify your answer.
3. What sources/resources of the ones you have used have been more useful when completing the translation? Why?

Before posting their finalised translations to the discussion boards, students were given the opportunity to meet up live in a Zoom session to work together/discuss their options and agree on a final version of the translation and questions. Once the translations and questions were finalised, they submitted their translation by posting them on the forum. The translations were then marked and returned to students with feedback and comments and posted below the original translation submitted by the group, so all could benefit from the comments received. Common areas for improvement were identified. Students were then asked to reflect and comment on their marked translations by providing a summary of those areas they needed to improve and stating how they intended to incorporate the feedback for future assignments.

7 Students' Perspectives: Data Analysis

A total of 27 students enrolled in the course completed the survey, comprising a mixture of closed and open-ended questions allowing us to analyse quantitative and qualitative data.

7.1 First Set of Questions

The first set of questions was aimed at addressing the students' perceptions of the suitability of translation into Spanish as a teaching activity in modern languages degrees. Results were surprisingly positive: 100% of students stated that translation into Spanish should be taught as part of a modern languages degree and that it is a useful means of learning Spanish and a skill in its own right. Regarding employability, 89% of students agreed that translating into Spanish is an important skill to acquire.

The respondents were also asked to rate the enjoyment they had derived from translation into Spanish from (1 to 5 Likert scale, 1 being not enjoyable and 5 being very enjoyable). One student gave the activity a rating of 1, 3 a rating of 2, 10 a rating of 3, and 8 and 5 gave it a 4 and a 5, respectively, meaning that the majority of students had a very encouraging attitude to translating into the target language. This was also confirmed in the next question, when rating whether translation into Spanish is a stimulating and intellectually challenging activity. The majority of responses were found in ratings 4 and 5 (14 and 12 students, respectively), with 1 student rating this at a 3. When asked to expand on why (or why not) translation into Spanish was a useful activity and should be (or should not be) part of the Year 2 language syllabus, similar themes were identified. Three students commented that translation into English should be prioritised as most translators translate into their stronger language (English in their case). One student also noted that they felt employers would prefer a native speaker of Spanish to undertake the task but acknowledged that translating into Spanish was more intellectually stimulating than translating into their mother tongue. On the other hand, 24 students were in favour of including translation into Spanish in their course:

* Thirteen students stated that translation into Spanish helped them identify new vocabulary and gave them opportunities to reflect on structural/grammatical differences between English writing and Spanish in a practical way.

- Four students specifically mentioned that translation into Spanish was key to learning a new language and as important as translation into English.
- Seven commented that being exposed to translation into Spanish in their course was very useful in terms of possibly pursuing a career in that direction and finding out more about the target culture, even if not studying a translation degree.

It is particularly interesting to note that even despite some ever-persisting views such as that translating into English exercises should be prioritised or that some employers prefer native speakers for this task are still present, the vast majority of students had a positive approach to translating into Spanish, also stating that it needs to be present in language degrees. They acknowledged this activity as beneficial to them not only from a language development point of view but also from an employability angle.

7.2 Second Set of Questions

The second set of questions targeted the students' views on the activities presented to them in their course. From the perspective of whether the exercises had been helpful in developing their language skills, 93% of students stated that they were. Students were also given a list of potential areas they had developed when undertaking the activities, being able to choose as many as they wished (or none at all). Only one student stated that the activities overall had not helped them. As per the rest of the responses:

1. The top three elements that were selected by students were enhancement of Spanish grammar and syntax (25 responses each) and vocabulary (24).
2. These responses were closely followed by development of register and style and knowledge of the target culture (receiving 18 and 17 responses, respectively); being more exposed to a wider range of

resources such as films, TV series, films in the target language (15); and becoming more (inter)culturally aware (13).

Regarding motivation, from a rating of 1 to 5 (with 1 being not motivating to 5 being very motivating), 5 students rated the activities at 2, while 22 rated them at 3 or more (10 responses for 3, 4 for 4, and 8 for 5). In terms of the activities being stimulating and intellectually challenging (from 1 to 5), the majority of students, 25, rated them at a 4 (15 responses) and a 5 (10 responses). One student rated the activities at 2 and another one at 3. The distribution of responses changed slightly in the next question where students were asked to rate whether they found the activities enjoyable. The majority rated them with a 4 and a 5 (10 and 7 responses, respectively), but we saw a slight increase in the other ratings, with 3 students giving the activities a 2 and 7 a 3.

In the following question, students were asked about the activities they found most useful and enjoyable from a given set list of items, from which they could choose as many as they wished. Ninety per cent of students selected the actual translation text with a contextual translation brief to tackle the translation. Sixty per cent chose activities related to videos to help them prepare and reflect on the translation text (using activities created with EdPuzzle, Genially, and YouTube videos), while 33% chose the reflective questions about the translation where they would discuss issues and translation strategies. Lastly, 22% selected assessment-related activities to understand the marking criteria and what was expected from students. It is important to note that although assessment-related activities were selected only by 22% for their enjoyability and usefulness, when students were asked directly about the assessment activities and how these helped them in preparing for assignments, the results obtained were very positive—as we will discuss later on in this section.

With regard to employability, 19 students rated the activities at a 4 and a 5 (13 and 6 students, respectively), stating that the activities had equipped them with adequate employability skills. Two students rated them at 2, while six gave the activities a rating of 3. To finish off this set of questions, we asked students to expand on how the activities were (or were not) meaningful for their language-learning experience, enabling them to add any comments on the translation-into-Spanish activities, the thematic topics selected, and the skills gained. Twenty-four positive responses were received, highlighting the quality of the feedback received in the tasks and the variety of texts presented. They also valued the cultural knowledge gained and the integration of the activities into their personal lives, as summarised by the students' comments below:

> I highly valued all feedback I have received based on the translations I have submitted, both in formative weekly exercises and summative assessments. It was always well-structured, insightful, and helpful. I liked being able to compare my own translations with others on the discussion board. I liked that the feedback was always personalised, provided to each work separately, and that the translations were not reviewed all together but individually for each person. I appreciated the extra materials often provided either to help understand the context of a given text better or to engage in further voluntary research on the particular topic. The variety of texts we have been given aided in broadening my knowledge of different aspects of the target culture, sparking my interest in it and getting me accustomed to the different forms of Spanish used in various forms of texts.
>
> I really enjoyed them much more than the translation into English activities. I enjoyed the range of different text[s] and the cultural knowledge I gained by researching them. It has given me an interest in translation into Spanish, so I often watch my favourite old English language TV shows with Spanish subtitles on. They can be really fascinating! I write down any sentences I find particularly interesting or useful for my future uni work. Not only have I worked hard towards my assessments, but I have integrated these activities into my personal life.

On the other hand, one student commented that they struggled to see the relation with employability directly, noting that they felt they did not understand how to translate in registers they would be likelier to use—for example, in business and marketing settings, where as they understand it, many language graduates end up. Regarding the format in which the activities were presented, two students also added that although they enjoyed reading texts and translating them, they did not particularly like posting them on the online forum as they preferred to bring them into class and work on them together.

7.3 Third Set of Questions

The last set of questions was designed to seek the students' views on the suitability of the translation activities regarding assessment and whether online translation boards had assisted them in engaging with the translation activities and in developing a sense of community.

When asked whether they felt that the translation-into-Spanish activities included in the course were aligned with the assessment for this component of the module, 96% of the students stated that this was the case. When prompted to answer if the exercises included in the course aided them in gaining a better understanding of what was expected from students in terms of assessment, 85% responded positively, noting a slight decrease compared to the first question but still very encouraging results. In terms of the suitability of the activities for helping students prepare efficiently for their final translation-into-Spanish assessments, 89% were satisfied with the quality and design of the exercises in this respect. This shows that although initially these activities were not selected as the most enjoyable/useful by students, they see their value and applicability to their assessments.

For the next question, students were presented with a list of activities related to assessment and were asked to select those that they had found to be the most useful, being able to choose as many as they liked or none at all. Seventy-seven per cent of students selected the reflective questions to identify aspects they struggled with in the translation and find strategies to resolve them. Thirty-five per cent chose marking their own translation into Spanish using the marking criteria provided, while 15% stated that blind marking translations from student peers using the marking criteria had been one of the most helpful exercises. For this question in particular, it is important to highlight how powerful reflective questions are for students and their learning as they are given opportunities to discuss these in groups and with the rest of the class as a whole. It is also interesting to note that there is a clear preference for marking their own work and not so much for marking peers' work.

Students were also given the opportunity to expand on how the activities were or were not useful in relation to assessment, and some interesting thoughts were shared. Of all comments received, 18 were supportive of the use of these activities and found them useful as they helped them to understand what the markers were looking for and prepare them for what to expect, as well as equipping them to identify common mistakes and apply changes to future pieces of work. They also praised self-reflection activities and being challenged to find strategies to resolve translation problems, adding that they felt more confident when it came to completing the work. As one student also points out:

> The tasks including marking others' translations and comparing them with others were helpful in the way that I was able to see different methods of translating the same text, experience how different people produce completely different translations of one text.

On the other hand, seven comments were submitted on how the activities did not quite work, with these students emphasising that they would have benefitted from undertaking more activities using the marking criteria and noting that they struggled to figure out their own individual strengths and weaknesses in translation. Comments also related to peer assessment and group translation work. One student suggested that peer assessment was not helpful at the university level. Another student suggested that they did not enjoy doing group translation work as members of the group tended to have very different translations and it was hard to come to an agreement.

Moving to the use of online translation discussion boards and whether these aided in enhancing the delivery of translation activities, rating answers from 1 to 5, we found that most students rated its use from 3 to 5 (12 responses for 3, 5 for 4, and 5 for 5). Three students rated the boards at a 3, while two gave them a 1. Students were also asked about how the online delivery of translation activities had changed their approach to learning. Four students did not provide us with an answer. Of those comments in favour of the use of online translation boards, being them 14 in total:

- Five students suggested that online translation discussion boards worked very well for them as they allowed them to work more inde-

pendently and flexibly. They also stated that the translation part of the module was the only one that they had found more helpful after having been moved online.
- Five students noted that they found working on their translations on their own and posting them to discussion boards more helpful than the manner in which the face-to-face translation classes had been conducted the previous year. This is due to the fact that they had access to others' translations where they could find new solutions and look for inspiration, and the feedback was visible to everyone, so they could see what the tutors thought about various methods adopted by other students.
- Two students noted that having been more exposed to technology, they had become more accustomed to adding notes to documents, justifying their translation choices more accurately.
- Two students mentioned that working with online discussion boards had helped them by enhancing their understanding of how the areas studied in the grammar classes proved helpful when they had to do translation tasks.

Seven comments stated that online translation discussion boards had not changed their approach to the translation-into-Spanish tasks:

- Four students stated that they found it really hard to engage and retain information when the delivery was not in person as the quality of the teaching was not the same. They did not find that discussion boards offered help at times when students were confused about a certain grammar aspect behind a translation choice.
- Three referred specifically to motivation, saying that they found it harder to stay motivated and it was much easier in person.

The impact of the use of translation discussion boards on the students' sense of community was found to be a very divisive issue. On the one hand, 55.6% stated that the discussion boards had helped and enhanced a sense of belonging in the translation classes, while, on the other hand, 44.4% mentioned that the discussion boards had not helped them in this respect. When asked to expand on why or why not they did not feel online discussion boards had assisted them, we noted some interesting comments:

- Fifteen students pointed out that they found the use of translation boards really helpful for sharing their views of problems with translation and as a forum to reflect on the questions posed for translation exercises. Six students also pointed out that they had had the opportunity to meet new people and get to speak with other students, allowing them as a class to build a sense of community. Five commented that the translations published on the discussion board were available for a long time, and students could always go back to them without worrying about losing them. They also emphasised that they could have access to the translations provided by their course mates in their entirety, not in fragments, without ever sensing any competition stemming from being able to access others' translations and the feedback provided to students by the tutors. The discussion board where they worked on translations as a group was a new experience, giving them the opportunity to co-create a translation for the first time, and they found it very helpful and inspiring to see how others dealt with certain aspects of the text.
- Twelve pointed out that the teaching felt more impersonal due to the online nature of the activities. As a result, they found it challenging to interact with other peers and build a community through digital formats, as compared to in-person interaction. Of these 12 comments, three students pointed out that they found it intimidating to have to post on the discussion board where everyone could see answers and mistakes. Two also remarked that they did not feel fully comfortable engaging in discussions with their classmates.

8 Conclusions

The arrival of the pandemic took the whole teaching community by surprise, requiring a swift response to continue delivering language programmes effectively. These changes enabled us to come up with innovative and creative approaches to teaching, encouraging us to be more flexible and inclusive with our teaching materials and assessment, as well as to create a more impactful experience for our students.

The introduction of online asynchronous activities in language programmes that were delivered fully face to face pre-pandemic posed a challenge for teachers and students alike (Pais Marden and Herrington 2022). This highlighted the importance of studying the impact of these activities in the students' language-learning process, emphasising the alignment between learning outcomes, teaching materials, and assessment. With this purpose in mind, in this chapter we have proven that the delivery of translation-into-Spanish activities and engaging students with assessment through the use of online translation discussion boards can be successful.

Gathering the students' views on these implemented activities has allowed us to corroborate our hypothesis that approaching translation into the foreign language through asynchronous activities and as a communicative and reflective process can be crucial in affecting how students value and perceive this skill. Not only did all students who responded to the survey state that translation into Spanish should be an integral part of their language degree, but they also saw it (contrary to popular belief) as a motivating, stimulating, and intellectually challenging activity which makes them more employable. These results are comparable to similar surveys undertaken by Carreres (2006) and Wagstaffe (2018) and show that the activities proposed progressively aid in changing their attitudes towards translation, dismantling the myth that translation into the foreign language is daunting and only for native speakers.

Students were also able to see that the assessment activities created were clearly aligned with the final assessment tasks, and this facilitated their understanding of the marking criteria and, thus, of what was expected of them. They particularly valued the reflective element in translation assessments, which boosted their confidence in finding strategies and problem-solving and gave them a feeling of completeness and achievement.

Online translation discussion boards can enhance the delivery of translation activities, as well as the students' experience. However, more work needs to be done in relation to developing a sense of community within their translation groups. While most students acknowledged that interacting via online translation discussion boards was a positive experience, many found it more impersonal and challenging to connect with teachers and students than in the face-to-face environment.

Moving forward, it is vital for teachers and researchers of pedagogy to learn from these experiences, incorporating all the positive elements identified into our teaching practices and working with the feedback provided by students to make their learning as meaningful as possible. Therefore, we conclude that providing opportunities to collaboratively work with formative assessment, utilising a space for students to reflect and exchange best practices, is paramount. Online translation discussion boards constitute an invaluable tool to facilitate that. We firmly believe that given the reflective nature of translation, translation online discussion boards can play a strategic role even as we return to fully face-to-face teaching. The pandemic taught us that there are more ways to make our teaching insightful to our students, so let us take this unique opportunity to take language teaching to the next level.

References

Blake, R.J., and A.G. Guillen. 2020. *Brave new digital classroom: Technology and foreign language learning*. 3rd ed. Washington, DC: Georgetown University Press.

Cardiff University. 2021. Blended learning framework, five key principles 2021–22. Version 2.2. https://intranet.cardiff.ac.uk/staff/supporting-your-work/teach-and-support-students/teach-and-assess-students/learning-and-teaching-development/digital-learning-framework/five-key-principles. Accessed 25 November 2022.

Carreres, A. 2006. Strange bedfellows: Translation and language teaching. The teaching of translation into L2 in modern language degrees: Uses and limitations. In Sixth Symposium on Translation, Terminology and Interpretation in Cuba and Canada. http://www.cttic.org/ACTI/2006/papers/Carreres.pdf. Accessed 21 November 2022.

Carreres, Á. 2014. Translation as a means and as an end: Reassessing the divide. *The Interpreter and Translator Trainer* 8 (1): 123–135. https://doi.org/10.1080/1750399X.2014.908561.

Carreres, Á., and M. Noriega-Sánchez. 2021. The translation turn: A communicative approach to translation in the language classroom. In *Innovative language pedagogy report*, ed. T. Beaven and F. Rosell-Aguilar, 83–89. Cambridge, MA: University of Cambridge. https://doi.org/10.14705/rpnet.2021.50.1240.

Carreres, Á., et al. 2017. Translation in Spanish language Teaching: The Fifth Skill/La traducción en la enseñanza del español: la quinta destreza. *Journal of Spanish Language Teaching* 4 (2): 99–109. https://doi.org/10.1080/23247797.2017.1419030.

———. 2021. Introduction: Translation and plurilingual approaches to language teaching and learning. *Translation and translanguaging in multilingual contexts* 7 (1): 1–16. https://doi.org/10.1075/ttmc.00066.int.

Chakowa, J. 2019. Engaging with peers, mentors and native speakers as language learning partners in an online environment. *Alsic* 22 (2). https://doi.org/10.4000/alsic.3864.

Cook, A. 2001. Assessing the use of flexible assessment. *Assessment & Evaluation in Higher Education* 26 (6): 539–549. https://doi.org/10.1080/02602930120093878.

Cook, G. 2010. *Translation in language teaching*. Oxford: Oxford University Press.

Council of Europe. 2001. *Common European framework of reference for languages: Learning, teaching, assessment*. Strasbourg: Council of Europe Publishing. https://rm.coe.int/1680459f97. Accessed 25 November 2022.

———. 2018. *Common European framework of reference for languages: Learning, teaching, assessment—Companion volume*. Strasbourg: Council of Europe Publishing. https://rm.coe.int/cefr-companion-volume-with-new-descriptors-2018/1680787989. Accessed 25 November 2022.

———. 2020. *Common European Framework of Reference for Languages: Learning, Teaching, Assessment—Companion Volume*. Strasbourg: Council of Europe Publishing. https://www.coe.int/lang-cefr. Accessed 25 November 2022.

Hall, G., and G. Cook. 2012. Own-language use in language teaching and learning. *Language Teaching* 45 (3): 271–308. https://doi.org/10.1017/S0261444812000067.

Haslam, C. 2018. How to be Spanish *The Sunday Times*. https://www.thetimes.co.uk/article/guide-how-to-be-spanish-sgf39ttgx. Accessed 25 November 2022.

Huertas Barros, E. 2011. Collaborative learning in the translation classroom: Preliminary survey results. *JoSTrans, The Journal of Specialised Translation* 16: 42–60. https://jostrans.org/issue16/art_barros.pdf. Accessed 25 November 2022.

Irwin, B., and S. Hepplestone. 2011. Examining increased flexibility in assessment formats. *Assessment & Evaluation in Higher Education* 37 (7): 773–785. https://doi.org/10.1080/02602938.2011.573842.

Joksimović, S., et al. 2015. The history and state of online learning. In *Preparing for the digital university: A review of the history and current state of distance, blended, and online learning*, ed. G. Siemens et al., 93–132. https://web.archive.org/web/20170829065215/http://linkresearchlab.org/PreparingDigitalUniv ersity.pdf. Accessed 25 November 2022.

King, A. 2016. *Blended language learning: Part of the Cambridge papers in ELT series*. Cambridge: Cambridge University Press. https://www.cambridge.org/us/files/2115/7488/8334/CambridgePapersinELT_BlendedLearning_2016_ONLINE.pdf. Accessed 25 November 2022.

Laviosa, S. 2014. *Translation and language education. Pedagogical approaches explained*. New York and London: Routledge.

Leonardi, V. 2010. *The role of pedagogical translation in second language acquisition: From theory to practice*. Bern: Peter Lang.

Malmkjaer, K. 2010. Language learning and translation. In *Handbook of translation studies*, ed. Y. Gambier and L.V. Doorslaer, 185–190. Amsterdam: John Benjamins.

Off Course (Perdiendo el norte). 2015. Directed by Nacho García Velilla [Film]. Spain: Warner Bros.

Pais Marden, M., and J. Herrington. 2022. Asynchronous text-based communication in online communities of foreign language learners: Design principles for practice. *Australasian Journal of Educational Technology* 38 (2): 83–97. https://doi.org/10.14742/ajet.7370.

Pintado Gutierrez, L. 2020. Inverse translation and the language student: A case study. *Language Learning in Higher Education* 10 (1): 171–193. https://doi.org/10.1515/cercles-2020-2013.

Pym, A., et al. 2013. *Translation and Language Learning: The role of translation in the teaching of languages in the European Union: A study*. Luxembourg: Publications Office of the European Union.

Talaván, N. 2013. *La subtitulación en el aprendizaje de lenguas extranjeras*. Barcelona: Octaedro.

———. 2019. Creative audiovisual translation applied to foreign language education: A preliminary approach. *Journal of Audiovisual Translation* 2 (1): 53–74. https://doi.org/10.47476/jat.v2i1.57.

Wagstaffe, Sally. 2018. Translation, motivation and the CEFR. Paper presented at UK Lingua 2018 in Durham, United Kingdom.

Wanner, T., et al. 2021. Flexible assessment and student empowerment: Advantages and disadvantages—Research from an Australian University.

Teaching in Higher Education. https://doi.org/10.1080/1356251 7.2021.1989578.

Wilkins, B. 2018. Asynchronous collaboration integrating online learning in the foreign language classroom. *The Journal of Language Learning and Teaching* 8 (2): 101–108. https://dergipark.org.tr/en/pub/jltl/issue/42266/508539. Accessed 25 November 2022.

6
Loops, Sayings, and Tongue-Twisters: How to Enhance Foreign Language Communicative Skills in Online Learning Environments

Livia Manzini

1 Introduction

The move to ERT during the COVID-19 pandemic made it necessary to rethink the materials and activities to be used to address language skills for the different levels of language proficiency. As previously mentioned by other authors in this collection and by Fiorucci in the introduction, directly transporting online what used to be done face to face (F2F) was simply not an option. Therefore, researchers and teachers have engaged in a debate on the use of digital educational tools that could, on the one hand, help academics in the delivery of online or hybrid classes and, on the other hand, support students in acquiring and improving language skills while maintaining their motivation and engagement. Among the language skills that students of foreign languages (FLs) must acquire, communicative skills play a fundamental role, and they have been widely

---

L. Manzini (✉)
University of Birmingham, Birmingham, UK

Alma Mater Studiorum - Università di Bologna, Bologna, Italy
e-mail: livia.manzini2@unibo.it

identified by teachers as a particular challenge in the context of online teaching.

In this chapter, I will illustrate and analyse the results of a research project that, on the one hand, aimed to define the core sounds of the Italian language that students of Italian FL must master to maintain intelligibility during communicative exchanges. On the other hand, the research had a wider scope, intending to ascertain the effectiveness of blended learning in the design of a specific teaching strategy, which aids students in improving their pronunciation and intonation skills and, more generally, their communicative competence in the target language. Thanks to the technological devices and virtual learning environments (VLEs) available, it is possible to verbally practise a foreign language in different communicative contexts even when teachers and students are not physically in the same room. Among the different strategies adopted by teachers to enhance the acquisition of communicative skills in online learning contexts, drama techniques are an effective option when combined with the appropriate technology, as I will show in this chapter. Conceived and developed in the context of an ERT environment, the results of my research project are relevant for the future, as they define effective strategies for the acquisition of communicative skills in both face-to-face and online foreign language teaching.

In the field of foreign language acquisition, the use of teaching activities based on different drama techniques, which evoke an emotional response in students, may boost their ability to memorise some specific aspects of the target language, even in distance-learning contexts. In this respect, Decoursey stated, drawing on Damasio (1994), that 'when there is an emotional response to a perception or some learning, the brain marks it as useful to the organism. So […] drama in the language classroom [allows us to] mark elements of language with emotion so that students will remember them' (2012, p. 7).

Since the second half of the twentieth century, with the increasing predominance of the communicative approach, drama activities have been widely integrated into foreign language classes. The communicative approach owed its great success to the adoption of techniques that privileged the development of communicative skills over translation abilities (Piazzoli 2011a, b). Therefore, many scholars (Slade 1954; Way 1967; Heathcote 1984; O'Neill 1995) developed methods based on the use of creative drama, which helps students prioritise and valorise spontaneity and freedom of expression over what they express and develop concentration, creativity, and sensibility. To achieve this, the drama techniques to be adopted should first be imitative of the real world, and second, they should enhance a realistic use of the language in plausible communicative contexts by engaging the performers (the students) actively and emotionally so that the performance itself could boost memory and learning.

Drawing on the previous theorisation and application of drama techniques in the foreign language classroom, I created materials to use drama techniques in FL teaching. To achieve my research aims, I designed a qualitative study involving an experimental phase, which consisted of a series of pronunciation and intonation sessions delivered during communicative skills sessions to different groups of students of Italian as a foreign language at different levels of Italian proficiency. Students were required to engage with the activities below (in class and at home) that were selected, devised, and explained by me as teacher-as-researcher:

1. Brief dialogues ('loops'), which require students to perform them an indefinite number of times and use different emotional statuses while they practise different linguistic elements (grammatical rules, specific vocabulary, idiomatic expressions, etc.).
2. Scenes taken from films linked to the main topic of the curriculum.
3. Dialogues taken from literary texts that have already been introduced to students during plenaries.

The activities based on drama techniques were delivered during online classes on Zoom. Students were required to perform some of them by means of Vocaroo, an online voice recording tool (which allows the recorded files to be stored) that was particularly effective for several reasons. First, by storing the audio files of the students' performances during the whole academic year, I could monitor progress and identify the linguistic aspects that required further practice—to give an example, Vocaroo proved to be valuable in spotting the phonological elements that needed further training for students to reach a higher level of linguistic competence, as I will illustrate below. The experience with Vocaroo during the recent pandemic could certainly be considered a valuable and successful example of good online training of pronunciation and intonation, which could be replicated in the future by universities and other academic institutions in order to include more efficient and effective teaching of communicative skills in their curricula. The same applied to students, as they could complete the exercises and practise specific communicative skills in a safe space (i.e. they could turn their Zoom cameras and microphones off while recording on Vocaroo), which allowed them to feel more self-confident as they practised the new linguistic aspects. Furthermore, the use of an online voice recording tool gave them the chance to listen to their recordings, to spot mistakes, and to record their performance again before sending the audio file to the tutor. In this way, students were able to become more aware of both the needs and strengths of their communicative competence. They could also record themselves as many times as needed to perform the exercise well, taking charge of their learning and feeling confident about the final product. Finally, the repeated use of an online tool for the practice of verbal skills allowed students to acquire digital skills, and this turned out to be particularly effective for subsequent forms of assessments (both formative and summative oral-aural), as they were conducted via Zoom and, without any prior practice, students might have had issues related to the use of digital tools for assessment purposes. The feedback I have received so far from students suggests that the creative drama activities allow them to practise skills which are not usually addressed in language courses in a motivating, enjoyable, and meaningful way. Moreover, the use of a variety of online teaching tools during the online sessions helped students to practise and experience them intensively and to become more aware of their language competence. More generally, acquiring and practising digital skills is now a crucial and necessary element of any course, regardless of its means of delivery.

The following paragraphs provide a detailed description of the participants and the teaching materials used and explain the findings that emerged from this research.

2   The Participants

The number of subjects in the experiment was 36 during the first year of the experimental phase and 7 during the second year. The participants were first-year (beginners and advanced) and second-year (intermediate and advanced) students of Italian as FL enrolled in a BA in Modern Languages at a Northern British university. Participants were selected on a voluntary basis and were a 'sample of convenience' (McKay 2006) since they were enrolled in courses I was teaching: they were subjects that I could 'get access to' (p. 37). Two further factors guided the selection of the experiment's subjects: first, students had different levels of language proficiency, and I was interested in investigating the role of pronunciation and intonation at different levels of linguistic competence and in identifying at which level of the foreign language-learning process students could obtain better learning outcomes and develop greater language awareness. Second, the size of the groups was relatively small, which allowed me to deliver the activities more efficiently and monitor the students' learning pace, needs, and outcomes more accurately. The experiment took place for the first time during 2020–2021 (February–April) and the second during 2021–2022 (February–April). During both phases, the experiment lasted 20 minutes per week, working exclusively on the pronunciation and intonation activities devised purposely for training that could be delivered F2F, hybrid, or online.

Before participants took part in the experiment, the framework and aim of the study were explained to enable them to give informed consent for their participation and the use of the data. Students were also told that the experiment would not be part of their exam and would not affect their final mark.

3 The Selection of Teaching Materials

Loops, tongue-twisters, and sayings (the focus of this chapter) were devised and deployed for the pronunciation and intonation training. A selection of dialogic texts taken from contemporary novels, theatrical pieces, and films was also included to provide a wider choice of teaching materials. Finally, a small number of poetic forms and songs were also incorporated. The selection of activities and texts was based on experience and on the evidence from different case studies (Dockalova 2011; Korkut and Çelik 2018; Tsybaneva et al. 2019). I opted for loops, tongue-twisters, and sayings, as many scholars (e.g. Korolkova et al. 2015; Turumi et al. 2016; Nurhasanah 2018) have identified them as useful teaching resources to train and improve students' phonological awareness. Moreover, the lack of research on the use of loops for the teaching and training of Italian segmentals and suprasegmentals was a reason in itself to test them in my study and to analyse the findings derived from their implementation in online communicative skills classes. Regarding the use of dialogic texts selected from contemporary novels, theatrical pieces, and films, this choice arose from a desire to avoid literary forms that could dampen the students' motivation and hinder their engagement with pronunciation and intonation training. In this respect, contemporary literary texts and films may prove easier for students in terms of both language and content, as they feature not only a broad variety of different uses of the target language but also a considerable number of cultural, social, and historical links that can positively affect the students' mastery of both linguistic and cultural awareness. Furthermore, the combination of reading activities with drama techniques, which require students to actively perform the written texts, can provide students with detailed insight into the verbal and non-verbal habits of native speakers of the target language. It also gives them the chance to practise verbal and non-verbal features of the target language in a safe place. Finally, songs and a limited number of poetic forms (e.g. futurist poems, haikus, and pattern poems) were selected to provide examples of peculiar combinations of sounds and prosodic characteristics. Thanks to their specific phonological characteristics, they can be helpful additional material for the training of pronunciation and intonation skills.

Due to space-related constraints, in this chapter I will analyse only the results that emerged from the online use of loops, sayings, and tongue-twisters. Moreover, I will explain the use of Vocaroo for the training of communicative skills—specifically segmental and suprasegmental traits of Italian—during the two-semester-long experimental phases of the research project.

4 The First Experimental Phase (March 2021–April 2021)

In this section, I will present the materials devised and used on Zoom during the first experimental phase, which was delivered during the second term of 2020–2021.

The pronunciation and intonation training sessions were delivered during the communicative skills classes, which took the form of two-hour sessions held once a week with two different groups of beginner first-year students, one group of intermediate second-year students, and one group of advanced second-year students. The materials used for the training presented specific segmental and suprasegmental features that I selected based on the answers of a focus group. This consisted of native English speakers who were studying or had previously studied Italian. They were asked questions about the segmental and suprasegmental traits they'd found particularly difficult to master while learning Italian. The sessions were thus focused on sounds and groups of sounds identified as particularly difficult to master by native English speakers.

The pronunciation exercises involved a variety of perceptive and articulatory exercises based on decontextualised words, loops, sayings, and tongue-twisters (see Appendix, Tables 6.4, 6.6, 6.8, 6.10, and 6.13) specifically devised or selected for the training of Italian segmentals and suprasegmentals, which are generally challenging for native English speakers (e.g. liquids, dentals, nasals, single vs double consonants, -gn, -gl, etc.). The students were required to listen to the teacher pronouncing the words/sentences twice and were then invited to use Vocaroo to record themselves.[1] The activities were chosen on the basis of their phonological characteristics, and the words used in the exercises were of common usage to ensure that students knew their meanings and could later put the pronunciation and intonation training into practice (e.g. during real communicative exchanges in class).

For the practising of suprasegmentals, famous Italian sayings and tongue-twisters were selected and included in the training (see Appendix, Tables 6.4, 6.6, 6.8, 6.10, and 6.13). The selection was based on the need to practise the segmental and suprasegmental traits that were trained during the drilling activity carried out with Vocaroo. Therefore, in addition to continuing to practise the segmentals during the first part of the session, students were also required to produce the same segmentals in a contextualised phonological situation, where the co-presence of different segmental features might have resulted in a more complex realisation of the sounds already trained during the 'listen and repeat' exercise. Using tongue-twisters in the sessions was useful for the training of intonation and phonological fluency. Tongue-twisters and nursery rhymes are characterised by specific sound patterns such as alliteration, consonance, repetition, assonance, and other juxtapositions of sounds requiring good control of the articulatory system. Therefore, tongue-twisters are useful, as they allow students to become accustomed to the prosody of the target language from a perceptive as well as a productive point of view and to improve their articulatory skills. This results in more fluency and naturalness when they speak the target language, that is, bringing it closer to how speakers pronounce words when addressing their interlocutors (Prosic-Santovac 2009). Finally, Gonzales Iglesias (2009, p. 4) states that tongue-twisters are a fun activity in the language classroom, and therefore their inclusion among the activities delivered to train communicative skills can be particularly effective and enjoyable for learners.

Nursery rhymes were also included among the activities specifically devised for the training of segmental and suprasegmental features of Italian. Nursery rhymes were either selected or written by me (as was the one reported below), and they combined some of the segmentals trained in the 'listen and repeat' exercises and encouraged students to articulate the segmental features previously practised in a different phonological context, where other sounds and groups of sounds were also present (to sum up: geminates, voiceless alveopalatal fricative, and voiced alveolar trill):

Un nuovo uovo fu comprato tra gli ingredienti
Per creare una torta niente male
Tuorli, zucchero e farina
Vanno messi in una terrina
Poi si inizia a mescolare e fra poco è da infornare.
Muovi i mescoli e prepara la torta non troppo amara
Aggiungi un po' di saccarosio per renderla di un sapor ancor più

Strepitoso.
Uomini e donne la mangeranno e dell'altra ne vorranno
Quindi due te ne convien preparare
Forza, sbrigati, che di lavoro ne hai da fare!

Moreover, the phonological and prosodic characteristics of nursery rhymes help students acquire a more natural way of speaking and encourage them to improve the mechanical articulation of specific sequences of sound patterns, which may at first prove difficult to pronounce properly.

The analysis of the recordings from the pronunciation and intonation trainings held during the first experimental phase brought to the surface both the segmentals already mastered by students and some incorrect phonological reproductions practised during the sessions. Out of all the segmentals practised, students had difficulty in properly articulating the voiced palatal lateral approximant and the voiced alveolar trill preceded by a consonant. Moreover, the audio files revealed articulatory issues with the voiced alveolar trill when it is in the post-consonantal position after the voiceless dental /t/ and when it is in pre-consonantal position before the voiceless bilabial plosive /p/. Furthermore, words presenting the same graphic appearance but whose meaning changes according to the different positions of the stress were particularly difficult to pronounce. Other problematic segmental features were geminates, especially when positioned in phonological contexts with more challenging phonological traits; the combination of the voiced alveolar trill with both consonants and vowels and in different positions (pre-consonantal, post-consonantal, post-vowel, etc.) was shown to be the most difficult segmental sequence to master. Moreover, the diphthong /uo/ was not correctly articulated, and geminates were not properly pronounced. The mispronounced sounds caused difficulties in listeners' understanding of the students' performance (see Appendix, Tables 6.5 and 6.11). In the first training session, students showed that they were able to articulate geminates properly when they were in single, decontextualised words. However, when the same words were placed in more challenging phonological contexts, students at this level of language proficiency were unable to master double consonants. More specifically, for intermediate students, some issues were spotted in the articulation of the voiceless dental /t/ and voiced dental /d/, where phonological interference from the students' native language, English, was detected. Advanced-level second-year students still struggled to distinguish the nasal palatal /ɲ/ and the nasal alveolar /n/. Table 6.14 reports the results shown by the recordings of the intermediate groups and the advanced group. The only segmentals to appear problematic for the intermediate students but not for the advanced ones are the sounds /ʃ/ and /sk/.

As concerns intonation, no relevant issues were detected during the phonological reproduction of the decontextualised words. However, the recordings of the tongue-twisters revealed some difficulties in pronouncing the selected segmental features in a more phonologically articulatory context. Even the segmentals that were pronounced correctly in the pronunciation activities, which involved single decontextualised words, were not properly articulated, and this resulted in a lack of fluency and in an unnatural oral performance. The students were not able to recognise the stress changes and missed marking the changes in stress position while performing the exercises. Because of this first analysis, it appears that the mastering of suprasegmental features was impeded by the difficulty of performing some specific segmentals, which negatively affected the overall performance from an intonation point of view. This limited the fluency and naturalness of the oral performance. In the case of intermediate students, despite the inaccurate pronunciation of both dentals (the voiceless /t/ and the voiced /d/), comprehension of tongue-twisters and nursery rhymes was not compromised. The use of the same activities devised for first-year beginners for both groups of intermediates was prompted by the need to ascertain whether certain segmental and suprasegmental features can be naturally picked up by students while they are improving their general language proficiency. The recordings showed that the pronunciation and intonation issues identified for first-year beginners seemed completely absent from the performances of second-year students (Table 6.12) and that advanced-level secondyear students mastered all of the segmental and suprasegmental traits practised during the pronunciation and intonation training (Table 6.14).

5 The Second Experimental Phase (March 2022–April 2022)

As already described for the first experimental phase, the pronunciation and intonation training sessions were delivered during the communicative skills class, which was a two-hour session held once a week with one group of intermediate second-year students. The students had already received the same type of pronunciation and intonation training during their first year when they were enrolled as beginners. The pronunciation and intonation training sessions in 2021–2022 were delivered online on Zoom. Due to the different allocation of students and teachers to the communicative skills groups in 2021–2022, I was only able to gather the new recordings for half of the students who had taken part in the research project in 2020–2021. Although the number of participants was subsequently reduced, the data collected are useful for two main reasons: (1) to determine whether the students who had been training for two years had improved their performance of segmental and suprasegmental features that were not yet mastered during the first trial and (2) to determine whether students who had been trained for two years had worse, equal, or better pronunciation and intonation skills when compared to the Core IV Intermediate students who were involved in the research project in 2020–2021 and who received segmental and suprasegmental training for one semester only. The sessions delivered during the second term in 2021–2022 featured the same activities used during the 2020–2021 academic year. The structure of the pronunciation and intonation training sessions had two main aims. The first was to compare the two groups of intermediate students (the 2020–2021 group vs the 2021–2022 group) in terms of their grasp of the same segmental and suprasegmental traits, with a view to detecting possible major issues. Moreover, the comparison helped to identify on a larger scale the phonological sequences that were still not mastered or still caused articulation issues at this level of language proficiency and those that were already acquired and correctly used in oral communicative contexts. The second aim was to compare the performance of second-year intermediate students to that of their first year as beginner students, in order to identify the segmentals and suprasegmentals that are naturally acquired by students as their overall language proficiency improves. My aim was also to identify the phonemes that still caused problems despite the advancing level of the students' language skills and despite the two years of training received. Consequently, all the sessions delivered to second-year intermediate students during 2021–2022 were identical to the two sessions delivered to both first-year beginner students and second-year intermediate students during the 2020–2021 academic year. The segmentals that were addressed during the first session and the structure of the sessions were the same as those described for the first session. The tongue-twisters used in the first pronunciation and intonation training session are listed in Tables 6.4, 6.6, 6.8, 6.10, and 6.13.

For the training of suprasegmentals, two Italian tongue-twisters were included in the training once again. As already specified in the previous analysis of the recordings, the selection of tongue-twisters was based on the need to practise the single consonants and geminates that were trained during the drilling activity carried out with Vocaroo. Therefore, in addition to practising the segmentals trained during the first part of the session, students were also required to pronounce the same segmentals in a contextualised phonological situation, where the co-presence of different segmental features might have resulted in a more complex articulation of the sounds already trained during the 'listen and repeat' exercise. Using tongue-twisters in the sessions was particularly useful for training intonation and phonological fluency.

As already pointed out in the introductory paragraph, this session aimed to define and compare the phonological traits that caused articulation issues for the participants during their first year at university. The recordings gathered during the second experimental phase reflected an overall level of segmental and suprasegmental mastery appropriate for students at this level of language proficiency. Most segmental features selected for the training were already acquired and well-articulated by students. However, despite the students' improvement in the level of pronunciation and intonation, the pronunciation of some of the segmentals in the exercises was still slightly inaccurate. For instance, some students showed some difficulties in discriminating between the pairs of sounds /ʃ/ and /sk/. In the tables, the improvements made by the participants can clearly be seen. Except for the discrimination between the sounds /ʎ/ versus /l/, the segmentals that were shown to be difficult to pronounce by Core II Beginners had now been acquired (Table 6.16). Some issues were spotted in the articulation of the voiceless dental /t/ and the voiced dental /d/, where phonological interference from the students' native language, English, was again detected.

As regards the suprasegmental features, no specific issue emerged, and despite the inaccurate pronunciation of voiceless dental /t/ and the voiced dental /d/, the understanding of tongue-twisters and nursery rhymes was not compromised. Also in this case, the main aim of using the same activities devised for first-year beginners for both groups of intermediate students was to ascertain whether certain segmental and suprasegmental features can be naturally picked up as students' general language proficiency improves. The results showed that second-year students at an intermediate level have overcome the phonological issues that beset first-year students at the beginner level. For instance, as illustrated in Table 6.18, most of the segmental and suprasegmental traits that were identified as problematic for first-year students were generally well performed by second-year students. Table 6.19 also outlines the improvements made by Core IV Intermediate students during the 2021–2022 academic year, compared to those made by Core IV Intermediate students during the 2020–2021 academic year.

6 Analysis of the Summative Oral-Aural Assessments

The analysis of the Vocaroo audio files brought to the surface the specific segmental and suprasegmental traits that students at different language levels are able or unable to pronounce when they are required to articulate them in specific phonological contexts. The tongue-twisters and nursery rhymes included in the sessions required the participants to focus on the articulation of single sounds or groups of sounds that were different in each session and located in specific phonological positions and communicative contexts. As mentioned above, although the tongue-twisters and nursery rhymes were authentic resources and thus engaging training for students, this formative assessment can only provide insight into the students' level of mastery of the sounds trained in specific phonological locations. Therefore, to have a more rigorous picture of the level of the students' mastery of segmentals and suprasegmentals in spontaneous communicative contexts, it is helpful to analyse the recordings of the oral-aural assessments where students were required to discuss a chosen topic, either in the form of a presentation or in the form of a monologue, and then spontaneously answer a series of unprepared questions from the teachers. The analysis of recordings of the oral-aural assessments provides insight into the students' spontaneous use of language and will help to determine whether, in unprepared phonological contexts, students still display the same phonological deficiencies as those detected in the Vocaroo audio files. The comparison between the results gathered from the analysis of the Vocaroo recordings and those collected from the summative oral-aural assessments will also help us identify the positive outcomes that a systematic implementation of pronunciation and intonation training sessions can bring to the level of phonological awareness of students at different levels of language proficiency.

6.1 Core II Beginners: Oral-Aural Assessments (May 2021)

The summative oral-aural assessment of Core II Beginners was divided into two parts. The first consisted of a discussion. Students were required to prepare a two- to three-minute presentation on a chosen topic and answer questions from their teachers. The second part involved the discussion of unseen material. Students were given two unseen pictures and a couple of minutes to familiarise themselves with them. Then, they were asked to describe both pictures and compare them; the description of the pictures was followed by Q&A.

Tables 6.21 and 6.22 report the data collected for each Core II Beginner student during the pronunciation and intonation training sessions. The analysis of the Vocaroo audio tapes enabled us to identify the sounds causing the main articulation problems for both groups of beginners from among all the sounds trained in the pronunciation and intonation activities. Students found it particularly challenging to discriminate between [/ʎ/] and [/l/]; [/ʃ/] and [/sk/]; the voiced alveolar sibilant fricative /dz/ and the voiceless alveopalatal fricative [/s/]; [/k/] versus [/ʧ/]; [/g/] versus [/dʒ/]; the articulation of the voiced alveolar trill [/r/] when preceded or followed by another consonant sound; and the geminates.

Then, Tables 6.23 and 6.24 report the data and analysis of the summative oral-aural assessment of each beginner student. They identified the segmentals and suprasegmentals that were still causing problems after the training sessions. As the tables show, the sounds that caused the main articulation problems during the exam were the same as those that had emerged from the analysis of the Vocaroo audio files. Students had the most pronunciation issues in the articulation of geminates, [/ʎ/], the voiced alveolar sibilant fricative /dz/, the voiceless alveopalatal fricative [/s/]; [/k/] versus [/ʧ/]; [/g/] versus [/dʒ/]; [/ʃ/] versus [/sk/]. The comparison between formative and summative assessment confirmed the complexity of the articulation of the sounds listed above for students at the beginner's level of Italian. However, the more spontaneous nature of the language used during the oral-aural assessment highlighted further phonological traits that were difficult for some of the participants. In particular, the pronunciation of the grapheme [gh] appears to be particularly confusing when it appears in words that contain other complex sounds, such as [/k/] versus [/ʧ/]; for example, the word *ghiaccio* (ice) was often mispronounced as *giaccio* [dʒaʧʧio], as if the hard sound [/g/] was assimilated with the following soft sound [/ʧ/] and consequently pronounced as [/dʒ/]. Another problematic segmental was the diphthong [au], which was often pronounced as [o]; for example, *causa* (cause) became *cosa* (thing) and *pausa* (pause) became *posa* (pose). In such cases, mispronunciation might cause misunderstanding, as the incorrect articulation of the diphthong changes the meaning of words completely. Lastly, errors in word stress and the influence of other languages' suprasegmental features (especially Spanish, for those students also learning Spanish) were detected during some students' performance. The incorrect use of these suprasegmental features negatively affected the speaking performance of students by making their spoken Italian sound less natural.

The comparison between the results gathered from the pronunciation and intonation training sessions and the oral-aural assessments confirms that a more systematic implementation of pronunciation and intonation training sessions from the very first stages of language acquisition could help students remember and acquire the phonological awareness necessary to remember the articulatory and muscular positions required to pronounce all the segmental features correctly while using the target language in different communicative contexts.

6.2 Core IV Intermediate: Oral-Aural Assessments (May 2021)

The summative oral-aural assessment for Core IV Intermediate students was linked to the digital project that students had to complete as part of their summative assessment at the end of the second semester. The digital project consisted of 600 words in a PDF document or PowerPoint selected from a series of posts students had completed during Term Two on the Discussion section of the module page on Canvas. For each student, a discussion page was created with the title 'Discussione attivata da…(name of the student)'. Over the second term, the students were required to choose a topic or topics linked to the content of the communicative skills hours. This included topics addressed in the textbook, activities in the course pack, and Year Abroad-related activities. The posts needed to show that the students had engaged in preliminary research on the selected theme. Students were asked to adopt a critical approach by analysing specific issues, leaving informed comments, and trying to persuade others of their viewpoint. They were also required to stimulate a debate among their fellow 'bloggers'.

The oral-aural assessment consisted of a short presentation (five to seven minutes) on one of the topics that students had proposed on the Canvas discussion page as 'topic leader'. The topic of the presentation had to be different from the topic that students had used for their digital project assessment. They were required to present the topic, specify why they were interested in it, and analyse a specific aspect. They were required to use PowerPoint slides and show that they had engaged in independent research. The students' presentations were followed by questions from the examiners.

Tables 6.25 and 6.26 show the data collected for each Core IV Intermediate student during the pronunciation and intonation training sessions and the summative oral-aural assessments. The sounds that caused articulation issues during the pronunciation and intonation training sessions delivered in class were [] /ʃ/versus [/sk/]; [/ʎ/] versus [/l/]; [/ɲ/] versus [/n/]; geminates; the consonant r and its specific phonological positions (before and after consonants); /ʧ/versus [/k/]; and word stress. Among the participants, out of 14 students, 3 participants in group 1 (students 1, 4, and 6) and 3 more in group 2 (students 2, 4, and 7) had no articulation issue either in the performance of the training sessions or in the oral-aural assessment. For the other students, the segmentals and suprasegmentals not mastered, as they emerged from the analysis of the summative assessments, reflected those that had already been highlighted by the data collected from the Vocaroo recordings. Only two sounds did not seem to be challenging during the pronunciation and intonation activities, while they had caused some issues during the oral-aural assessment: the voiced alveolar sibilant fricative /dz/, either geminated or single, was not mastered by some of the students. In particular, the sound /dz/ was often mistaken for the voiceless alveolar sibilant [/s/]. This pronunciation issue might be caused by the influence of Spanish phonology on Italian for students of Spanish. Moreover, some students had intonation issues specifically related to the interference from Spanish suprasegmental features, which affected their Italian pronunciation. Despite the articulation issue related to the pronunciation of /dz/, the emergence of the same problematic sounds reveals that the pronunciation and intonation exercises devised for the Intermediate groups were well-tailored to the students' phonological needs. Obviously, the small amount of time devoted to the specific training of pronunciation and intonation did not allow for the overcoming of the articulation problems detected.

6.3 Core IV Advanced: Oral-Aural Assessments (May 2021)

The summative oral-aural assessment for Core IV Advanced students was structured in the same way as the one already analysed for the intermediate level of the 2020–2021 academic year. The only difference was in the required number of words for the digital project (750). Table 6.27 reports the data gathered for each Core IV Advanced student during the pronunciation and intonation training sessions and the summative oral-aural assessments. Unlike the results obtained for the Intermediate students, with the Advanced group, it was clear that when students were required to focus on specific segmental and suprasegmental features, their mastery of the phonological traits had drastically improved. Except for students 3 and 5, who had articulation issues when required to distinguish between [/ɲ/] and [/n/], no other relevant phonological errors were detected. However, when students were required to use the language in a more spontaneous communicative context and when they were not explicitly asked to focus on the articulation of sounds, more pronunciation and intonation mistakes were identified. Although mispronunciations did not interfere with the intelligibility of the students' speech, imprecisions were detected concerning the articulation of geminates and the correct location of word stress; articulation issues also emerged for the voiced alveolar sibilant fricative /dz/ and the voiced alveolar trill [/r/] and in the distinction between /ʃ/ and [/sk/]—see Table 6.27.

The comparison revealed that students were physically able to master the majority of sounds trained during targeted formative assessments. Therefore, the mistakes detected during the individual performances at the summative assessment were not caused by articulatory impediments. What emerged from the analysis, again, was the students' difficulty in remembering the place where the trained sounds are articulated. The difficulty to memorise the articulatory and muscular movements necessary to pronounce the sounds correctly reflects their lack of phonological awareness, which, at this advanced stage, was not strong enough to guarantee the correct articulation of the more difficult sounds. When students were not explicitly required to focus on the articulation of specific sounds, even students who did not make any mistakes during the training sessions mispronounced sounds that they could master in a more defined communicative context, such as the one provided by the pronunciation and intonation exercises during the communicative skills hours. A possible reason could be the very limited time specifically devoted to the training of pronunciation and intonation and to the novelty of this practice (students only attended two training sessions and had never previously received specific training or guidelines on pronunciation and intonation).

These comparative analyses in Tables 6.31 and 6.32 suggest that a more systematic and appropriate phonological training might help students to implicitly memorise the movements of the articulatory apparatus and to apply them consistently while speaking the target language without the need to focus on how to pronounce a particular sound or group of sounds. Therefore, this class for the implementation of the teaching of segmentals and suprasegmentals in the curriculum should occur from the very first year to get the students practising their phonological skills in step with the other linguistic skills acquired and honed during the communicative skills classes. Furthermore, the introduction of phonology from the beginning of their academic experience might also help the students to avoid mispronunciation mistakes that could become fossilised and subsequently be difficult to correct.

6.4 Core II Advanced: Oral-Aural Assessment (May 2021)

To better determine the students' phonological improvements associated with the pronunciation and intonation training sessions delivered in class, it was crucial to have a group of students uninvolved in the training sessions, which could therefore highlight the benefits provided by the segmental- and suprasegmental-focused activities. The benefits are not to be understood exclusively as the actual improvements in the students' phonological skills. The benefits of the segmental and suprasegmental training sessions must also work as boosters for the development of phonological awareness in both students and teachers. Phonological awareness on the part of both agents involved in the foreign language learning process would improve the students' attitude towards the acquisition of the basic phonological skills necessary to avoid misunderstandings during communicative exchanges with other speakers. It would, moreover, also lead to change, improvement, and enriching of languages curricula in Higher Education.

The Core II Advanced module was not involved in the pronunciation and intonation training sessions for two main reasons—one being that the level of Italian proficiency of this group was notably akin to the proficiency of those on the Core IV Intermediate level. Therefore, a comparison between the two was seen as useful to show the difference in the main segmental and suprasegmental issues between trained and untrained students. The analysis of the assessments followed the same procedures used for the other modules' recordings. Each student was given a number to minimise the chances that personal data might leak from the study. While listening to the recording, the phonological issues or errors that could cause misunderstanding during communicative exchanges were recorded and analysed by comparing them to the results of the analysis of the video tapes of the Core IV Intermediate summative oral-aural assessments.

The summative assessment was structured in a manner corresponding to that already highlighted for the Core IV Intermediate Group (research presentation on relevant cultural element, delivered with digital aids, followed by Q&A). Except for three students who had native speaker-like proficiency and whose performances were therefore excluded from the phonological analysis, the recordings revealed phonological issues that mirrored the results already highlighted during the analysis of the Core IV Intermediate recordings and summative assessments. For Core II Advanced as well, the phonological traits that emerged as problematic were: [/ɲ/]; consonant /r/ and its specific phonological locations (before and after consonants); and word stress. Moreover, the voiced alveolar sibilant fricative /dz/, either geminated or single, was not mastered by some of the students. In particular, the sound /dz/ was often mistaken for the voiceless alveolar sibilant [/s/]. Another problematic segmental was the diphthong [/au/], which was often pronounced as [/o/]. The only segmentals that did not cause relevant issues in this group of students were the geminated sounds, which had been identified as problematic phonological traits for the Intermediate group. The results reveal that phonological issues were also present among students who had a high level of language proficiency.

Therefore, as already pointed out, without specific pronunciation and intonation training, students may keep on mispronouncing sounds and causing misunderstandings during communicative exchanges with other speakers. A more systematic inclusion of phonological training and the introduction of the study of phonology from the very beginning of the students' journey might counter this.

6.5 Core IV Intermediate (Ex Core II Beginners): Oral-Aural Assessment (2021–2022)

The summative oral-aural exercise for Core IV Intermediate consisted of a chosen topic, presented in the form of either a presentation or a monologue, followed by a few unprepared questions from the teachers, which students had to answer spontaneously. Core IV Intermediate students were the only group who had received pronunciation and intonation training during both 2020–2021 and 2021–2022 Term Two. Hence, an analysis of the oral-aural assessment of some of the Core IV Intermediate students' exam recordings, comparing these with the results of the analysis of the same students' Vocaroo audio files, will provide a comprehensive picture of outcomes. In the analysis of the 2021–2022 recordings, each student is named by using the same identification number already used in the analysis of the Vocaroo audio files and the oral-aural assessment recorded in the 2020–2021 academic year.

The analysis identified the positive outcomes that a systematic, appropriate, and longer-term implementation of pronunciation and intonation training sessions can bring to the level of phonological awareness of students. Furthermore, the analysis of recordings of the oral-aural assessments provided insight into the students' spontaneous use of the language and helped to determine whether, in unprepared phonological contexts, students still made the same phonological errors as those that emerged from the data collected through the Vocaroo audio files.

Tables 6.28, 6.29, and 6.30 in Appendix report the data collected for students during the pronunciation and intonation training sessions and the summative oral-aural assessments in 2021–2022. The sounds that caused articulation issues during the pronunciation and intonation training sessions delivered in class were /ʃ/ and /sk/; [/ʎ/] versus [/l/]; [/ɲ/] versus [/n/]; geminates; the consonant r and its specific phonological locations (before and after consonants); /tʃ/versus [/k/]; and word stress.

Unlike the analysis of the 2020–2021 recordings, all 2021–2022 students presented articulatory issues either in their performance in the training sessions, in their oral-aural assessment, or in both. The unmastered segmentals and suprasegmentals that emerged from the analysis of the summative assessments match those that have already been highlighted in the data collected from the Vocaroo recordings (Tables 6.30, 6.31, and 6.32). The comparison between the results from the pronunciation and intonation training sessions and the oral-aural assessments revealed that students had similar but fewer articulation issues in more spontaneous communicative exchanges (i.e. unprepared answers to the questions during the exam) than in predetermined communicative contexts (i.e. tongue-twisters and nursery rhymes). Only in a very small number of cases did the audio tapes of the summative oral-aural assessments highlight segmental and suprasegmental features that caused articulation issues and, in some cases, misunderstandings only during spontaneous speech that had not emerged during the formative training sessions. In general, the oral-aural assessment recordings showed a significant improvement in the students' pronunciation skills. For example, in the first group, student 2's oral-aural assessment tape showed that the student only had repeated issues in distinguishing between /ʃ/ and /sk/, while the other segmental features identified as not mastered in the Vocaroo recordings seemed to have been mastered in the oral-aural exercise. Similarly, student 5 still had articulation issues with the sound [/r/] when placed before another consonant, but they seemed to have overcome the other pronunciation inaccuracies that were noticed during the training sessions. Similar results also emerged from the analysis of group 2's oral-aural assessment recordings. Student 6 still had issues with the articulation of the sound [/l/] but demonstrated that s/he could master the sound [/ɲ/] during the oral-aural assessment; student 7 did not appear to have any of the articulation issues highlighted during the analysis of the Vocaroo audio tapes but still had difficulties with the suprasegmental features of Italian; and student 9 still showed inaccuracies in word stresses, but none of the articulation issues that had surfaced in the Vocaroo files were still present in their oral-aural assessment. The only exception was student 4—although the recording of their exam shows that they were able to master the sound [/ʎ/], there were still frequent inaccuracies when pronouncing the sounds [/r/] and [/t/], and they also mispronounced the sound [/ɲ/], which did not emerge as an unmastered segmental during the analysis of the Vocaroo recordings.

Despite the exception of student 4 from group 2, the analysis of the oral-aural assessment recordings highlights the students' acquisition of the segmental and suprasegmental traits that had caused issues during the training sessions.

To lend further support to the hypothesis that the prolonged and systematic training of segmentals and suprasegmentals positively affects students' phonological awareness and skills, it is relevant to compare the results of the analysis of the oral-aural assessment collected during 2020–2021 with the results from the summative oral-aural exercise conducted in 2021–2022. As already pointed out, the sample of students analysed during 2021–2022 had already been analysed in 2020–2021, and these students were the only ones who had received training over two years during their communicative skills hours (Tables 6.31 and 6.32).

The tables sum up each student's progress over the two years of pronunciation and intonation training, showing how each participant had improved their pronunciation skills by overcoming at least some of the pronunciation issues that had emerged at the end of the first pronunciation and intonation training session. Several factors may have contributed to the development of greater phonological competence and skills—for instance, the higher level of language proficiency of students, greater self-confidence while speaking the target language, a motivation to improve their language skills before their year abroad, and increased cultural competence gained during the classes.

7   The Students' Feedback

The respondents who filled in the questionnaire were 12 in total (gender: 11 females and 1 male; ethnic background: 10 white British, 1 white Irish, 1 white other background (Croatian), and 1 white/Asian; first language: 11 native English speakers and 1 native Croatian speaker). Out of the 12 respondents, 3 students were first-year beginners, 8 students were second-year intermediates, and 1 student was second-year advanced. The results of a Four-point Likert scale Questionnaire for students on the role of pronunciation and intonation in learning Italian as a foreign language, delivered at the end of the two-year-long training, reveal that learners do believe that these skills play a crucial role in their final learning outcomes and consider activities aiming at their development very useful. More precisely, the answers provided to the question 'In your perception, could specific pronunciation- and intonation-training be useful to improve your ability to master the sounds listed above? Please tick (✓) how useful specific pronunciation training is for you (1: NOT USEFUL; 2: SLIGHTLY USEFUL; 3: USEFUL; 4: VERY USEFUL)' show that: one student considered the training very useful; three students considered the training useful and were interested in it; one student considered the training useful, and they were very interested; seven students considered the training very useful and they were very interested in it. The answers collected confirm that generally students, despite their different levels of language proficiency, consider the implementation of pronunciation and intonation training positively and are interested in doing specific activities and exercises in order to acquire or improve their pronunciation and intonation skills. Therefore, a systematic and appropriate teaching of segmental and suprasegmental features would be appreciated by students of modern languages, as the long-form answers reported below suggest:

[1] I feel more confident when speaking and reading in front of others however I am yet to master or become overly familiar with certain sounds.
[2] My pronouncing has improved massively with speaking exercises but I feel I need more practice/immersion to sound like a native speaker.
[3] Because I think that I have improved on areas that I found difficult (like double consonants) but I definitely still have a bit of an English accent when speaking.
[4] Some of my pronunciation/intonation has improved but other sounds aren't as understandable.

The answers provided by the respondents suggest that they have developed a level of pronunciation and intonation awareness that allows them to better define the segmentals and suprasegmentals that still need some practice in order to be fully mastered. Another aspect emerging from the answers is the negative influence that unmastered sounds can have on learners' confidence, especially during oral communicative exchanges with native speakers. This is another reason why pronunciation and intonation training should be introduced systematically and appropriately in modern languages curricula—students can then practise and improve the phonological features that may negatively interfere with their use of the target language, both in class and in more natural communicative contexts.

Similarly, the students' answers to the mid-term evaluation survey for 2020–2021, which have been reported in the table below, revealed that learners appreciated the use of drama techniques during the communicative skills classes as they found them to be particularly enjoyable and effective exercises. Chiefly, students confirm that these activities helped them to actively learn the language (in particular, speaking and listening skills) in a rather relaxed and friendly environment.

> [1] I really like the incorporation of music into the modules, I like the pronunciation and speaking practice as it's very useful, I also enjoy having a smaller class as I feel more involved and everyone can participate easily.
> [2] I enjoy when teachers allow us to be creative, such as creating a scenario using the vocabulary we've just learned.
> [3] The discussion topics are interesting; we learn interesting vocabulary; pronunciation exercises.
> [4] Friendly environment, attention to increasing vocabulary, fun activities like dialogues and acting.

The students' feedback also confirms, from the learners' perspective, the validity of exercises based on drama techniques for the training of pronunciation and intonation and of communicative skills more generally.

8 Conclusions

One of the aims of my research was to define the core sounds of the Italian language that learners of Italian FL must master in order to maintain intelligibility during communicative exchanges in the target language. The relevance of pronunciation and intonation training is maintained by many scholars, as noted above, and this was also one of the beliefs which inspired this study. Moreover, the interviews conducted before the start of this research with native English speakers who studied/study Italian during their university years pointed out some of the most difficult Italian sounds to master—for example, double consonants which indicate a difference in meaning; the rolling /r/, dentals (/t/ vs /d/), /ɲ/, /ʎ/, /tʃ/ vs /k/, /ʃ/ vs /sk/ Starting from that list and taking inspiration from Jenkins' Lingua Franca Core (Jenkins 2002), I designed specific teaching materials to be used during both online and blended teaching sessions, such as loops, sayings, tongue-twisters, and nursery rhymes; I also selected literary texts, in particular dialogic texts, from contemporary novels, theatrical plays, and movies, as well as songs and specific forms of poetry which, however, have not been tested during this research project, but which represent examples of accepted good practice for language tutors. Finally, I created activities and exercises to be undertaken using an online recording voice tool named Vocaroo, which greatly helped students to practise pronunciation and intonation skills autonomously and which allowed me to keep track of the students' progress over the two-year research project. The drama activities delivered on Zoom and supported by the use of Vocaroo did not only help students to improve their communicative skills and cultural awareness but also provided them with the necessary digital skills to successfully complete online summative oral-aural assessments. In fact, the activities done online during the two experimental phases of this research project acted as a relevant and targeted training for students to feel more self-confident and at ease while learning through virtual learning environments. As a result, they also felt more confident when being assessed online, also thanks to the expertise gained with technological devices and digital tool functions (e.g. Zoom) through the online-only delivery of communicative skills classes over an extended period of time. Drama techniques helped them to practise how to use their voice and para-verbal and non-verbal elements which may be used differently in communicative exchanges delivered online. Thus, I suggest the inclusion in academic curricula of online sessions where students are required to learn and actively perform—for instance, through the use of creative drama activities. Online learning could be beneficial for them not only in terms of their learning outcomes but also in terms of final results in summative assessments.

The findings revealed that regular and appropriate online training of segmentals and suprasegmentals positively affected students' phonological awareness and more general communicative skills. As far as the pronunciation of single sounds or groups of sounds is concerned, it has been possible to identify specific segmentals that generally cause articulation issues for students of Italian FL, for instance, the rolling /r/, dentals (/t/ vs /d/), /ɲ/, /ʎ/, /tʃ/ vs /k/, /ʃ/ vs /sk/, geminates. However, teachers who are willing to introduce systematic pronunciation and intonation training sessions among their classes are advised to ask their students directly which segmental and suprasegmental traits they personally find difficult to master—since FL classes may include a variety of linguistic backgrounds, it would be more inclusive (and, hence, motivating) to adapt the segmental and suprasegmental training to the learning needs of every student.

Intonation appeared to be the most difficult phonological skill for students to master, as data revealed that 'unnatural' intonation was one of the issues that emerged most frequently from the analysis of the recordings. However, more intense and consistent intonation training based on the use of materials that encourage the development of suprasegmental traits (i.e. dialogues taken from contemporary novels, films, and theatrical pieces, or the use of a variety of poetical forms and songs) could improve students' mastery of intonation as well. For improvements to happen and to make communicative skills exercises meaningful within the overall FL learning process, teachers must select sources and devise new materials that combine the practice of specific segmental and suprasegmental traits with the training of other language skills. To link the language acquisition process closely to the acquisition of cultural awareness, pronunciation and intonation training sessions should be thematically linked to the topics addressed in the academic curricula. In this way, phonological training would benefit from the use of materials that students are familiar with from plenaries and seminars, and the training of segmentals and suprasegmentals that characterise specific and technical vocabulary related to certain topics could improve students' self-confidence when addressing those topics in the target language.

Appendix

Table 6.1 Linguistic analysis of the Core II Beginners' recordings – Group 1 and Group 2, Term 2 – Academic Year 2020/2021

Date	Segmentals mastered	Segmentals not mastered	Intonation
01/03/2021	Double consonants /r/ /t/ /ɲ/	/br/ /ʎ/	Single words are generally pronounced correctly
04/03/2021	/r/	/ʎ/ vs /l/ /ɲ/ vs /n/ Stress Double consonants	Students are not able to reproduce all segmentals; they just focus on the segmentals trained at that time
18/03/2021	/rv/	Stress /rl/ /tr/	
22/03/2021	/rv/	–/rd/ –/rf/ –/rt/ –/rl/ /ʃ/ vs /sk/ Double consonants	
24/03/2021	/t/	–/sbr/ –/uor/ –/rn/ –/rt/ –/tr/ –/uo/ Double consonants	

6 Loops, Sayings, and Tongue-Twisters: How to Enhance... 179

Table 6.2 Linguistic analysis of the Core IV Intermediate's recordings – Group 1 and Group 2, Term 2 – Academic Year 2020/2021

Date	Segmentals mastered	Segmentals not mastered	Intonation
08/03/2021	/ʎ/ vs /l/ /dʒ/ vs /g/ /tʃ/vs /k/ Double consonants /r/	/ʃ/ vs /sk	
18/03/2021	/tr/ /r/	/t/, /d/	
22/03/2021	/rv/	n.a.	
25/03/2021		n.a.	

Table 6.3 Linguistic analysis of the Core IV Advanced's recordings – Term 2 – Academic Year 2020/2021

Date	Segmentals mastered	Segmentals not mastered	Intonation
04/03/2021		/ɲ/ vs /n/	
24/03/2021	/r/ /ʎ/ vs /l/ /tr/ /rv/		

Table 6.4 Core II Beginners (group 1)—segmentals trained during training sessions 1 and 2 – Term 2 – Academic Year 2020–2021

	Single vs geminated /l:/ vs /l/ /s:/ vs /s/ /m:/ vs /m/	Voiced alveolar trill in post-consonantal position. /pr/ /br/ /tr/	Geminated voiced alveolar trill. /r:/	The nasal palatal /ɲ/	The nasal palatal /ɲ/ vs the nasal alveolar /n/	Voiceless dental (single, double and in the middle of a word and post-consonant) /t/ /t:/ /rt/	The voiced alveolar sibilant fricative(at the beginning of a word, in the middle of a word) /dz/ /ndz/
Voiced palatal lateral approximant /ʎ/	paLLa vs paLa caSSa vs caSa caMMino vs caMino	Prato liBRo Trono	aRRivare coRRere maRRone	coGNome Gnocchi Gnomo	CampaGNa CampaNia	Tavolo teTTo toRTa	Zucchero Zanzara melanZana
coniGlio							
taGLiare							
imbroGLiare							

Geminates /l:/ /s:/ /n:/	Voiced palatal lateral approximant /ʎ/	Voiceless alveopalatal fricative + voiceless velar plosive /ʃ/ vs /sk/	Voiced alveolar trill /r/
Un'antica stele era ricoperta di stelle incise con uno scalpello ed un martello, e dipinte così bene che sembrava che avessero usato un pennarello al posto di un pennello.[a]	Io cercavo l'erba–voglio, tra le foglie, sotto il tiglio, ma ho trovato solo miglio, un cespuglio di cerfoglio, fiori rossi di trifoglio. Ma non c'era l'erba-voglio.[b]	Ho in tasca l'esca ed esco per la pesca, ma il pesce non s'adesca, c'è l'acqua troppo fresca. Convien che la finisca, non prenderò una lisca! Mi metto in tasca l'esca e torno dalla pesca.	Sei tu quel barbaro barbiere che barbaramente barbasti la barba a quel povero barbaro barbone? Remo rema sul Reno con remi di rame.

[a]This tongue-twister was devised by the researcher
[b]Unless devised by the researcher, all material used for training consisted of well-known Italian tongue-twisters and rhymes. See Web References section for information

6 Loops, Sayings, and Tongue-Twisters: How to Enhance... 181

Table 6.5 Core II Beginners (group 1)—results for the segmentals trained during training sessions 1, 2, and 3 – Term 2 – Academic Year 2020–2021

Date	Segmentals mastered	Segmentals not mastered	Intonation
01/03/2021 and 04/03/2021	Geminates /r/ /t/ /ɲ/	/br/ /ʎ/ vs /l/ /ɲ/ vs /n/	Single words work fine. Issues were detected with tongue-twisters
25/03/2021	/t/	–/sbr/ –/uor/ –/rn/ –/rt/ –/tr/ –/uo/ Geminates	Issues with more complex phonological patterns were detected

Table 6.6 Core II Beginners (group 1)—tongue-twisters used during training sessions 1 and 2 – Term 2 – Academic Year 2020–2021

Stressed words	Geminates /p:/ /t:/ /r:/ /k:/ /n:/ /tʃ/	Geminates vs single consonants /s:/ vs /dz/ /l:/ vs /l/ /r:/ vs /r/	Voiceless alveopalatal fricative	Voiced alveolar trill /r/
Per colpa di un accento/un tale di Santhià/ credeva d'essere alla meta/ed era appena a metà./ Per analogo errore/un contadino a Rho/ tentava invano di cogliere/le pere da un però./ Non parliamo del dolore/di un signore di Corfù/ quando, senza più accento,/il suo cucu non cantò più (Rodari 2010).	Appendiamo un cappotto marrone ad un attacca-panni di legno ed ottone.	Il vecchio e caro carro portava a casa una cassa che conteneva una pala ed una palla.	Se la serva non ti serve, a che serve che ti serva di una serva che non serve? Serviti di una serva che serve, e se questa non ti serve, serviti dei miei servi. Se oggi seren non è, doman seren sarà. Se non sarà seren, si rasserenerà.	Treno troppo stretto e troppo stracco stracca troppi storpi e stroppia troppo.

Table 6.7 Core II Beginners (group 1)—results for the tongue-twisters used during training sessions 1 and 2 – Term 2 – Academic Year 2020–2021

Date	Segmentals mastered	Segmentals not mastered	Intonation
18/03/2021 and 24/03/2021	/s/ /r/ –/rv/	–/rp/ –/tr/ Stress changes and geminates	Issues with more complex phonological patterns were detected

Table 6.8 Core II Beginners (group 2)—segmentals trained during training sessions 1 and 2 – Term 2 – Academic Year 2020–2021

Sound discrimination	Drilling of consonants	Training of geminates	Intonation
The nasal palatal /ɲ/ vs the nasal alveolar /n/; Voiced palatal lateral approximant /ʎ/ vs voiced alveolar lateral approximant /l/ Voiceless palatal affricate /tʃ/ vs voiceless velar plosive /k/ /ɲ/ vs /n/ Il compagno di Melania ha sognato di accompagnare sua cognata in campagna, in Campania, per farle compagnia in caso di bisogno (This tongue-twister was devised by the researcher) /ʎ/ vs/ l/ Sul tagliere l'aglio taglia, non tagliare la tovaglia; la tovaglia non è aglio, se la tagli fai uno sbaglio /tʃ/ vs /k/ Il cuoco cuoce in cucina e dice che la cuoca giace e tace perché sua cugina non dica che le piace cuocere in cucina col cuoco.	Voiceless alveopalatal fricative /s/ Voiced alveolar trill. /r/ –/S/ Sa chi sa se sa chi sa, che se sa non sa se sa, sol chi sa che nulla sa, ne sa più di chi ne sa –/R/ Trentatrè Trentini entrarono a Trento tutti e trentatrè trotterellando. Sopra la panca la capra canta, sotto la panca la capra crepa. Tigre contro tigre.	Voiced alveolar lateral approximant /l:/ Voiceless dental /t:/ The voiced alveolar trill when preceded by the voiced dental fricative /tr/ /T:/, /TR/ Stanno stretti sotto i letti sette spettri a denti stretti.–DOPPIE Apelle figlio di Apollo fece una palla di pelle di pollo. Tutti i pesci vennero a galla per vedere la palla di pelle di pollo fatta da Apelle figlio di Apollo.	No particular suprasegmental-related issues were detected

6 Loops, Sayings, and Tongue-Twisters: How to Enhance... 183

Table 6.9 Core II Beginners (group 2)—results for the segmentals trained during training sessions 1 and 2 – Term 2 – Academic Year 2020–2021

Date	Segmentals mastered	Segmentals not mastered	Intonation
08/03/2021	/ʎ/ vs /l/ /ɲ/ vs /n/ /dʒ/ vs /g/ /tʃ/ vs /k/ Double consonants /r/	/ʃ/ vs /sk/	No particular suprasegmental-related issues were detected

Table 6.10 Core II Beginners (group 2)—tongue-twisters used during training session 3 – Term 2 – Academic Year 2020–2021

Geminates /l:/ /s:/ /n:/	Voiced palatal lateral approximant. /ʎ/	Voiceless alveopalatal fricative /s/	Voiced alveolar trill. /r/
Un'antica stele era ricoperta di stelle incise con uno scalpello ed un martello, e dipinte così bene che sembrava che avessero usato un pennarello al posto di un pennello.[a]	Io cercavo l'erba–voglio, tra le foglie, sotto il tiglio, ma ho trovato solo miglio, un cespuglio di cerfoglio, fiori rossi di trifoglio. Ma non c'era l'erba-voglio.	Ho in tasca l'esca ed esco per la pesca, ma il pesce non s'adesca, c'è l'acqua troppo fresca. Convien che la finisca, non prenderò una lisca! Mi metto in tasca l'esca e torno dalla pesca.	Sei tu quel barbaro barbiere che barbaramente barbasti la barba a quel povero barbaro barbone? Remo rema sul Reno con remi di rame.

Un nuovo uovo fu comprato tra gli ingredienti
Per creare una torta niente male
Tuorli, zucchero e farina
Vanno messi in una terrina
Poi si inizia a mescolare e fra poco è da infornare.
Muovi i mescoli e prepara la torta non troppo amara
Aggiungi un po' di saccarosio per renderla di un sapor ancor più
Strepitoso.
Uomini e donne la mangeranno e dell'altra ne vorranno
Quindi due te ne convien preparare
Forza, sbrigati, che di lavoro ne hai da fare![b]

[a]This tongue-twister was devised by the researcher
[b]This nursery rhyme was devised by the researcher

Table 6.11 Core II Beginners (group 2)—results for the tongue-twisters used during training session 3 – Term 2 – Academic Year 2020–2021

	Date	Segmentals mastered	Segmentals not mastered	Intonation
First-year Core II Beginners	25/03/2021	/t/	/sbr/ /uor/ /rn/ /rt/ /tr/ /uo/ Geminates	Issues with more complex phonological patterns were detected

Table 6.12 Comparison between the results of Core II Beginner's (Group 1 and Group 2) and Core IV Intermediate's (Group 1 and Group 2) – training sessions 1 and 2 – Term 2 – Academic Year 2020–2021

	Date	Segmentals mastered	Segmentals not mastered	Intonation
First-year Core II Beginners	18/03/2021 and 22/03/2021	/s/ /r/ /rv/	/rp/ /tr/ Stress changes and geminates	Issues were detected in relation to more complex phonological patterns
Second-year Core IV Intermediates	18/03/2021	Geminates /tr/ /r/ /rp/	/t/ /d/	No particular suprasegmental-related issues were detected
	22/03/21	/rv/	n/a	

Table 6.13 Core IV Intermediate (Group 1 and Group 2)—segmentals trained during training sessions 1, 2, and 3 – Term 2 – Academic Year 2020–2021

Sound discrimination	Drilling of consonants	Training of geminates	Intonation
The nasal palatal /ɲ/ vs the nasal alveolar /n/ Voiced palatal lateral approximant /ʎ/ vs voiced alveolar lateral approximant /l/ Voiceless palatal affricate /tʃ/ vs voiceless velar plosive /k/	Voiceless alveopalatal fricative /s/ Voiced alveolar trill /r/	Voiced alveolar lateral approximant /l:/ Voiceless dental /t:/ The voiced alveolar trill when preceded by the voiced dental fricative /tr./	No particular suprasegmental-related issues were detected
/ɲ/ vs /n/ Il compagno di Melania ha sognato di accompagnare sua cognata in campagna, in Campania, per farle compagnia in caso di bisogno.[a]	/s/ Sa chi sa se sa chi sa, che se sa non sa se sa, sol chi sa che nulla sa, ne sa più di chi ne sa	/t:/, /tr/ Stanno stretti sotto i letti sette spettri a denti stretti. –double consonants Apelle figlio di Apollo fece una palla di pelle di pollo. Tutti i pesci vennero a galla per vedere la palla di pelle di pollo fatta da Apelle figlio di Apollo.	

[a]This tongue-twister was devised by the researcher

Table 6.14 Comparative analysis of the results of Core IV Intermediate (GRoup 1 and GRoup 2) and Core IV Advanced—training session 1 – Term 2 – Academic Year 2020–2021

	Date	Segmentals mastered	Segmentals not mastered	Intonation
Core IV Advanced	04/03/2021	All segmental features	n.a.	No particular suprasegmental-related issues were detected
Core IV Intermediate	08/03/2021	/ʎ/ vs /l/ /ɲ/ vs /n/ /dʒ/ vs /g/ /tʃ/ vs /k/ Double consonants /r/	/ʃ/ vs /sk/	No particular suprasegmental-related issues were detected

Table 6.15 Comparative analysis of the results of Core II Beginner (Group 1 and Group 2), Core IV Intermediate (Group 1 and Group 2), and Core IV Advanced—all training sessions – Term 2 – Academic Year 2020–2021

	Date	Segmentals mastered	Segmentals not mastered	Intonation
Second-year Core IV Advanced	24/03/2021	/r/ /ʎ/ vs /l/ /tr/ /rv/	n.a.	No particular suprasegmental-related issues were detected
Second-year Core IV Intermediates	18/03/21 22/03/21	Geminates /tr/ /r/ /rp/ /rv/	/t/ /d/ n.a.	No particular suprasegmental-related issues were detected
First-year Core II Beginners	18/03/21 22/03/21	[/s/] [/r/] /rv/	/rp/ /tr/ Stress changes and geminates	Issues were detected in relation to more complex phonological patterns

Table 6.16 Comparative analysis of the results of Core II Beginner (Group 1 and Group 2) and Core IV Intermediate (Group 1 and 2) – training sessions 1, 2, and 3 – Term 2 – Academic Year 2020–2021

Date	Segmentals mastered	Segmentals not mastered	Intonation
Core IV Intermediate Academic year 2020–2021			
04/03/2021	/dʒ/ vs /g/ /tʃ/ vs /k/ double consonants /r7 /ʃ/ vs /sk/	/ʎ/ vs /l/	Stress issues related to unknown words
18/03/2021	/tr/ /r/ /t/, /d/	/ʎ/ vs /l/	Stress issues related to unknown words
25/03/2021	All segmentals included in the exercises were mastered by the students	n.a.	Stress issues related to unknown words
Core II Beginners Academic year 2020–2021			
01/03/2021	Double consonants /r/ /t/ /ɲ/	/br/ /ʎ/	Single words work fine
04/03/2021	/r/	/ʎ/ vs /l/ /ɲ/ vs /n/ Stress Double consonants	Students are not able to reproduce all segmentals; they just focus on the segmentals trained in each session
18/03/2021	/rv/	Stress /rl/ /tr/	
22/03/2021	/rv/	/rd/ /rf/ /rt/ /rl/ /ʃ/ vs /sk/ double consonants	
25/03/2021	/t/	/sbr/ /uor/ /rn/ /rt/ /tr/ /uo/ Double consonants	

Table 6.17 Core IV Intermediate (Group 1 and Group 2)—results for the segmentals trained during training sessions 1, 2, and 3 – Term 2 – Academic Year 2020–2021

Core IV Intermediate			
date	Segmentals mastered	Segmentals not mastered	Intonation
08/03/2021	/ʎ/ vs /l/ /dʒ/ vs /g/ /tʃ/ vs /k/ Double consonants /r/	/ʃ/ vs /sk/	
18/03/2021	/tr/ /r/	/t/, /d/	
22/03/2021	/rv/	n.a.	
25/03/2021		n.a.	

Table 6.18 Comparative analysis of the results across the two academic years for Core II Beginner (Group 1 and Group 2, 2020–2021) and Core IV Intermediate (Group 1 and Group 2, 2021–2022)

	Date	Segmentals mastered	Segmentals not mastered	Intonation
Core IV Intermediate Academic year 2021–2022	04/03/2022	/dʒ/ vs /g/ /tʃ/ vs /k/ Double consonants r /ʃ/ vs /sk/	/ʎ/ vs /l/	Stress issues related to unknown words
Core II Beginners Group 1 Academic year 2020–2021	01/03/2021	Double consonants /r/ /t/ /ɲ/	/br/ /ʎ/	
Core II Beginners Group 2 Academic year 2020–2021	04/03/2021	/r/	/ʎ/ vs /l/ /ɲ/ vs /n/ Stress Double consonants	Students are not able to reproduce all segmentals; they just focus on the segmentals trained from time to time

6 Loops, Sayings, and Tongue-Twisters: How to Enhance... 189

Table 6.19 Core IV Intermediate (Group 1 and GRoup 2)—results across the two academic years 2020–2021 and 2021–2022

	Date	Segmentals mastered	Segmentals not mastered	Intonation
Core IV Intermediate Academic year 2021–2022	18/03/2022	/tr/ /r/ /t/, /d/ /ʎ/ vs /l/	n.a.	Stress issues related to unknown words
Core IV Intermediate Academic year 2020–2021	08/03/2021	/ʎ/ vs /l/ /ɲ/ vs /n/ /dʒ/ vs /g/ /tʃ/ vs /k/ Double consonants	/ʃ/ vs /sk/	No particular suprasegmental-related issues were detected

Table 6.20 Core IV Intermediate (Group 1 and Group 2) and Core II Beginner (Group 1 and Group 2) results across the two academic years 2020–2021 and 2021–2022

	Date	Segmentals mastered	Segmentals not mastered	Intonation
Core IV Intermediate Academic year 2021–2022	25/03/2022	All segmentals included in the exercises were mastered by the students	n.a.	Stress issues related to unknown words
Core II Beginner Academic year 2020–2021	25/03/2021	/t/	/sbr/ /uor/ /rn/ /rt/ /tr/ /uo/ Geminates	Issues with more complex phonological patterns were detected

Table 6.21 Core II Beginners (Group 1)—comparative analysis of each student's performance during training sessions 1 and 2 – Term 2 – Academic Year 2020–2021

Group 1 Pronunciation and intonation training sessions		
Student	Segmentals and suprasegmentals not mastered 01/03/2021	Segmentals and suprasegmentals not mastered 22/03/2021
Student 1	/ʎ/ /rt/ Some geminates (*marone, corere*)	Distinction between single consonants and geminates (*maronne, ottonne*) /ʃ/ vs /sk/
Student 2	Voiceless alveopalatal fricative [/s/]—	n.a.
Student 3	n.a.	n.a.
Student 4	/ʎ/ Voiceless alveopalatal fricative /s/	/ʎ/ vs /l/
Student 5	Voiceless alveopalatal fricative /s/ /br/	/rt/ /gr/ /tr/ /ʃ/ vs /sk/
Student 6	n.a.	Distinction between single and geminated voiceless alveopalatal fricative /s/

6 Loops, Sayings, and Tongue-Twisters: How to Enhance... 191

Table 6.22 Core II Beginners (Group 2)—comparative analysis of each student's performance during training sessions 1, 2, and 3 – Term 2 – Academic Year 2020–2021

Group 2 Pronunciation and intonation training sessions			
Student	Segmentals and suprasegmentals not mastered 04/03/2021	Segmentals and suprasegmentals not mastered 18/03/2021	Segmentals and suprasegmentals not mastered 25/03/2021
Student 1	n.a	Absent	Absent
Student 2	n.a.	n.a.	n.a.
Student 3	/tr/ /ʎ/ the voiced alveolar sibilant fricative /dz/	/k/ vs /tʃ/ /g/ vs /dʒ/	/ʎ/ vs /l/
Student 4	/pr/ /br/ /tr/ /rt/ /r/ /ʎ/ Distinction between the single consonant and the geminate /s/	/kr/ /r/ /r:/ /ʎ/ /rl/ /rd/ /rv/ /tr/	/tr/ /pr/ /rt/ /br/ /r/ /ʎ/
Student 5	/rt/ /tr/ Geminates (venero) the voiced alveolar sibilant fricative /dz/ (antasi, succhero)	n.a.	Geminates (done) /uor/
Student 6	n.a.	n.a.	n.a.
Student 7	the voiced alveolar sibilant fricative /dz/ (succhero)	n.a.	Geminates (penelo)
Student 8	Absent	/rt/ /tr/ /rp/ /l/ vs /l:/	/uor/ /rn/ /rt/
Student 9	Absent	Absent	/r/ the voiced alveolar sibilant fricative /dz/ (succhero)

Table 6.23 Core II Beginners (Group 1)—comparative analysis of each student's summative oral-aural assessment – Academic Year 2020–2021

Summative oral-aural assessment (05/05/2021)	
Segmentals and suprasegmentals not mastered	
Student 1	Geminates (succeSo)
Student 2	/s/ (impreSSa)
	geminates (imbaLaGio, faTo, doNa, freDo)
	word stress (albèri, cìtta)
Student 3	/z/ vs /dz/ (alteSSa, sforSo)
	/k/ vs /tʃ/ (ghiaKKio)
	/g/vs /dʒ/ (dʒiaccio, inGLaterra)
	/au/ (diphthong—cOsa)
	Geminates (inghilteRa)
Student 4	/ʎ/(tagliatelle)
Student 5	/r/ (when placed before another consonant sound: formula, peRchè)
	/t/
	word stress (capàcita)
Student 6	/ʎ/(miLiore, famiLia)
	/ɲ/ (camapNia)

Table 6.24 Core II Beginners (Group 2)—comparative analysis of each student's summative oral-aural assessment – Academic Year 2020–2021

Summative oral-aural assessment (05/05/2021)	
Segmentals and suprasegmentals not mastered	
Student 1	Word stress (perche, pandèmia)
	/t/ vs /d/ (aiuDare)
	/z/ (infanCia)
	Both segmental and suprasegmental features are affected by interference from Spanish
Student 2	/ʎ/ (li)
Student 3	/e/ at the end of words is pronounced as /i/
	/z/ (vacanSa)
	/kw/ vs /k/ (cinKe)
	/sk/ (eXcursione)
	/au/ (diphthong—pOsa)
	] /ʃ/ vs /sk/(preferiSCIo)
Student 4	/r/ (completely omitted)
	/t/ (chiefly when it is followed by /r/)
	– /ɲ/ (spaNia)
	word stress (pandèmia)
Student 5	/au/ (diphthong—cOsa)
	(g/ (inGLaterra)
	/ʎ/ (miLiore)

(continued)

6 Loops, Sayings, and Tongue-Twisters: How to Enhance… 193

Table 6.24 (continued)

Summative oral-aural assessment (05/05/2021)	
	Segmentals and suprasegmentals not mastered
Student 6	/l/ (is pronounced as in Slavic languages)
	/ʎ/ (voLiono)
Student 7	/z/ (vacanSa)
	word stress (abàzzia)
	/ʎ/ (voLio)
Student 8	/z/ (vacanSa, preSo)
	geminates (preZo)
	/ʎ/ (miLiore)
	/r/ (chiefly when it precedes another consonant sound: aeropoRto)
	word stress (tavòli)
Student 9	–/tʃ/ vs /k/ (camiKa)

Table 6.25 Core IV Intermediate (Group 1 and Group 2)—comparative analysis of each student's performance during training sessions 1, 2, and 3 – Term 2 – Academic Year 2020–2021

Group	Student	Segmentals and suprasegmentals not mastered 08/03/2021	Segmentals and suprasegmentals not mastered 22/03/2021
Group 1	Student 1	n.a.	n.a.
	Student 2	/ʃ/ vs /sk/	Stress
		/ʎ/ vs /l/	/ɲ/ vs /n/
	Student 3	/ʎ/ vs /l/	/ɲ/ vs /n/
			/s/ vs /s:/
	Student 4	n.a.	Absent
	Student 5	n.a.	/r/
			/r:/
			/tr/
			/kr/
			/rf/
			/rv/
	Student 6	n.a.	n.a.
	Student 7	/ʎ/ vs/l/	Absent
		/ɲ/ vs /n/	

(continued)

Table 6.25 (continued)

Group	Student	Segmentals and suprasegmentals not mastered 08/03/2021	Segmentals and suprasegmentals not mastered 22/03/2021
Group 2	Student	Segmentals and suprasegmentals not mastered 18/03/2021	Segmentals and suprasegmentals not mastered 25/03/2021
	Student 1	/ʎ/ vs /l/ Geminates (*marone, capoto*)	n.a.
	Student 2	n.a.	n.a.
	Student 3	Stress /ʎ/ vs /l/ /ʃ/	n.a.
	Student 4	n.a.	n.a.
	Student 5	/tʃ/ vs /k/ Stress /r/ vs /r:/ /rf/ /rv/	Absent
	Student 6	/ʎ/ vs /l/	Absent
	Student 7	Absent	n.a.

Table 6.26 Core IV Intermediate (Group 1 and Group 2)—comparative analysis of each student's summative oral-aural assessment – Academic Year 2020–2021

		Core IV Intermediate. 2020–2021 Summative oral-aural assessment (04/05/2021)
Group 1	Student	Segmentals and suprasegmentals not mastered
	Student 1	n.a.
	Student 2	/s/ vs /dz/ (appreSSata) Word stress Mispronunciation of many words
	Student 3	/tʃ/ (speZialmente)
	Student 4	n.a.
	Student 5	/r/ (vedeRe, veRona, peR) /z/ vs /dz/ (sensa) /t/ (Tra, capuleTi)
	Student 6	n.a.
	Student 7	/au/ (Diphthong: Otentico) /e/ at the end of words is pronounced as /i/ /ɲ/ /dz/ (Samboni) Word stress (cìtta)

(continued)

6 Loops, Sayings, and Tongue-Twisters: How to Enhance... 195

Table 6.26 (continued)

		Core IV Intermediate. 2020–2021 Summative oral-aural assessment (04/05/2021)
Group 2	Student 1	Geminates (capaNe) Word stress (profùghi) Intonation is greatly influenced by Spanish
	Student 2	n.a.
	Student 3	/r/ (parlare, foRma, ripercoRRere) /dz/ /e/ at the end of words is pronounced as /i/ (introduzionI, regionI)
	Student 4	n.a.
	Student 5	/dr/ (suqDRa) /rm((foRma) /rt/ (paRte) /t/ /r/
	Student 6	Geminates (beLezza, aBracciato) Word stress (città)
	Student 7	n.a.

Table 6.27 Core IV Advanced—comparison between the results of each student's performance during training sessions 1 and 2, and each student's summative oral-aural assessment – Term 2 – Academic Year 2020–2021

Student	Training session Segmentals and suprasegmentals not mastered 04/03/2021	Segmentals and suprasegmentals not mastered 22/03/2021	Oral-aural assessment Segmentals and suprasegmentals not mastered 06/05/21
Student 1	n.a.	Absent	/uo/ (diphthong) (Omo) Word stress (contemporanèa)
Student 2	n.a.	n.a.	n.a.
Student 3	/ɲ/ vs /n/	Absent	/dz/ vs /z/ (firenZe, senZa) Geminates (metaLi) Word stress (proietìle)
Student 4	n.a.	Absent	/r/ (when located before consonants: gioRnali, distRarre) Geminates (proietaTo, DistraRe)
Student 5	/ɲ/ vs /n/	n.a.	n.a.
Student 6	Absent	n.a.	Geminates (beLezza, GambardeLa) Word stress (citta) /a/ (the vowel is pronounced as it is in French: Anche) Strong influence of French on intonation
Student 7	Absent	Absent	/ʃ/ vs /sk/ (Scematica) Word stress (stereotìpi) /e/ at the end of words is not pronounced (interpretazion) Strong influence of French on intonation

Table 6.28 Core IV Intermediate (Group 1, former Core II Beginners)—comparative analysis of each student's performance during training sessions 1 and 2 (Term 2, Academic Year 2020–2021) and training sessions 1, 2, and 3 (Term 2, Academic Year 2021–2022)

Pronunciation and intonation training sessions					
Student	01/03/2021	22/03/2021	04/03/2022	18/03/2022	25/03/2022
Student 2	Voiceless alveopalatal fricative /s/—	n.a.	/tr/ in new words	/ʎ/ vs /l/ /tr/	/uo/ /rl/ /n:/ /tr/ /ʎ/ vs /l/ /ʃ/ vs /sk/
Student 5	Voiceless alveopalatal fricative /s/ /br/	/rt/ /gr/ /tr/ /ʃ/ vs /sk/	/br/ /ʎ/ The stress is pronounced incorrectly in some words (càmino vs camìno)	/ʎ/ /gr/	n.a.

Table 6.29 Core IV Intermediate (Group 2, former Core II Beginners)—comparative analysis of each student's performance during training sessions 1, 2, and 3 (Term 2, Academic Year 2020–2021) and training sessions 1, 2, and 3 (Term 2, Academic Year 2021–2022)

Student	04/03/2021	18/03/2021	25/03/2021	04/03/2022	18/03/2022	25/03/2022
Student 4	/pr/ /br/ /tr/ /rt/ /r/ /ʃ/ Distinction between the single consonant and the geminate /s/	/kr/ /r/ /r:/ /ʃ/ /rl/ /rd/ /rv/ /tr/	/tr/ /pr/ /rt/ /br/ /r/ /ʃ/	/pr/ /br/ /tr/ /rt/ /r/ /ʃ/ Distinction between the single consonant and the geminate /s/	/ʃ/ vs /l/ /str/ /tr/ /kr/ /t / /t/ The stress is pronounced incorrectly in some words (campania vs campània)	/ʃ/ vs /l/ /tr/ /pr-/ /r/ /r/ when associated with other consonants /t/
Student 6	n.a.	n.a.	n.a.	/l/ Stress in new words	/ɲ/ vs /n/	n.a.
Student 7	voiced alveolar sibilant fricative /dz/ (zucchero)	n.a.	Geminates (penelo)	n.a.	/tʃ/ vs /k/	n.a.
Student 9	Absent	Absent	/r/ the voiced alveolar sibilant fricative /dz/ (zucchero)	Absent	Absent	/ʃ/ Distinction between the single consonant and the geminate /s/ /ʃ/ vs /sk/

6 Loops, Sayings, and Tongue-Twisters: How to Enhance... 199

Table 6.30 Core IV Intermediate (Group 1 and Group 2)—comparative analysis of each student's summative oral-aural assessment (–Academic Year 2021–2022)

Core IV Intermediate—second term. 2021–2022 Summative oral-aural assessment	Student	Segmentals and suprasegmentals not mastered
Group 1 06/05/2022	Student 2	/ʃ/ vs /sk/ (miSCHela) Some sporadic inaccuracies: /ia/ (ma_ale vs maiale) /v/ vs /b/ (proBengono, proBiene) – /tʃ/ vs /dz/ (commerZializzazione) Word stress (satùri)
	Student 5	/r/ (when placed before another consonant sound: palare vs paRlare; pesone vs peRsone; formula vs formula) Some sporadic inaccuracies: /ʎ/ (meLio) /s/ (anZia) geminates (generaLLe)
Group 2 06/05/2022	Student 4	/r/ (completely omitted) /t/ (mainly when it is followed by r) /ɲ/ (Nocchi) Some sporadic inaccuracies: word stress (adìge) /kw/ vs /k/ (ki vs qui) /ʎ/ vs /l/
	Student 6	/l/ (is pronounced as the palate-alveolar /lʲ/))
	Student 7	word stress (invano) Unnatural intonation
	Student 9	word stress (città, società, antasia) Some sporadic inaccuracies: /sf/ (traSFeriva) /sk/ (traSCorreva) /ai/ (a_uto vs aiuto) Geminates (guiDDano)

Table 6.31 ((Core II Beginner (Group 1) and Core IV Intermediate (Group 1, former Core II Beginner)—comparative analysis of each student's oral-aural assessment results across the two academic years 2020–2021 and 2021–2022

Student	Segmentals and suprasegmentals not mastered
Core II Beginner—second term. 2020–2021 Summative oral-aural assessment (05/05/2021) Group 1	
Student 2	/s/ (impreSSa) geminates (imbaLaGio, faTo, doNa, freDo) word stress (albèri, città)
Student 5	/r/ (when placed before another consonant sound: formula, peRchè) /t/ word stress (capàcita)
Core IV Intermediate—second term. 2021–2022 Summative oral-aural assessment (06/05/2022) Group 1	
Student 2	/ʃ/ vs /sk/ (miSCHela) Some sporadic inaccuracies: /ia/ (ma_ale vs maiale) /v/ vs /b/ (proBengono, proBiene) /tʃ/ vs /dz/ (commerZializzazione) Word stress (satùri)
Student 5	/r/ (when placed before another consonant sound: palare vs paRlare; pesone vs peRsone; formula vs formula) Some sporadic inaccuracies: /ʎ/ (meLio) /s/ (anZia) geminates (generaLLe)

6   Loops, Sayings, and Tongue-Twisters: How to Enhance…   201

Table 6.32 Core II Beginner (Group 2) and Core IV Intermediate (Group 2, former Core II Beginner)—comparative analysis of each student's oral-aural assessment results across the two academic years 2020–2021 and 2021–2022

Student	Segmentals and suprasegmentals not mastered
Core II Beginner—second term. 2020–2021 Summative oral-aural assessment (05/05/2021) Group 2	
Student 4	/r/ (completely omitted) /t/ (mainly when followed by r) /ɲ/ (spaNia) word stress (pandèmia)
Student 6	/l/ (is pronounced as in Slavic languages) /ʎ/ (voLiono)
Student 7	/z/ (vacanSa) word stress (abàzzia) /ʎ/ (voLio)
Student 9	/tʃ/ vs /k/ (camiKa)
Core IV Intermediate—second term. 2021–2022 Summative oral-aural assessment (06/05/2022) Group 2	
Student 4	/r/ (completely omitted) /t/ (mainly when followed by r) /ɲ/ (Nocchi) Some sporadic inaccuracies: word stress (adige) /kw/ vs /k/ (ki vs qui) /ʎ/ vs /l/
Student 6	/l/ (is pronounced as in Slavic languages)
Student 7	word stress (invano) Unnatural intonation
Student 9	word stress (cìtta, socìeta, fantàsia) Some sporadic inaccuracies: /sf/ (traSFeriva) /sk/ (traSCorreva) /ai/ (a_uto vs aiuto) Geminates (guiDDano)

Note

1. The segmentals addressed during the first pronunciation training session were: the voiced palatal lateral approximant /ʎ/; the phonological distinction between single consonants and their geminated counterparts in words which have similar spellings—/l:/ vs /l/, /s:/ vs /s/, /m:/ vs /m/; the voiced alveolar trill preceded by a consonant—/pr/, /br/, /tr/; the geminated voiced alveolar trill /r:/; the nasal palatal /ɲ/; the nasal alveolar /n/; the voiced dental fricative /t/, the geminated voiced dental fricative /t:/, and the voiced dental fricative in post-consonantal position /rt/; the voiced alveolar sibilant fricative/dz/and in post-consonantal position /ndz/. See Tables 6.4, 6.6, 6.8, 6.10, and 6.13.

References

Damasio, A. 1994. *Descartes' Error—Emotion, Reason and the Human Brain*. New York: G. P. Putnam's Sons.

Decoursey, M. 2012. Dramatic art for second language education: Appropriate process objectives for Hong Kong schools. *Asia-Pacific Journal for Arts Education* 11 (11): 250–270.

Dockalova, B. 2011. Loops: A multi-purpose drama technique for the language classroom. *Scenario* 1: 66–74.

Gonzales Iglesias, N. 2009. *Learning English with tongue twister*. Morrisville, NC: Lulu Press.

Heathcote, D. 1984. The authentic teacher: Signs and portents. In *Collected writings of Drama and education*, ed. D. Heathcote et al. London: Hutchinson.

Jenkins, J. 2002. A sociolinguistically-based, empirically researched pronunciation syllabus for English as an International Language. *Applied Linguistics* 23 (1): 83–103.

Korkut, P., and Ö. Çelik. 2018. Developing pronunciation through creative drama. *The Language Learning Journal* 49 (2): 147–159. https://doi.org/10.1080/09571736.2018.1491058.

Korolkova, Y.V., et al. 2015. Effective techniques for working with the tongue twister in the elementary level of training Russian as a foreign language. *Procedia - Social and Behavioral Sciences* 215: 102–106.

McKay, S. 2006. *Researching second language classroom*. Mahwah, NJ: Lawrence Erlbaum Associates.

Nurhasanah, Y. Zainil. 2018. Tongue twister as a technique to help students solve their difficulties in pronouncing /s/, /ʃ/ at junior high school. *Journal of English Language Teaching* 7 (4): 654–660. https://doi.org/10.24036/jelt.v7i4.101317.

O'Neill, C. 1995. *Drama worlds: A framework for process Drama*. Portsmouth: Heinemann.

Piazzoli, E. 2011a. Didattica process drama: principi di base, estetica e coinvolgimento. *Italiano Linguadue* 3 (1): 439–462. https://doi.org/10.13130/2037-3597/1243.

———. 2011b. Process drama: The use of affective space to reduce language anxiety in the additional language learning classroom. *The Journal of Applied Theatre and Performance* 16 (4): 557–573. https://doi.org/10.1080/13569783.2011.617104.

Prosic-Santovac, D. 2009. The Use of Tongue Twisters in EFL Teaching. *The Annual of the Faculty of Philosophy* 34: 159–169.

Rodari, G. 2010. *Filastrocche per tutto l'anno*. Einaudi.

Slade, P. 1954. *Child drama*. London: University of London Press.

Tsybaneva, V., et al. 2019. *Using drama in teaching intonation*. Amsterdam: Atlantis Press. https://doi.org/10.2991/ismge-19.2019.128.

Turumi, Y.L., Jamiluddin, and Salehuddin. 2016. Using tongue twister to improve the pronunciation of grade VIII students. *E-Journal of English Language Teaching Society (ELTS)* 4 (2): 1–12.

Way, Brian. 1967. *Development through drama*. London: Longmans.

Web References

https://aforismi.it
https://learnamo.com
https://www.amicideltedesco.eu
https://www.fabulinis.com
https://www.filastrocche.it

Part III

Intercultural Competence and Community in Online Settings

7

Developing an Online Community and Intercultural Competence: Travelling Virtually to China

Wissia Fiorucci, Ru Su, and Alvise Sforza Tarabochia

1   Introduction

In the last two decades of the twentieth century, scholars were already indicating that technologies could help students and teachers by providing further opportunities to network with native speakers of the target language, which would boost motivation (e.g. Chapelle and Jamieson 1986; Sullivan 1993; Warschauer 1996). In the following two decades, and prior to COVID-19, the idea of an 'online learning community' subsequently became the focus of copious literature, and within language education, it was broadly defined as 'a community of learners who meet online for their common interest in language and culture learning' (Cai and Zhu 2012). Thorne et al. (2009), for instance, reviewed studies that explored the impact of online communities on foreign language learning.

W. Fiorucci (✉) • R. Su • A. S. Tarabochia
University of Kent, Canterbury, UK
e-mail: w.firoucci@kent.ac.uk; R.Su@kent.ac.uk; A.Sforza-Tarabochia@kent.ac.uk

© The Author(s), under exclusive license to Springer Nature Switzerland AG 2023
W. Fiorucci (ed.), *Language Education During the Pandemic*,
https://doi.org/10.1007/978-3-031-35855-5_7

They confirmed that students felt particularly motivated by the increased opportunities to interact with others via both their native tongue and the studied language. Compared with traditional classes, studies furthermore argued that online learning communities can be an effective tool to encourage the sharing and honing of knowledge (Ke and Hoadley 2009), boost critical thinking and autonomous learning, and cultivate more confident learning approaches (e.g. Gazi 2009).

During the COVID-19 emergency, as the chapters in this collection demonstrate, technologies provided the necessary resources and activities for both synchronous and asynchronous teaching and learning. In terms of motivation and engagement, however, specific strategies had to be employed that would target the peculiar conditions in which learning was happening and teaching delivered. The 'online community', that is, was no longer a somewhat optional aspect of learning that would possibly lead to an increase in student motivation. Social restrictions of varying intensity meant that, by and large, across the world, there was no learning community outside of online learning communities, and hence their role and scope evolved with respect to previous theorisations—sharing and accessibility of knowledge was not enough. Experiences during the pandemic drastically changed the way in which we look at the notion of 'learning community'. The importance of a learning community can be approached from two mutually reinforcing (and converging) angles. We now know that, on the one hand, 'creating a sense of community among students via digital platforms is a vital component of effective online teaching' (Gibson 2020). This became clear once buildings were closed when it became immediately obvious in many institutions around the world that a resilient and well-established 'online learning community' did not exist; this was something institutions had to swiftly grapple with from the ground up. On the other hand, we also know that a sense of online community is a vital component of any effective learning experience. Mirroring social interactions outside of the educational space, learning has long ceased to happen exclusively within a physical space and has become more and more reliant on digital tools. Yet, as the pandemic has taught us, using digital tools is not enough—technology-enhanced learning (TEL) is only as effective as the sense of community developed within it.[1] Although theoretically recognised for a long time, it has now become relatively common knowledge that the design of online learning should do more than 'merely provide access to information' (Geer and Wing 2003, p. 376). Online learning design needs to rope in the participants through active interaction so that students 'are challenged to shift from passive learners, who were a feature of traditional distance education, to active participants who engage in their own construction of knowledge' (Geer and Wing 2003, p. 376)—Doerr and Zanola have given us an example of this, as they have explored the use of an online self-assessing tool that de facto offsets the circular model of the so-called Teaching Unit, and it simultaneously stimulates student engagement.

In language education, technology can reduce distances and provide effective tools for students to interact with native speakers and access authentic materials more easily, which can have a very positive impact on motivation (see Cai and Zhu 2012). Although a sense of community is fundamental to all learning and teaching regardless of the subject matter, there are aspects of language learning that made social restrictions very detrimental to language education in particular—the asset of being able to travel, for example, which was abruptly curbed, as well as aspects that have been addressed by other authors in this collection, who have investigated and analysed solutions in response to the impossibility of developing communicative skills in the traditional, face-to-face (F2F) way (e.g. Manzini and Heinrich on pronunciation and, thus, speaking).

Our project of setting out to establish an exchange agreement with a Western Chinese university meant, first and foremost, providing students from both institutions with more learning opportunities aimed at increasing their motivation, and hence engagement, by bridging both cultural and geographical barriers. When the details of the project came to be defined just as the first lockdowns were implemented, our ultimate goal then became to build an online language community. Our research more specifically addressed the following questions:

RQ1: Can we successfully embed intercultural communication training utilising TEL?
RQ2: What are the best strategies to engage and motivate students to achieve the above?

RQ3: What are the fundamental elements of an online language learning community?

In the next section, we will explain how we formulated the project so as to be able to answer these questions, including our justification for the selection of activities and the way we obtained feedback from students to evaluate its success.

2   The Project

Connection across borders has been a crucial driving force of this project since its inception in 2018. Our starting point was the aim of expanding an existing partnership with the Western Chinese university, with a view to motivating students through more direct access to native speakers and opportunities for intercultural communication. Let us here briefly take a step back and look at what we mean by 'intercultural communication' and associated expressions such as 'intercultural awareness' and 'intercultural competence'.

Intercultural communication involves, at a very basic level, communication within and between different cultural contexts, and it will involve the use of one or more languages that are not everyone's native tongues. For successful intercultural communication, intercultural awareness is paramount: we cannot simply speak the language of our interlocutor; we also need to develop an attitude of openness and positive receptivity towards those differences and subtleties that differentiate cultural contexts on a level that is not solely linguistic. Intercultural competence is therefore the 'ability to communicate effectively and appropriately in intercultural situations based on one's intercultural knowledge, skills', attitudes—that is, 'adroitness' in communication skills and 'sensitivity' towards cultural differences, and awareness—that is, 'cognitive aspect of understanding cultural differences' (Deardorff 2006, p. 249). Besides providing the platforms and opportunities to hone language skills and acquire intercultural knowledge, an active training of that knowledge and skills within different contexts is needed for the development of intercultural competence.

To make this intercultural training possible, the grounds for collaboration among teachers and students were laid soon after the partnership was initiated in 2018 with the goal of developing a programme of cultural exchange. Our first agreed plan was for the University of Kent (UoK) to offer a Mandarin Trainee Teacher programme for aspiring teachers of Mandarin (newly graduated from the Chinese university). This was the first step towards the devising of the final programme, and it was prompted by experiences within the same Language School, where a language training programme has existed since 2016 for aspiring teachers of romance and European languages (this programme was awarded the University of Kent Humanities Teaching Prize in 2019).

2.1 The International Training Programme

Literature on the topic of teaching exchanges tends to focus on secondary schools, but studies on higher education (HE) exchanges do exist and, importantly, results are generally consistent across stages. These experiences focus on attaining language-teaching skills and developing intercultural awareness for all involved (Paik et al. 2015; Baecher and Chung 2020), and these are the outcomes that guided our agreement with the KaDaGaoXin University of Xi'an.

At a fundamental level, teachers' exchanges across borders positively influence their practices and benefit student learning outcomes with immediate effect. For instance, exposure to diverse student bodies and different institutional cultures in the host country tends to result in more interactive and equitable teaching delivery for all involved. Likewise, we have seen students gaining direct access to native speakers who bring the direct and very recent experience of the relevant country (or countries) has been identified as a major contributing factor towards increased motivation. This was particularly important given COVID-19 restrictions, when the lack of a visible learning community, along with a diminished teaching presence, was identified as among the most common and detrimental barriers to both students' attainment and well-being.

Exchanges can, in general, have a transformative influence on promoting flexibility and innovation within teaching and learning environments.

The first three trainees joined the UoK virtually in 2020–2021 and were able to follow and actively participate in all classes remotely via Teams. The training took the form of co-teaching, following Cook and Friend's model (1995), but adapting it to a remote setting: co-teaching involves 'two or more professionals delivering substantive instruction to a diverse, or blended, group of students in a single physical space' (p. 2). In our case, the space was virtual, not physical. Yet, the presence of the trainees followed Cook and Friend's theoretical approach, where the rationale for co-teaching is to accomplish increased 'instructional options for all students', 'improve program intensity and continuity', and 'increase support for teachers' and for students 'with special needs' (p. 3). With learning happening exclusively online, two types of co-teaching were implemented. In one scenario, one taught and the other assisted; thus 'both educators [were] present, but one [took] a clear lead in the classroom while the other [observed] students' (p. 5), which in an online setting meant that the trainee would operate the main chat as well as conversing with individual students separately. One-to-one conversations could be initiated by either a student or the trainee—in the latter case, so as to check in with somebody who was seen as struggling or not seen at all (e.g. camera off). The other utilised model was that of 'parallel teaching' (see Cook and Friend, p. 7), taking place during group-work activities, as the two teachers would each observe and help different groups of students. Given the limited size of language seminars, the presence of two teachers meant that when students were divided into groups and 'sent' to breakout rooms, a teacher would also be present at almost all times, which contributed towards maintaining a reliable teaching presence.

Three more teachers joined in 2021–2022 and three more in 2022–2023. Over the course of the last two years, as teaching gradually resumed in F2F format, the trainees joined the classes in hybrid mode, but the main aspect of their training would consist of meeting with students in separate, online sessions, where they would focus on linguistic and intercultural aspects that needed attention, as identified by the main teacher: in this configuration we did not implement co-teaching, as the main instruction was 'delivered primarily in [the] classroom […] space' and the main teachers coordinated 'instruction (for example, plan[ning] an integrated unit together) but deliver[ing] it to separate groups of students in separate locations' (Cook and Friend 1995, p. 3)—in our case, online.

The outcomes of the training at the end of 2020–2021 were measured using mixed methods, in line with existing research on the topic (prior studies mostly use qualitative research methodologies, as well as mixed methods, with prominence given to reflexive data collection and analysis of perceptions before and after the exchanges). Feedback and interviews were gathered from the Chinese teacher trainees, too, by their own university, but we do not have access to these. However, as a tangible outcome of the project, as soon as travel was permitted again (spring 2022), they were all given the possibility of applying for a paid working experience in the UK. As a result, one of the former online trainees is currently working at the UoK as a trainee language lector.

Outcomes for students in the UK were evaluated with a short survey administered at the end of 2020–2021. The survey comprised 5-point Likert-scale questions and two open-ended questions. Twenty-five students responded, amounting to 79% of students impacted by the presence of the trainees. Overall, students indicated that:

1. They found the trainees' presence helpful in the virtual classroom (47% strongly agreed, 51% agreed, and 2% were undecided).
2. They felt that the extra sessions delivered by the trainees helped to boost their language skills (45% strongly agreed, 44% agreed, 4% were undecided, and 3% did not attend).
3. They felt that the extra sessions delivered by the trainees helped to boost their motivation (28% strongly agreed, 58% agreed, 11% were undecided, and 3% did not attend).

4. They felt their knowledge of Chinese culture had increased (51% strongly agreed, 39% agreed, 7% were undecided, and 3% did not attend).

Students responded to the first open question ('How has the trainees' work impacted your learning experience?') by focusing on two main aspects[2]:

1. They felt the extra cultural sessions helped with their immersion in Chinese culture.
2. They felt that the extra language sessions helped with their confidence in the regular seminars.

Among the most detailed comments were the following: 'Comprehensive range of tools available to facilitate learning. Additional online seminars with trainee teachers to expand on Chinese culture and drastically improve Mandarin pronunciation', and 'the inclusion of assistant Mandarin tutors doing additional online seminars I feel creates a wonderful multicultural atmosphere and fosters greater appreciation for Chinese culture and fortifies correct pronunciation'. Furthermore, no negative comments were offered.

Interestingly, the comments also focused on an aspect of the training which was not teacher- but student-led and which had not been formally planned: namely, the use of WeChat[3] with the trainees. We could summarise it with one representative comment, 'I value the WeChat group chat we have [with] the trainee teachers as we can easily communicate with them at any time of the day'. Integrating social media into teaching and learning activities, both formally and informally, can be helpful in supporting education (Cole et al. 2017). In the past decade, studies confirmed the meaningful impact that the use of online social media might have on academic performance through its contribution to forming a learning community (Greenhow 2011a, b; Zhu 2012). A 2013 report on 233 HE students from an undisclosed university commented that social media supported students in cooperative learning, and it increased self-confidence—especially for those (the majority, in this study) who prefer communication technology to F2F or verbal interactions (Voorn and

Kommers 2013). More recently, Ansari and Khan (2020), conducting an empirical investigation, confirmed the 'application and usefulness of the social media in transferring the resource materials, collaborative learning and interaction' among both peers and teachers, which facilitates students' motivation and engagement. That said, negative aspects of social media in education have also been considered over the years (Summers and Svinicki 2007; Kirschner and Karpinski 2010; Paul et al. 2012; Wu and Cheng 2018; Masood et al. 2020). David and Paul, for instance, explored the risk of diminished academic performance (David et al. 2012; Paul et al. 2012). Le Roux and Parry (2017) similarly stressed that time spent on social media could be problematic and adversely affect academic success—their research is based on the premise that students now spend less time socialising in person compared to their social media interactions, which would reduce their communication skills. Other negative outcomes stemming from social media use in education that have been investigated and discussed include information and/or communication overload, fatigue, stress (Masood et al. 2020), and lack of self-regulation (Purvis et al. 2016; Whelan et al. 2020).

While COVID-19 restrictions were in place, the amplified institutional use of platforms such as Teams, which have their own messaging function, allowed for the increase in social media-type features such as communication features and their infiltration into the academic context—as the language used in chats tends to follow messaging 'etiquette' rather than that of emails, this type of communication can be regarded as a hybrid, bridging the gap between formal and informal communication in academia (see Schneider 2020). At the same time, social media is widespread and common use; Facebook and WhatsApp (WeChat in our case) were also used at the instigation of both teachers and students—while this had already been happening pre-pandemic, the phenomenon unsurprisingly increased dramatically during the pandemic. In our case, those students who did comment on the use of the WeChat group were very positive about it and stressed that the chat allowed them to have ongoing communication with, and thus easy access to, the trainee teachers. The trainee teachers could thereby establish a reliable teaching presence (the felt loss of which was, as we saw in the Introduction to this volume, one of the aspects students struggled most with worldwide during the pandemic). Although our sample of participants and respondents is too small to draw any definitive conclusions, the overall feedback students offered for the project as a whole was very positive, as we will see below. The trainees' *reliable* presence, achieved via social media, was part of that success, and insomuch as it was a student-led initiative and only a marginal aspect of the programme, it only contributed positively to it without incurring any of the perils highlighted above.

That said, students responded to the second question ('What suggestions would you have to improve the programme?') by focusing on two main areas:

1. They indicated that they would prefer a mixture of in-person, blended, and hybrid sessions once travelling resumed.
2. They indicated they would like more cultural sessions.

Although teaching and travelling have resumed, we have not yet been able to invite the aspiring teachers for in-person training for several reasons (e.g. Visa permits). However, undeterred by travel restrictions, following theme 2 identified in the students' answer to question 2 ('What suggestions would you have to improve the programme?), *Travelling Virtually in Xi'an* was created and launched in November 2021. This was a series of online cultural workshops in which Chinese students provided unique insights into topics such as the city's history, culture, food, and entertainment.

By organising the programme, as abovementioned, our two foremost aims were to provide a platform for intercultural communication and subsequently to increase motivation among students, at a time when social restrictions prevented travelling and made establishing the presence of a reliable learning community more challenging.

2.2   The Cultural Programme

This part of the project was integral to the Chinese students' degree programme since they were reading to become teachers and it was compulsory for them as teaching practice. For the British students, the introduction of peer-learning was based on the assumption that 'peer-learning schemes promote and empower autonomous learning [and] enhance engagement'; they also help towards building 'community', 'intercultural awareness', and 'cross-cultural integration' (Keenan 2014). Furthermore, according to Ody and Carey (2013, p. 301), peer-led academic learning would, inter alia, facilitate a collaborative and active type of learning through a student-centred approach to education; support individual confidence; foster the notion of academic community; and become an extra mechanism for communication and feedback between teachers and students. Keenan further suggests that 'there are wide-ranging approaches to the organisation and operation of peer-led academic learning schemes' (2014). In fact, since its first appearances in the early 1990s, peer-led learning schemes have become systematic practice in many institutions worldwide, with new and innovative approaches being adopted. For example, '[t]he move to online peer-assisted learning programs (PAL) has been trialled in universities in Australia and overseas' (Crowley-Cyr and Hevers 2021).

Travelling Virtually in Xi'an, China, the Ancient Capital of 13 Dynasties was a student-led online programme. It gave participants first-hand viewpoints on ordinary Xi'an people's lives, food, history, ancient and modern archaeology, ancient music and traditional Piying drama (shadow puppets), and its more modern developments. With support but not direction from their teachers, students from the Xi'an prepared bespoke live-streaming and video recordings for the British students.[4] By assessing British students' intercultural knowledge via formative assessments during regular class time, the teachers of Mandarin had identified areas where opportunities for intercultural knowledge development were needed and passed the information on to the Chinese students. Although the focus was on cultural content, linguistic skills were also addressed in the form of reading and listening practice. All the video interviews were conducted in Mandarin with English subtitles—immersion in the language itself was however provided, within the context of our programme, through the presence of the trainee teachers, whilst the cultural sessions focused on intercultural skills.

The first workshop was delivered on 10 November 2021 and the last on 2 February 2022.[5] First, the Chinese students would introduce the content of the workshop, and then a video (of varying lengths, between 25 and 40 minutes long) would be streamed live. After the streaming, the Chinese students would test their British counterparts' understanding of the video contents through a seminar-style session, which would include games, quizzes, open questions, vocabulary exercises, and so on. Participants were encouraged to use the chat function at all times to ask questions as well as to talk to one another, comment on the video, and more. We have not systematically analysed engagement with the Teams chat, but we noted that each session concluded with various conversations having taken place via messaging, on the topics of the video, among participants from both countries. The language of communication was English, but participants also regularly shared live reactions to the videos and chat comments with emojis—unsurprisingly, reactions and emojis were in fact very popular: they not only mirror digital conversations in daily life but also represent a sort of international lingua franca for swift communication (Leonardi 2022) and are especially effective for conveying emotions (as their name suggests). Obviously, even emojis can be understood differently not only cross-culturally but also between speakers of the same language (Leonardi 2022). That said, there was a strong prevalence of emojis such as 'clapping hands', 'smileys', 'thanks', and 'hearts', which communicated definite positive feelings and appreciation.

Three workshops featured as many as 60 students, whilst 15 students attended all of them. This bespoke programme was also made available to staff, so as to develop a wider sense of 'learning community', which would include both students and teachers.[6] (Unfortunately, staff presence varied considerably from session to session and, therefore, we decided not to include them in our end-of-programme surveys.) We started gathering feedback from students as the programme unfolded to make sure we were delivering enjoyable and thus motivating experiences. Aware of potential survey fatigue (between the end of autumn module evaluation forms and the National Student Survey (NSS) starting early in the spring term), we only asked them to provide comments if they had any to make. We received seven comments via a Microsoft form, four of which focused specifically on the quality of the material prepared for them, while the rest complimented its contents.[7] Three students spontaneously provided video feedback to express their appreciation to their Chinese counterparts, both during and at the end of the workshops. This spontaneous initiative highlighted feelings of gratitude towards their Chinese peers, admiration for the quality of work produced, and enthusiasm for the kind of learning provided, which was not only tailor-made but also produced by peers with first-hand experience.[8]

At the end, we formally evaluated the success of the cultural programme through a survey that focused on reflexive data and analysis of perceptions after the exchanges. We included two sections with 5-point Likert-scale questions—one section with multiple-choice answers and one last section with two open questions.[9] What emerged from the analysis of the data obtained from 26 respondents will be described in the next section.

3   Analysis of End of Project Survey

The first, Likert-scale section (typical five-level Likert items from strongly disagree to strongly agree), was designed to provide us with data regarding student perceptions of their learning experience, with some crucial questions (e.g. on intercultural learning) being crossed-checked with the ones in the last section.

One hundred per cent of student respondents strongly agreed that their Chinese peers had been 'very good at explaining things and have made the subject interesting'. The same percentage strongly agreed that they 'had opportunities to explore ideas and concepts in depth and apply what [they] learnt outside of the sessions'. Exact 83.3% strongly agreed that their communication skills improved (16.7% agreed). Finally, 79% strongly agreed that the learning environment was 'engaging, and [they] found it easy to participate' (15% agreed).

The second section confirmed the results of the first to a certain extent. To the multiple-choice question (where two options could be ticked) 'What do you feel you have mostly gained from the programme?': 75% answered that they had 'learned extensively about Chinese culture' and 100% 'knew more about Xi'an, China' at the end of the programme. (This particular question reveals the limits of the survey as we could not cross-reference these answers with numbers of events attended and which ones.) Yet, while 100% of students had previously strongly agreed on their improved communication skills, only 37.4% declared that they felt they had 'improved Chinese language skills'. This leads us to think that participants may have found the sessions helpful for their communication abilities in general (validating the Likert-scale questions) but felt that they had not provided enough training specifically in the Chinese language. Then, 62.5% 'felt more motivated to learn Chinese', but to the multiple-choice question 'How do you feel about attending the Summer camp in Xi'an?', 87.5% responded they felt 'excited', only 12.5% said 'I need to know more', and 0% said they were 'not interested'. These two sets of answers seem somewhat at odds since a prerequisite for qualifying for the summer camp was an intermediate level of Chinese, and language learning was part of the programme. What we have inferred from this disparity is that while few students felt their language skills in Chinese had improved, and 62.5% of respondents felt more motivated to learn the language (which is a relatively low percentage compared to the 87.5% excited about the summer camp), the intercultural learning and the perception of improved communication skills were major driving factors for the summer camp question. There is a strong indication here that participants felt very positively about their learning in this programme with regard to its intercultural contents and application outside of the sessions, as well as about their own improved communication skills, thanks to an engaging learning environment.

Finally, the last section comprised two standard open-ended questions. The first one was: 'Did you enjoy the programme and, if so, why?' Unfortunately, we only had six students completing this part of the survey. The comments confirmed the analysis of answers above, about students' appreciation of the gained intercultural knowledge, their excitement at the prospect of going to Xi'an, and the quality of the teaching.[10] Obviously, answers from all the participants would have strengthened this last point, as the sample is very limited. That said, none of the students provided suggestions for improvements, which was the second question. Two of them said that everything was 'perfect', and they 'would not change anything' or 'I have nothing to suggest as each session was amazing'. Yet, there were no comments on the learning of the Chinese language, which confirms our aforementioned views about this aspect of the programme: there were too few opportunities for Chinese language learning, but the students nonetheless enjoyed the programme in view of the other learning outcomes they felt they had achieved.

4   Conclusions

In this last section, we will consider each of our research questions. The first one was: 'Can we successfully embed intercultural communication training utilising TEL?' Through our cultural programme, we have established a successful practice for making this possible. Utilising e-learning platforms (e.g. Moodle and Teams) to both share materials and conduct synchronous sessions, we have provided students with the opportunity to gain first-hand insights into the country where their language of study is spoken. Data gathered from the interim and final surveys confirmed that students felt that both their intercultural knowledge and communication skills (e.g. intercultural awareness) had increased, these being crucial components of intercultural competence. The presence of the trainees was indicated as an element that facilitated this.

The second question was about 'the best strategies to engage and motivate students to achieve' intercultural competence through online intercultural training. We first introduced online co-teaching, which has been indicated by students as a positive addition to their regular classes. In fact, as a result of comments deriving from the first teacher-training experience in 2020–2021, we have not only established a systematic online programme for the trainees but also reached an agreement with the Chinese university to physically host a visiting lecturer. (We do not yet know what the outcomes of this latest addition to our programme will be, as both lecturer and lector have only recently arrived for the current academic year.) The lecturer will deliver extra cultural sessions since this is the aspect of the programme students have been most enthusiastic about, and they had also indicated, in the first survey, that they would prefer a mixture of online and in-person sessions. In general, our goal for the teachers' exchange was to increase students' motivation by providing more opportunities for direct access to native speakers, which we have implemented both in-person and online.

Other crucial factors for the successful online training of intercultural skills are the quality of material and an effective use of technology. Besides the basic necessities (e.g. a reliable internet connection, identified as a major issue worldwide during the pandemic), cultivating the sensory aspects of learning—visual and aural—through proficient use of technology and well-designed material is also of paramount importance for engaging students and maintaining that engagement. The quality of material is therefore connected to the effective use of technology. One of the respondents specifically remarked that 'the presentation[s] are beautiful and executed very professionally which makes *learning about the culture even more interesting*' (our emphasis). In general, comments about the quality of material have been many, relative to the small sample, confirming that 'well-designed audio-visual learning media will help [in] achieving learning goals' (Fuady and Mutalib 2019, p. 1). In our case, considering the contents of the audiovisual material prepared by the Chinese students, we also conformed to Pribadi's theorisation (2004) that 'audiovisual media is widely used to teach a learning experience that cannot be seen directly, this is because audiovisual media have the potential to show parts of an object realistically'. This was, we believe, fundamental to the success of our project because it was conducive to a learning experience that, offsetting geographical barriers (and social restrictions), allowed for immersion within the described cultural setting, as also indicated in some of the comments, for example: '[It] really feels like you can go to Xi'an and meet these people and speak about the same topics in depth'.

Finally, the third research question was more ambitious in that we wanted to figure out 'What are the fundamental elements of an online language learning community?'. As we can gauge from our experiences and the comments highlighted above, the word (or related variants) that keeps recurring when we speak of 'online community' is 'reliability'—reliability of an online internet connection so that communication is not (easily) disrupted; reliability of teaching; reliability of the learning community presence. If we consider that a reliable internet connection is that which allows access to the virtual space, then we can say that an online community will be reliable when both space and participants maintain a steady presence and are easily accessible. An online community these days is no longer merely an addition to regular, face-to-face teaching (and obviously, for distance-learning degrees, we would need to tackle the argument from a different perspective). A reliable online learning community is necessary not only to make sure educational structures are resilient, and hence remain themselves reliable, in case of further closures due to (however unlikely) causes of *force majeure*. A reliable online community is also necessary because, on the one hand, it can favour inclusivity on a very broad level. Easy access to materials and teachers must be a given in the context of HE, where demographics are swiftly changing—we have more and more students studying part-time; mature (and non-mature) students with caring duties; and the rising cost-of-living crisis may make commuting easier than living in student accommodation on campus. This means varying student attendance patterns (Payne Miller et al. 2017), which calls for a stable presence (of space and people) independent of the physical spaces of the classroom and of the office (e.g. a commuting student might be able to attend classes but be unable to go to a teacher's office hours, for instance—accessibility is not just about seminar attendance).

On the other hand, before the pandemic, technological innovations had already been drastically changing the way we learn—in a way that is not limited to how we learn, for example, acquire, exchange, and produce knowledge, but also extends to how we communicate and interact with others both within the learning process and outside of it (Schwab 2016). If we have learnt something from emergency remote teaching (ERT) during COVID-19, it is that education structures worldwide have not yet adapted to this reality (Sofi-Karim et al. 2023). After COVID-19, it is obvious that we can no longer postpone a sustainable response to these changes, which should take the form of embedding technology and the kind of communication and interactions it shapes and allows within teaching practices. Therefore, an online learning community is not only helpful in increasing learning opportunities, which is how its potential was mostly viewed in the late 1990s and 2000s. Today, education can be truly transformative only if 'educators construct essential teaching and learning environments [that] foster students' abilities of analysis, imagination, inventiveness, critical thinking, and metacognition'. To this end, 'online teaching has been applied in various ways worldwide and is currently expanding exponentially' (Sofi-Karim et al. 2023).

An online learning community is a requirement of successful education strategies to develop and hone the skills necessary in today's world, and it will comprise several elements. Through our project, we have identified some of these elements, though obviously the narrow scope of our research does not allow for any decisive conclusions, but only for reflections and suggestions based on what worked well for us. Hence, circling back to our initial point above, what makes an online community effective? The first answer is reliability. We can achieve reliability, first, through a systematic sharing of materials and resources via a platform that is accessible to all. In this respect, it is important that teachers utilise not many, but one or two platforms at most so that all participants will always know where to access content. Furthermore, the setup of the programme also made it possible and easy for teachers and students to come together to share knowledge, regardless of where they were based geographically. This confirms that while in traditional classrooms, it is one individual who does most of the teaching, TEL renders co-teaching easier by means of learning platforms, bringing with it the advantages highlighted above—among which are more learning opportunities for students and an increased teaching presence (e.g. in breakout groups or in extra activities such as the cultural sessions). This has a bearing on reliability as well. The programme has also proven sustainable because the model on which it has been created can be repeated—in fact, it is being repeated—within a context of F2F teaching with online elements, offsetting some of the limits of traditional in-person learning. (To ensure sustainability, central coordination and institutional commitment are also imperative: programmes of this kind need to be supported, as individual teachers will not be able to overcome the bureaucratic hurdles connected with organising international exchanges involving travelling.)

Finally, the use of non-institutional social media among peers from different continents has been indicated by British students as a very effective tool for their learning. They specifically mentioned the possibility to communicate with the trainees in their daily lives, just as they would socially, outside of academia. For this to be successful, we would recommend use of social media only if it is embedded as a student-led initiative to avoid risks of communication and information overload.

Improving intercultural communication competences was—if not the foremost—one of the key learning outcomes of this programme, and to this end we set up an engaging and friendly environment for all students, who would learn (and teach, in the case of Chinese students) independently and with minimal teacher's guidance. Research shows that autonomous learning can boost students' motivation and engagement (Gazi 2009; Ushioda 2011) and these are, in turn, fundamental to the development of a community. After only seven sessions, and an ocean apart, students felt their intercultural knowledge and communications skills had improved (12.5% of them even indicated that they had made new friends, answering the question about what they felt they had gained most in the programme). One aspect of the cultural programme we will revisit is the prominence of the Chinese language within it. In fact, though the Chinese students conducted most of their communication in English, the British students did not have as many opportunities to speak Mandarin as would have led to perceived improvements—they learnt new vocabulary and possibly improved their listening skills but rarely elected to converse in Mandarin, as this was not required by the format of the programme. A possibility would be to ask the British students to produce a number of videos in Mandarin in the same vein as the ones made by their Chinese counterparts. To achieve similar standards, this should be made part of their assessment pattern so as to motivate them and make sure there is adequate engagement while avoiding an increase in workload that would detract from other academic endeavours. For now, we will continue making improvements to the programme without significant alterations, as we are currently developing the in-person teacher training for the lector, as well as a suitable programme for the visiting teacher. We hope that the increased presence of native speakers within the department and in their leading of the activities will lead to tangible improvements in the students' language skills (e.g. in pronunciation) and, as a result, increase students' confidence.

Notes

1. An example of TEL is Mobile Assisted Language Learning (MALL). This is formal or informal learning mediated by handheld devices that must be available anytime, anywhere. MALL can be effective as an additional tool for enhancing the four language skills (speaking, writing, reading, and listening), and it is fundamentally useful for boosting motivation, engagement, and autonomy—which, as highlighted in the Introduction, are indissolubly connected elements of learning. However, one issue with MALL is that many apps exist out there whose focus will be on one skill or another. Many apps will, for instance, focus on vocabulary. There is, in the main, not a single app for language learning that adopts a truly holistic approach. Even those that claim to be more complete than others fall short, at least when it comes to the subject of this chapter: community.
2. The questionnaire was administered via Microsoft Forms. The students had been informed of the scope of the study, and anonymity was granted by the complete absence of any personal details request in the form, as well as by the functionality in Microsoft form, which allows for complete anonymity of respondents.
3. WeChat is a Chinese instant messaging, social media app, first released in 2011. In 2018 it became the largest standalone mobile app in the world.
4. The recordings can be found here: https://www.kent.ac.uk/language-centre/events/14671/travelling-virtually-in-xian
5. At both the beginning and the end of the programme, virtual ceremonies were held, with the presence of senior members of faculty from the Chinese university and equivalent-level colleagues from the UoK. This was meant to impress on both students and staff participants an appreciation for the project from senior figures, with the intention of signalling senior management's appreciation and support. The ceremonies were also meant to make students feel part of a bigger community by introducing people involved in the making of the project, who did not necessarily attend all seminars but who contributed in a different way (e.g. administratively and organisationally). In this respect, it is worth clarifying that the three authors of this chapter had different roles within the project. Wissia Fiorucci handled the administrative side of the cultural programme set-up and the ensuing learning agreement. Ru Su led

conversations with our Chinese partners and oversaw the running of the programme itself in all its components, with help from Wissia Fiorucci who is also in charge of lectors' training. Alvise Sforza Tarabochia gathered and analysed data from the surveys, as well as taking part in official ceremonies. The chapter was co-written and research was conducted by all authors.

6. Its success led to our being invited to the online International Chinese Education Conference, hosted by the Chinese Cultural Institute–Chinese Plus, in December 2021. We introduced our project and university to the participants at the conference, which featured academics from all over the world. This exposure also allowed us to use the programme as a case study to negotiate with the Chinese Centre for Language Education and Cooperation, which eventually agreed to fund a new exchange agreement between the two universities.
7. For instance: 'I love the presentations of Xi'an culture on Wednesday afternoon […]. The presentation are beautiful and executed very professionally which makes learning about the culture even more interesting'.
8. Transcripts from the videos: 'The programme has been outstanding, … really feels like you can go to Xi'an and meet these people and speak about the same topics in depth…hope there are more this kind of culture exchanges to come./Every teacher and student at [the Chinese] university has done a fantastic job./I hope to study abroad in China one day, … I think this gives me a taste of what it would be like and I really appreciate the kind of insider knowledge that I could find out from the programme./The culture and the history of China and how big Xi'an is because I haven't actually heard of the city Xi'an before, … so I really enjoyed that'.
9. To protect student anonymity, and given the small numbers that could render identification easy, we did not include any questions that could lead to identifying the student respondent, and hence we do not have data available for analysis of aspects through cross-referencing (e.g. we do not know if students who attended certain seminars rather than others feel they had developed intercultural knowledge to a lesser or greater degree).
10. Comments are reported here in their entirety: 'The inclusion of the opportunity to work in China as well as the impressive cultural exchange seminars were amazingly done and wonderfully inclusive and expressive of Chinese culture./ I love the Wednesday sessions with training teachers

in China, it is a very helpful revision session as well as learning about Chinese (especially Xi'an) culture./ As an extra I love the presentations of Xi'an culture on Wednesday afternoon and I am very much excited for having the opportunity to visit Xi'an potentially in the spring./The presentation are beautiful and executed very professionally which makes learning about the culture even more interesting./ The cultural sessions were amazing and I enjoyed them a lot./ I really enjoyed every workshop. It was executed at a very professional level and all of the students and staff involved have done an amazing job!! I do not have any suggestions for improvement as I think everything went very well./ They were perfect, I wouldn't change anything./ I don't have nothing to suggest as each session was amazing, so professional and interesting. They have enriched my heritage'.

References

Ansari, J.A.N., and N.A. Khan. 2020. Exploring the role of social media in collaborative learning. The new domain of learning. *Smart Learning Environments* 7 (9). https://doi.org/10.1186/s40561-020-00118-7.

Baecher, L., and S. Chung. 2020. Transformative professional development for in-service teachers through international service learning. *Teacher Development* 24 (1): 33–51. https://doi.org/10.1080/13664530.2019.1682033.

Cai, S., and W. Zhu. 2012. The Impact of an Online Learning Community Project on University Chinese as a Foreign Language Students' Motivation. *Foreign Language Annals* 45: 307–329. https://doi.org/10.1111/j.1944-9720.2012.01204.x.

Chapelle, C., and J. Jamieson. 1986. Computer-assisted language learning as a predictor of success in acquiring English as a second language. *TESOL Quarterly* 20: 27–46.

Cole, D., E. Rengasamy, S. Batchelor, et al. 2017. Using social media to support small group learning. *BMC Med Educ* 17: 201. https://doi.org/10.1186/s12909-017-1060-7.

Cook, L., and M. Friend. 1995. Co-teaching: Guidelines for creating effective practices. *Focus on Exceptional Children* 28 (3): 1–16. https://doi.org/10.17161/foec.v28i3.6852.

Crowley-Cyr, L., and J. Hevers. 2021. Using peer assisted learning to improve academic engagement and progression of first year online law students. *Journal of University Teaching & Learning Practice* 18 (1): 10.53761/1.18.1.2.

David, O.N., et al. 2012. Model of perceived influence of academic performance using social networking. *International Journal of Computer and Technology* 2: 24–29.

Deardorff, D.K. 2006. Identification and assessment of intercultural competence as a student outcome of internationalization. *Journal of Studies in International Education* 10 (3): 241–266.

Fuady, R., and A.A. Mutalib. 2019. Audio-visual media in learning. *Journal of K6 Education and Management* 1 (2): 1–6. https://doi.org/10.11594/jk6em.01.02.01.

Gazi, Z.A. 2009. Implementing constructivist approach into online course designs in Distance Education Institute at Eastern Mediterranean University. *The Turkish Online Journal of Educational Technology* 8 (2): 68–81.

Geer, R., and A. Wing. 2003. The online learning community: Strategies, problems and issues. In *Proceedings of the International Conference on Computers in Education 2002*, vol. 1, 376–377. IEEE. https://doi.org/10.1109/CIE.2002.1185951.

Gibson, M. 2020. Creating a welcoming and inclusive online learning community. https://www.timeshighereducation.com/campus/creating-welcoming-and-inclusive-online-learning-community. Accessed 27 November 2022.

Greenhow, C. 2011a. Online social networks and learning. *On the Horizon* 19 (1): 4–12.

———. 2011b. Youth, learning, and social media. *Journal of Educational Computing Research* 45 (2): 139–146. https://doi.org/10.2190/EC.45.2.a.

Ke, F., and C. Hoadley. 2009. Evaluating online learning communities. *Educational Technology Research and Development* 57 (4): 487–510.

Keenan, D. 2014. Mapping student-led peer learning in the UK. *Advance HE*. https://www.advance-he.ac.uk/knowledge-hub/mapping-student-led-peer-learning-uk. Accessed 21 November 2022.

Kirschner, P.A., and A.C. Karpinski. 2010. Facebook® and academic performance. *Computers in Human Behaviour* 26 (6): 1237–1245. https://doi.org/10.1016/j.chb.2010.03.024.

Le Roux, D.B., and D.A. Parry. 2017. In-lecture media use and academic performance: Does subject area matter? *Computers in Human Behaviour* 77: 86–94. https://doi.org/10.1016/j.chb.2017.08.030.

Leonardi, V. 2022. Communication challenges and transformations in the Digital Era: emoji language and emoji translation. *Language and Semiotic Studies* 8 (3): 22–44. https://doi.org/10.1515/lass-2022-2003.

Masood, A., et al. 2020. Adverse consequences of excessive social networking site use on academic performance: Explaining underlying mechanism from stress perspective. *Computers in Human Behaviour* 113 (106476): 106476. https://doi.org/10.1016/j.chb.2020.106476.

Ody, M., and W. Carey. 2013. Peer education. In Morgan, M. (ed.) *The student engagement handbook: practice in higher education*. Bingley: Emerald Group Publishing Ltd.

Paik, S.J., et al. 2015. Intercultural exchange among global teachers: The case of the teaching excellence and achievement study abroad program. *International Journal of Intercultural Relations* 49 (November): 100–113. https://doi.org/10.1016/j.ijintrel.2015.06.011.

Paul, J.A., et al. 2012. Effect of online social networking on student academic performance. *Computers in Human Behaviour* 28: 2117–2127. https://doi.org/10.1016/j.chb.2012.06.016.

Payne Miller, E., et al. 2017. Changing demographics and needs assessment for learning centres in the 21st century. *Learning Assistance Review* 22 (1): 21–36.

Pribadi, B.A. 2004. Ketersediaan dan pemanfaatan media dan teknologi pembelajaran di perguruan tinggi. *Jurnal Pendidikan* 5 (2): 145–156.

Purvis, A., et al. 2016. Engagement or distraction: The use of social media for learning in higher education. *Student Engagement and Experience Journal* 5(1): 1–5. https://doi.org/10.7190/seej.v5.i1.104. Accessed 27 November 2022.

Schneider, C. 2020. Setting up a language learning environment in Microsoft Teams. *Studies in Self-Access Learning Journal* 11 (3): 263–270. https://doi.org/10.37237/110312.

Schwab, K. 2016. *The Fourth Industrial Revolution*. World Economic Forum.

Sofi-Karim, M., A.O. Bali, and K. Rached. 2023. Online education via media platforms and applications as an innovative teaching method. *Educ Inf Technol* 28: 507–523. https://doi.org/10.1007s10639-022-11188-0.

Sullivan, N. 1993. Teaching writing on a computer network. *TESOL Journal* 3: 34–35.

Summers, J.J., and M.D. Svinicki. 2007. Investigating classroom community in higher education. *Learning and Individual Differences* 17: 55–67. https://psycnet.apa.org/doi/10.1016/j.lindif.2007.01.006.

Thorne, S.L., R.W. Black, and J.M. Sykes. 2009. Second Language Use, Socialization, and Learning in Internet Interest Communities and Online Gaming. *The Modern Language Journal* 93: 802–821. https://doi.org/10.1111/j.1540-4781.2009.00974.x.

Ushioda, E. 2011. Why Autonomy? Insights from Motivation Theory and Research. *Innovation in Language Learning and Teaching* 5 (2): 221–232.

Voorn, R.J., and P.A. Kommers. 2013. Social media and higher education: Introversion and collaborative learning from the student's perspective. *International Journal of Social Media and Interactive Learning Environments* 1 (1): 59–73.

Warschauer, M. 1996. Motivational aspects of using computers for writing and communication. In *Telecommunication in foreign language learning: Proceedings of the Hawaii symposium*, ed. M. Warschauer, 29–46. Honolulu: University of Hawai'i, Second Language Teaching and Curriculum Centre.

Whelan, E., et al. 2020. Applying the SOBC paradigm to explain how social media overload affects academic performance. *Computers & Education* 143. https://doi.org/10.1016/j.compedu.2019.103692. Accessed 27 November 2022.

Wu, J.-Y., and T. Cheng. 2018. Who is better adapted in learning online within the personal learning environment? Relating gender differences in cognitive attention networks to digital distraction. *Computer Education* 128: 312–329. https://doi.org/10.1016/j.compedu.2018.08.016.

Zhu, C. 2012. Student satisfaction, performance, and knowledge construction in online collaborative learning. *Journal of Educational Technology & Society* 15 (1): 127–136.

8

Developing a Sense of Community Online Through Intercultural Communication: A Gamified Approach

Patricia Díaz-Muñoz and Laura Stecca

1   Introduction

The state of health emergency due to COVID-19 afflicted education around the world. In March 2020, educational institutions were forced to adapt their syllabi to online didactics. Further complicating matters as regards language teaching were the already existing need for training learners in intercultural dialogue—to avoid prejudices and stereotypes that are harmful to language learning itself and prevent effective intercultural communication. Although many scholars (Dervin 2009; Balboni and Caon 2014, 2015; Balboni 2015), to mention but a few, have worked on teaching intercultural competence, the pandemic brought about the need to develop innovative materials and tools to raise intercultural awareness within an online setting.

P. Díaz-Muñoz
Complutense University of Madrid, Madrid, Spain
e-mail: patrid02@ucm.es

L. Stecca (✉)
Italian Language School, London, UK

Hence, the aim of our research is twofold. Moving from a localised to a wide-ranging goal, on the one hand, we aimed to create a sense of intercultural community among students in the time of COVID-19. On the other, we intended to develop effective online tools to develop the intercultural competence of B1 students of Italian and Spanish.[1] A constructivist and gamified approach was followed to develop the study.

Gamification consists of 'using game design elements in non-game contexts' (Deterding et al. 2011, p. 9), in this case education. We also wanted to ascertain whether gamification could be a fruitful methodological strategy in multicultural settings. We based our work on two fundamental premises. First, in addition to helping to create a desired sense of intercultural community, gamification can boost students' motivation and engagement in online lessons due to the component of fun it borrows from video games (Alsawaier 2018). Furthermore, the cooperative nature of gamification may encourage mutual understanding among students from different cultural backgrounds (Cassany 2004).

In carrying out our research during the COVID-19 emergency, we aimed to address the following questions:

RQ1: What are the effects of gamification on intercultural competence within online teaching?
RQ2: To what extent is gamification effective in the creation of a sense of intercultural community among students from different cultural backgrounds?

The present chapter is divided into five sections, including this introduction, which outlines the objectives of the study as well as the main premises. In Sect. 2, a theoretical background will be provided to elaborate on intercultural competence teaching and gamification. Section 3 will include a brief description of the gamified activities designed for the purposes of the study and of the participants—B1 students of Italian and Spanish. In Sect. 4, the results and findings from the application of these gamified activities in the classroom will be compared and discussed qualitatively. Finally, conclusions will be given alongside suggesting possibilities for further research and future directions on the topic.

2 Theoretical Background

This section is divided into four subsections to introduce theoretical notions that were necessary to develop the study, namely intercultural communicative competence and gamification.

2.1 Intercultural Communicative Competence

It is often thought that the most effective way to communicate with a person of a different nationality is to find a common language or to study the language spoken in their country. Sometimes we even consider body language as a universally understandable way to communicate (Balboni and Caon 2015), for example, when we give information to tourists.

However, while conversations are made up of verbal and non-verbal language, codes, words, and gestures are not always shared by the speakers, not even if they do speak the same language. These differences do not only depend on the language in use but also depend on the country of origin, the belonging to an ethnic group or religion, or different social background. Thus, a word, a supposition, or any type of belief that we take for granted acquires an added value deriving from other people's understanding of it. When we do not take these differences into account, we expose ourselves to potential misunderstandings and miscommunication. When the communicative misunderstanding is determined by a cultural factor, from a social perspective this can be received as a much worse mistake than a grammatical one—within a classroom context it can, for instance, jeopardise an individual's sense of belonging, understood as their idea of connectedness to the community (Keyser et al. 2022, p. 2), as also explained in the Introduction to this volume.

Communicative competence (Balboni and Caon 2014)—the set of skills and knowledge that we put into practice when using a language—is what connects our mind to the world and allows us to express our thoughts in communicative events. According to Balboni and Caon (2015), communicative competence consists of linguistic components, extra-linguistic components, and contextual components (which include intercultural knowledge).[2]

In other words, it is not only what we say that represents a message, but everything that we are, that we use, the position and movements of our bodies, and many other elements. These all contribute to the success—or failure—of the communicative act. Intercultural competence and its concepts are in continuous development (Dervin 2010), and as Dervin (2016) reports, a point of view is not a given. Because of these factors, even if it 'is a vital competence in our contemporary world' (Dervin 2010, p. 158), it is impossible to create a manual with all the characteristics of a universal cultural communicative competence.

2.2 Intercultural Misunderstanding and Its Consequences

According to Grant, in his preface to Corner's *Education in Multicultural Societies*:

> Multicultural education is still widely regarded as a 'problem', as something to do with racial or linguistic minorities (or 'immigrants'), no doubt worth enough but peripheral to the main concerns of the educational system. Even when action is taken, it is more often than not conceived as remedial action, such as teaching more English (or French, or German or whatever) to non-native speaking pupils, helping them to fit into the majority society, […] with little attempt to find out what languages they actually speak; they are defined by what they lack rather than by what they have. (Grant p. 8 in Corner, 1984)

Here, a first critical point emerges: ethnic and/or linguistic minorities seem to be the true subjects of intercultural projects. But why should we sensitise only the ethnic minorities to the national culture instead of involving the majority cultures in the project of inculturation as well?: 'If multicultural programs were prepared for the majority (which would be highly logical) or if they covered all children without distinction'—says Bottani, head of the research plan on inter-sectoral policies for children and the OECD[3]—'there would be no ethnic dilemma' (1989, p. 21). Intercultural education cannot be a unilateral activity aimed at imposing the language, values, and traditions of a dominant culture on minorities.

The prefix *inter* in intercultural (from Latin: 'between') implies a bilateral movement, between culture and culture, between person and person. As Porcher (in CERI 1989, p. 30) has it, 'if the intercultural policy is to be consistent and effective it must be adopted generally and for everyone'. We should all connect to other cultures, relying on relations of cooperation and coexistence.

Cultural misunderstandings can lead to stereotypes and prejudice (which are meant to be a physiological mechanism to protect us from the unknown): intercultural education plays a fundamental role in preventing this, and this is especially the case within language teaching since its main purpose is to allow students to effectively communicate with people from different backgrounds.

2.3 Intercultural Education in the Online Setting

Troncarelli (2004) affirms that language learners seem particularly advantaged by distance learning, having access through the network to online dictionaries and conjugators, explanations and patterns of grammar rules, automatically corrected activities, and phonetic or video transcriptions with pronunciation. Research on language education during the pandemic also supports this point in terms of online learning (see Fiorucci's Introduction to this volume).

Another essential aspect of online language teaching is the possibility of having a direct connection with the country, culture, and native speakers of the language learned. The materials and the resources to which we have access are often authentic, designed to be usable by native speakers; teachers may themselves come from the country whose language and culture are being studied and can transmit a natural and spontaneous communication. As Bonfiglio (2013, p. 16) puts it: 'Si costruisce un ambiente virtuale, ma non per questo meno reale, dove avviene l'interazione'.[4]

Within language education, however, teaching intercultural communicative competence is a hard task since it includes too many variables and is continuously being modified and developed (Balboni and Caon 2014).[5] In Alm's words:

> The contact with people of different cultural backgrounds, especially in computer-mediated communication, does not necessarily lead to increased intercultural awareness and [...] on the contrary can contribute to creating more stereotypes, negative and positive representations about the self and the other. (2016, p. 26)

Still, it is possible to educate students by offering tools that can lead to an increasingly autonomous discovery of the cultural characteristics they may encounter, for example, helping them familiarise themselves with a process of 'lifelong observation dei problemi di comunicazione interculturale' (Balboni 2015, p. 138).[6] The continuous training in empathy and the constant analysis of others' culture and behaviour, as well as ours, can reduce the risk of misunderstandings every time you encounter different languages and cultures (Fiorucci et al.'s study in this volume offers an example of sustained cultural training).[7] The use of video calls in teaching mediated by technology, for example, can enable students to observe themselves and their counterparts, as it removes 'distraction' from the environment and lets us focus on the interlocutor and on ourselves. Regarding this matter, Celentin (2007) reminds us how, in addition to the interlocutor's image (even if limited to the half-length), it is possible to see our image while we interact, which helps us to analyse the situation on an intercultural level (gestures, expressiveness, use of accessories or jewels, way of dressing, and so forth).

It seems, however, that it is not uncommon for students to experience a socio-psychological block, which may cause them to refuse to speak during class, as reported by Ming (2004). The reasons are various, and they include the learner's personality, the presence of learning disabilities, or the student's origin, among other factors. The author deduces that some students are not inclined to participate in the lesson because they feel inferior to their peers, since they believe they have an inferior language level. The opposite may also occur. That is, students do not want to appear arrogant because they speak better than their peers.

Although this happens commonly also in face-to-face settings, the insecure student is likely to resort to available tools and strategies rendered possible by an online setting, such as communicating mainly in asynchronous mode (which allows them to reflect for longer and feel more confident before making their contribution). As for the more competent students, one of the advantages of group teaching (relevant to gamification) can come into play: the use of the expertise of the course participants in an online setting (Bonfiglio 2013). The learners who can be considered 'experts' would not risk being addressed as arrogant when demonstrating their ability but would support those who have difficulties and thus become support figures who can make the whole group progress. Although Bonfiglio (2013) refers to online settings, this might apply to any teaching context.

Gamification has been selected as the methodological strategy to overcome these difficulties. A definition for gamification will be provided in the next section, where it is introduced together with some important notions and nuances concerning this methodological strategy.

2.4 Gamification as a Methodological Strategy

As Díaz Antillanca (2016) highlights, as children, we learn and discover the world by playing. However, the playful nature of human beings has, until very recently, been under-explored and has even been suppressed within school settings, as the author claims—which deprives students and teachers of powerful learning tools. One of the most innovative methodological strategies related to games and playing is *gamification*. Gamification is the use of 'game design elements in non-game contexts to motivate and increase user activity' (Deterding et al. 2011, p. 9).

Foncubierta and Rodríguez (2014) clarify the distinction between video games and gamification in educational settings[8]: while video games are conceived for users' enjoyment, gamification aims at engaging students and creating a sense of autonomy. It means that gamification focuses on student learning rather than fun in itself. In the same vein, Alsawaier (2018, p. 62) states that '[g]amification is not when learning is changed into a computer game but rather when adding a design layer of game elements to enhance learning, increase engagement, and encourage positive behavior'. Examples of some game elements that are usually employed to design gamified activities are rewards such as points or badges, overcoming and unlocking different levels, narrative structures, use of personal or group avatars, role-taking, competition, and so on (Alsawaier 2018; Pujolà and Herrera Jiménez 2018).

That said, it is important to point out that teachers must consider students' specific needs and the selected learning outcomes to choose the proper elements to include in their gamified activities (Lee and Hammer 2011; Pujolà and Herrera Jiménez 2018). It means that gamification entails careful and thorough design of the activities. In addition to focusing on learning outcomes, Pujolà and Herrera Jiménez (2018) claim that one of the keys to gamifying effectively is to know what kind of player the students are. In this regard, Marczewski (2015) proposes six gamification user types based on Bartle's (1996) initial classification:

1. Philanthropists: they are altruistic and willing to give without expecting a reward.
2. Socialisers: they want to interact with others and create social connections.
3. Free spirits: they like to create and explore within a system.
4. Achievers: they seek to progress within a system by completing tasks or prove themselves by tackling difficult challenges.
5. Players: they will do anything to earn a reward within a system.
6. Disruptors: they tend to disrupt the system either directly or through others to force negative or positive changes. They like to test the system's boundaries and try to push further.[9]

Considering the difficulty of identifying types of players among students, Pujolà and Herrera Jiménez (2018) propose including gamified activities that can attract the largest possible number of players to make the most of the gamified activities at hand.[10]

According to Foncubierta and Rodríguez (2014), a well-designed set of gamified activities can promote communicative behaviour even beyond the classroom. This makes gamification a very useful and profitable methodological strategy in online lessons, where students might find it difficult to establish social bonds with their peers and teachers. The cooperative and communicative nature of gamification has the potential to create that desired sense of community among foreign language students, which is vital for them to feel comfortable in class. Moreover, Cassany (2004) emphasises the positive effects of cooperative activities on the development of students' intercultural awareness, for students from different cultural backgrounds need to cooperate to carry out tasks. Hence, gamification could help break down barriers such as the isolation that students may experience in online lessons or the communicative misunderstandings among students from different cultural contexts.

Alsawaier (2018) highlights the importance of distinguishing between motivation and engagement: while 'motivation is linked to psychological elements that drive behaviour and choice-making' (2018, pp. 67–68), '[e]ngagement indicates the passion and emotional involvement in participating and completing learning activities' (2018, p. 69). Thus, a combination of both motivation and engagement would be necessary to create a sense of community among the students, for they need to stick to their roles and rules within their group to attain the group's objectives—they are, that is, invested with a sense of responsibility for their group's performance, which can motivate them and hence develop engagement.

To encourage motivation and engagement, Alsawaier (2018) proposes the creation of challenging activities according to students' level and resources. This idea is related to Csikszentmihalyi's flow theory (1988, 1990, 1992), which consists in challenging students to the point that the task itself becomes the sole focus of their attention (Abio 2006). Nevertheless, this flow state or boost of motivation and engagement is difficult to achieve in online lessons since students are isolated at home, perhaps keeping their cameras off and lacking learning stimuli. Here is where gamification proves to be a profitable resource again, for it 'borrows from video games the element of fun not only to gain the learners' engagement, but also to positively increase their motivation' (Alsawaier 2018, p. 74).

To summarise, gamification provides teachers and students with learning tools to encourage motivation and engagement and to subsequently stimulate a sense of community during online lessons. However, teachers must carefully choose the elements they are going to use in their gamified activities to trigger these positive effects.

The next section will discuss and explain in depth the elements and the gamified activities selected to develop the current research.

3 Methodology

The goal of this section is to describe the gamification elements and the procedure followed to develop and implement the gamified activities. A description of the participants, as well as the ethical considerations, will be provided. Hence, the section is divided into two subsections: participants and didactic proposal.

3.1 Participants

The present set of gamified activities was designed to be applied in online foreign language lessons within a university context. Specifically, the participants of the study were undergraduate students of Italian and Spanish in their first year at a Southern British University. In addition to being foreign language learners, the participants came from different cultural backgrounds, which highlights the importance of training their intercultural competence.

Firstly, it is worth mentioning that special attention has been drawn to the ethical considerations since asking for third parties' collaboration always entails an intrusion into their private lives (Cohen et al. 2017). Thus, it is necessary to guarantee the protection and anonymity of students' identities through the anonymity attached to their answers. Furthermore, students were aware that they were taking part in a research project before doing the activities, although they did not know the nature and the specific goal of the study so as not to condition their answers. The participants also filled in a consent form to meet the ethical requirements for analysing and disclosing the data obtained from their responses.

That said, students of Italian had a B1 level, but two students were native speakers of Italian, and two others were considered bilingual because one of them had attended high school in Italy and the other was a heritage speaker. Consequently, B1 level students felt discouraged from participating in class due to this difference in their level and the isolation brought about by COVID-19. Moreover, the students did not seem to have established any social bonds within the group, which also affected their performance in the Italian lessons. There were three Italian trainees who helped them complete their tasks in class and participated in the gamified activities to make them flow more smoothly.

In the Spanish module, all the students had a B1 level, with no remarkable differences among them. However, students would also find it difficult to participate in class because of lacking social bonds within the group, except for a group of French Erasmus students who were friends. Unlike the students in the Italian module, the students of Spanish did not have any trainees to help them complete the activities.

3.2 Didactic Proposal

This subsection presents the procedure followed in designing the gamified activities, as well as the activities themselves. According to Pujolà and Herrera Jiménez (2018), there are three phases to follow when defining didactic proposals (including gamified activities), namely, planning, development, and evaluation. Hence, this subsection has been divided into three different parts, one for each of the three phases.

Planning Phase

When creating a set of gamified activities, the designer must consider their target students, the time, and the space available, the materials to be employed, the people who are to conduct the activities, and the goal of the activities (Redondo Juárez 2021). Given the students in our sample, we set ourselves the aim of breaking cultural and online teaching barriers in the time of COVID-19.

Once the objectives of the gamified activities had been set, we had to consider the gamification elements used to design the activities at hand. In the first place, the students were asked to work in teams to promote cooperation. Each team consisted of three students from different cultural backgrounds, wherever possible, and they were assigned different roles: a spokesperson, a secretary, and a time and points checker. In this way, all the students could feel important and make their own particular and needed contributions to the team. Furthermore, it could help keep them engaged since the students knew they had a responsibility and a mission to accomplish. The students were also given the possibility of choosing a team name so they could identify themselves with the team, which would consolidate the group identity.

In addition to promoting cooperation, working in teams also promotes competition. The decision of making them compete against other teams was made to save time, given that all the activities needed to be conducted in two sessions. At the same time, competition may boost motivation because the activity entails a goal, that of winning, which is more immediately tangible than the learning goals themselves. To make the competition more interesting, points were given to each team for finding the correct answer to each activity. Even though the points system has been criticised for being too basic, Tulloch (2014) proves it to be very useful and states that it does not only serve to increase motivation through competition, but it also allows students to measure their progress during the activity.

Another way for students to track their own progress throughout the gamified activities is to overcome different levels of difficulty (Tulloch 2014). Thus, each activity was called a 'level' and required a higher degree of reflection on cultural issues from the students as they progressed. Moreover, students had to find the correct answer to unlock and continue to the next activity or 'level'. In addition to maintaining the intrigue surrounding what would come next, the levelling system helped students to acknowledge their progress and feel encouraged to finish all the activities.

Finally, as Pujolà and Herrera Jiménez (2018) claim, teachers must consider the kinds of players their students are when designing gamified activities to adapt the activities to their needs and wants. Given that it is not always possible to identify the type of players, they suggest including at least one element related to each of the six types of players to attract the largest possible number of students. Having designed the gamified activities and the gamification elements to be included, the next step was to apply the activities in class. The next section deals with the content and description of each of the activities and an explanation of the way they can attract students as players.

Development Phase

In the first place, the students were divided into three groups in the Italian class and into four groups in the Spanish class. Then, the teachers explained they were going to cooperate in teams to engage with a set of activities (or 'levels') related to (inter)cultural matters. They were also told they would receive points for each correct answer, which was an important reward since they had to compete against the other teams too. As previously mentioned, the points system was included for students to track their own progress and to engage those who were considered *players*[11] according to Marczewski's (2015) classification. In the same way, the activities turned into 'unlockable levels' for *achievers* to face them as challenges and boost their motivation. Moreover, cooperation and competition can be used as bait to involve *socialisers*.

Before starting the first activity, the students were encouraged to choose a team name and to assign roles: spokesperson, secretary, and points and time checker. Apart from boosting students' engagement, these different roles were created to attract *philanthropists*, for they had to carry out a task that suited them well to help their teammates achieve their goals. Once the students knew what they had to do and the time limit they had to complete each level, they started carrying out the activities.

The first activity was conducted *in plenum* as a starting point for teammates to get acquainted with each other and to familiarise themselves with the dynamics of the gamified activities. In this activity, the teachers shared their screens in the virtual platform Teams and showed a video.[12] This was about Italian and Spanish people talking about what they were going to do when the pandemic of COVID-19 would be over, including routines in their daily lives. The students had to find out who these people were and what their daily lives were like. Then, the teachers showed the video again for students to describe these people's moods using as many adjectives as possible.

After the warm-up, Teams breakout rooms were created for the students to start working in groups. Then, they moved to the second activity, which consisted of five trivia questions dealing with content and vocabulary from the video (see Appendices 1 and 2). They had to discuss all five questions in teams and select the correct answer. As soon as they finished, the teams received feedback *in plenum* and the answer to all the questions. Each team obtained two points for each correct answer.

As they finished, the teams went on to the third activity in their breakout rooms. In this jigsaw puzzle-like activity, the students had to order words to form sentences from the video. Again, each group received feedback at the end of the activity, and they were awarded five points for each correct sentence. Once the third activity was finished, the students were asked to complete fourth activity. This activity consisted of five speeches given during COVID-19 by the presidents or prime ministers of different countries: France, Germany, the UK, the USA, and Italy/Spain. The fourth activity was an open answer activity to attract *free spirits*' attention and to make the students think about cultural features. Hence, each group had to find the keywords of the five speeches and deduce cultural features from them. For each feature they could find and explain to their classmates, they received two points. Moreover, they had to add two more common cultural features related to the aforementioned countries. Finally, the students were asked to discuss in their teams to what extent the pandemic and the lockdown had affected the creation and development of a sense of community. The teacher would circulate among Teams breakout rooms to supervise the activity, with the implementation of 'parallel teaching' (see Cook and Friend 1995, p. 7) when teacher trainees were present (see Fiorucci et al.'s chapter).

Lastly, in the fifth activity each team was asked to write a short speech to thank people for the effort made during the pandemic. The speeches should be as intercultural as possible to reach more citizens. Afterwards, the students were encouraged to reflect on the cultural aspects that their team and the other teams had included in their speeches and on the impact of these cultural aspects on the sense of community. These last reflections were made *in plenum* and, at the end, the students had to vote for their favourite speech. The team that had created the speech with the most votes was given the last crucial points, very likely becoming the winning team. The voting system was included so that *disruptors* felt that they could manipulate and alter the outcome of the activities to some extent. In addition to attracting disruptor users, the voting system allowed the students to evaluate and judge their own work, promoting their critical thinking and their intercultural awareness.

Evaluation Phase

After the implementation of the gamified activities in the Italian and Spanish classes, the outcomes were discussed and compared during the evaluation phase to check whether the initial objectives had been accomplished and to examine the effects of gamification on students' intercultural awareness and the creation of a sense of intercultural community in online teaching lessons. In addition to the academic implications of gamification in online settings, students' opinions were also considered by means of a post-activities questionnaire to assess their perception regarding their intercultural competence. The questionnaire submitted to students consisted of four sections: continuous learning, interpersonal engagement, psychological and attitudinal skills, and linguistic skills (verbal and non-verbal).[13] For each of the questions, the students had to tick the most suitable option to describe their personal situation in a numerical range from one to five. At the end of each of the four sections, they were given the possibility of leaving a comment to explain their choice or give further information on their intercultural experience. The results and findings obtained from this phase will be discussed in the following section.

4   Results and Findings

In this section, we intend to present the analyses that were formulated, as well as the results, both positive and negative, of what we observed, providing recommendations to carry out the lesson more efficiently.

After the activity had been completed, we spoke with the teacher who oversaw the delivery of material in the Spanish course.[14] We analysed how everything had been put into practice, how the students had reacted in terms of community and group work, and their response to some of the activities. We also discussed the material used and our initial responses to the activities and their functioning in the virtual classroom.

First, it is important to note that the general impression was positive since the activity had been dynamic and entertaining and had allowed everyone to participate in the execution of most of the tasks. Regarding this last aspect in the Italian module, even if all the students had previously studied the language, some of them were native speakers, graduated from high school in Italy or had an Italian family. Therefore, they regularly spoke the language at home. For this reason, communication and conversation activities were often difficult to carry out during the academic year. The students whose level was more representative of the B1 level often felt embarrassed when performing tasks in front of their classmates because of the language disparity and hence needed more support and stimuli. For this reason, throughout the year, and in the carrying out of this activity, the help of the trainees was valuable, for trainees were acknowledged by students as support figures and they were not too intimidated to ask for their help. In an in-class setting, it would have been easier for the teacher to monitor every student in their individual and group work, but this becomes relatively complicated online, given that, although it is possible to enter the breakout rooms individually, it is not possible to have a simultaneous view of all the groups. Hence, the teacher and the students felt reassured by the presence of the trainee teachers, who could provide immediate feedback and hence ensured what Fiorucci has referred to in this volume as a reliable teaching presence. This, Fiorucci et al. explain in their chapter, is a fundamental component of a learning community (online or otherwise).

In the Spanish class, on the other hand, there was a group of French students who already knew each other before the beginning of the module. For this reason, the other students, who did not share the same familiarity, sometimes felt uncomfortable. It is important to keep in mind that in a F2F setting it would be possible for students to talk or interact with the people sitting next to them in the classroom by, for instance, commenting on the lesson or asking for help. In the online classroom, or at least with most of the software used by schools and institutions, students can communicate one-to-one via chat, but they get to choose their interlocutor—which can reinforce existing relationships but does not help in forming new ones. As interactions with the group are mostly one-to-everyone, teacher-to-single student or student-to-teacher, it can be hard for students to get to know their classmates unless they are somehow forced to engage in dialogue with classmates they do not know. Therefore, the first element a teacher needs to address to elicit a sense of learning community is participation in seminar activities. In our case, a positive factor was certainly that of carrying out the activities in two sessions: the first activities (1 and 2) being completed and corrected *in plenum*, students were able to gradually approach the gamified and the intercultural components of the activity. In this way, they did not immediately find themselves thinking about the score and the goal of the proposed exercises. Rather, they had the necessary time to do it without pressure, having first acquired a certain degree of confidence in the topic and specific vocabulary. In the second part, and in activity 4, with the focus on gamification and intercultural competence, they worked well together to reach a common goal and think about cultural differences by observing and taking notes. In particular, the activity and the achievement of the intercultural objective have proven successful in those groups where participants were more diverse in terms of origin and personal background. A balanced communication was attained, rather than a judgement on the culture of the countries where the target language was spoken. The native speakers and/or people who knew the country the most became positive leaders within the group, but the 'responsibility' for success did not exclusively rely on them.

The activity involved describing and comparing different countries (Italy, Spain, France, Germany, the UK, and the USA), not only one of their target language or the country in which the students reside. In addition, students were then asked to think of other examples from around the world. In this way, everyone felt they could contribute something to the class, relying on and sharing their knowledge.

The last exercise (activity 5) especially saw the class adapt to the game modes and competitiveness. In the first stage, the students, who were supposed to create a speech, initially voted their own speeches as the best ones. In the second stage, they chose one from another team, as per game rules.

Considering the feedback and the contexts in which the students found themselves performing the activities—with a disparity of level, outside the in-class setting, and, in some cases, not knowing each other well—it can be concluded that the aim of creating a sense of community within the online class was achieved. This happened, however, more within the individual teams than as a class group, in an environment that might have been considered 'safer' in terms of preserving students' socio-psychological characteristics. In our view, the most successful activity was the one in which the students were asked to look for at least two cultural characteristics that may be present in the words of each of the Heads of State. This was indeed the activity in which there was greater collaboration within the teams, and everyone was able to use their knowledge in their team's favour. The least successful, however, was the first one, as the students still felt intimidated and probably not sure enough of themselves to share their impressions with their classmates, for the reasons previously explained.

On the other hand, a negative aspect was that the students in the Spanish class did not turn on their cameras during the activities. This was a recurring problem throughout the semester. It was not easy to ask students to turn on the cameras, since they were either studying in a common area of their accommodation and/or in a decidedly different context from that of the campus and the physical classroom. This is a common issue with ERT, even when the activities, such as in this case, are purposely designed for online delivery and thus not in emergency mode but within a forced remote learning environment. Within this setting, non-verbal and body language would certainly have favoured communication, both in breakout groups and *in plenum*, as it would have been possible for the students and the teacher to see facial expressions and understand if the instructions were clear. The sense of collaboration among the participants would certainly have been greater, not having to 'imagine' the faces and emotions of others. Thus, we can see here how when we speak of reliability regarding space—for example, the internet connection and the space through which this connection is provided—we are identifying a crucial element for the building of an online community (see Fiorucci et al.'s and Coderch's chapters, in this volume).

In light of these considerations, some aspects could be improved if the materials were to be repeated: it would be appropriate to find videos of the same type for both the Italian and Spanish classes. The video in Spanish is taken from a campaign that a governmental body, the municipality of Madrid, carried out to thank its citizens for the commitment and strength shown during lockdowns, while the video in Italian had the same purpose but was produced by Barilla, a multinational company in the food sector. The criticism made by students of Italian, especially those who were near-native or who knew the company better, was that the video exploited the situation for commercial purposes, and it was therefore not appreciated. In short, it would be better to use videos from governmental bodies in both cases or videos in which the message is delivered for similar purposes.

Further, students should be required to turn on their cameras, as non-verbal communication would certainly have helped and facilitated dialogue and increased complicity between the participants of each team. Even if it had been possible to complete all the activities, we would probably have needed more time, specifically to receive feedback from the students and to have a discussion on the questionnaires completed at the end of the project. Due to time constraints, students had to complete the questionnaire on their own after the second lesson and send it back to their teachers, while it would have probably been more functional to have some more time in class for students to answer questions individually and to lead a group feedback session as a final step.

Answers to the questionnaire revealed, as expected, that all students spoke at least one foreign language and, hence, they had met people from other cultural contexts. None of the students indicated a '1' (*minimum*) as an answer, and all seemed to be inclined towards and interested in communication and interaction with the other. This could be due to the high percentage of students residing in the UK but coming from other countries and to the fact that in most cases they were language students taking the course because they were interested in the language and culture of the countries where these languages are spoken. Quoting one of the students taking part in the research: 'I am always interested in other cultures, and I travel a lot and lived abroad so I like to learn to know other's cultures, languages, and so on. And I have many friends from other countries and boyfriend also from another country'.

Students felt they were not aware of norms such as kinesics and proxemics whether in their culture of origin or in other cultures, even if, in many cases, they showed an interest in cultural aspects such as the differences between their culture of origin and that of an L2. One of the students declared: 'I want to familiarise and learn what it is to assimilate with other cultures'.

Most of the students appreciated the proposed activities and indicated that the level of awareness of the differences between different cultures or nuances of one same culture has increased. As admitted by students, their approach to culture and intercultural traits is rather informal as it often derives from acquaintances and friends. For this reason, a more formal statement—for example, the words of politicians and state representatives as in the conducted activities—has made them discover that cultural aspects are reflected in all aspects of our life, even those that may be seen by young students as remote or exceptional.

As previously mentioned, everyone valued feeling themselves to be experts in something, despite their different origins, cultural backgrounds, and level of language competence and despite the final score achieved by the teams. Strong collaboration arose among the participants of each team, especially if made up of people from different cultural backgrounds or who knew each other previously, for the reasons analysed above. Consequently, there was a good level of competition between the teams, so the choice of using gamification to achieve an intercultural goal and motivate students to communicate with each other to reach a common purpose was fruitful.

5   Conclusions

The present study has examined the impact of gamification on intercultural competence within an online training setting. A set of gamified activities has been implemented in Italian and Spanish B1 classes to raise students' intercultural awareness and to create a sense of intercultural community among them, addressing some of the main challenges posed by the COVID-19 pandemic.

On the one hand, gamification has been proven to have many positive effects on students' intercultural competence. Firstly, it has helped with students' participation, encouraging those who did not feel comfortable in previous lessons to cooperate and contribute and turning native or near-native students into positive leaders for their teams. Moreover, all the students felt responsible and important in carrying out the roles they had been assigned and when sharing their own reflections with their teammates in the open answer activities. In addition to making all students feel they were experts in something, hence enhancing their motivation, cooperation in open answer activities served to make students think about cultural features and differences. Reflecting and sharing opinions on cultural matters enabled them to take a more critical stance towards cultural prejudices and stereotypes, promoting the development of their intercultural competence and the understanding between students from different cultural backgrounds. Finally, as a deeper understanding was reached between teammates, the sense of competition between teams increased, boosting students' motivation and engagement. The boost in motivation and engagement was also triggered by the points and levels systems.

The positive effects of gamification in online classes contributed to the creation of a sense of community or belonging among the students, which confirms the second hypothesis. Proof of this came from the evolution of the students throughout the activities: they started the first activity with the expected imbalance in participation and confidence, but by the end they were cooperating actively with their teammates and feeling comfortable in their teams. It is worth mentioning that this evolution was even more evident in teams with more cultural diversity. However, it was observed that this understanding and sense of community was kept within the teams rather than spreading to the whole class.

Once the effectiveness of gamification in creating social and intercultural bonds between students in multicultural online lessons has been proven, it would be interesting to see—with further studies and research on the topic—how students maintain and develop the social bonds created within each team as the course continues. Furthermore, it also seems necessary to conduct more gamified and cooperative activities from time to time or even gamify an entire module to try to extend this sense of community to the whole class, which could not be done in this study due to its limited scope. This would favour the much-desired motivation and participation on the part of the students in online lessons and lay the basis for a more systematic implementation of both online and gamified activities.

Appendices

Appendix 1: Didactic Material in Spanish

Nivel 1

a. Escucha el audio*. ¿Quién crees que son estas personas? ¿Cómo crees que es su día a día? Toma notas.
*El audio corresponde al vídeo 'Porque estar separados, jamás nos había unido tanto', publicado en el canal de YouTube de la Comunidad de Madrid:
https://www.youtube.com/watch?v=ee_QuFri_cM
b. Las personas que aparecen en el vídeo son habitantes de Madrid, que volverán a sus rutinas después de la pandemia del COVID-19. Mira de nuevo el vídeo y di cuál es su estado de ánimo. Escribe todos los adjetivos que se te ocurran para describirlos.

Nivel 2

a. Señala la respuesta correcta.–2 puntos a tu equipo por cada respuesta correcta.

a. ¿Qué tipo de vídeo es?

   – Una campaña política.
   – El tráiler de una película.
   – Una campaña publicitaria.

b. ¿Cuál es el propósito del vídeo?

   – Hacer ver la belleza de Madrid.
   – Vender cerveza.
   – Agradecer a los habitantes de Madrid el esfuerzo que están haciendo.

c. ¿Qué significa 'castiza' en el vídeo?

- Alegre.
- De Madrid.
- De España.

d. ¿Qué significa tomar una 'caña'?

- Ir a pescar.
- Beber una cerveza.
- Estar con los amigos.

e. ¿Qué pasa si un lugar está 'abarrotado'?

- Está prohibido entrar.
- Es un lugar de fiesta.
- Está lleno de gente.

Nivel 3

a. Algunas oraciones sacadas del vídeo se han desordenado, ¿podrías ponerlas en el orden correcto?
   5 puntos a tu equipo por cada oración correcta:

a. a/pronto/ser/volverás/tú.
b. Puerta del Sol/nuevo/la/de/abarrotaremos.
c. caña/volveremos/una/a/de/reunirnos/alrededor.
d. la/mano/volveremos/Gran Vía/la/a/cogidos/de/subir.

Nivel 4

a. Lee los siguientes extractos sacados de los discursos de diferentes presidentes europeos sobre el COVID-19. ¿Cuál te llama más la atención?

b. Señala las palabras clave del texto.—2 puntos por cada característica cultural que puedas explicar a tus compañeros.

c. ¿Qué características culturales se reflejan en cada texto? ¿Podrías añadir dos características más sobre cada país?

d. ¿De qué manera crees que puede haber influido la cuarentena en la creación y el desarrollo del 'sentido de comunidad'? ¿Conoces ejemplos similares de otros países?

Nivel 5

a. Escribid un breve discurso para animar y agradecer a vuestros conciudadanos el esfuerzo realizado durante la pandemia.
5b. Leed y reflexionad sobre el discurso que habéis escrito, ¿qué aspectos culturales habéis tenido en cuenta para realizarlo?
5c. Compartid vuestras ideas con vuestros compañeros y escuchad sus discursos. Atribuid 20 puntos al discurso que os parece más eficaz y que más os ha gustado.

Appendix 2: Didactic Material in Italian

Livello 1

a. Ascolta l'audio*. Chi sono, secondo te, queste persone? Come le immagini? Prendi appunti.

L'audio è quello del video 'quando finisce tutto.', pubblicato sul canale YouTube Il signor Franz e reperibile al link: https://www.youtube.com/watch?v=wQAOjfjU6kU.

Per questa attività si useranno i minuti da 00:00 a 01:04.

b. Le persone che hai sentito nell'audio sono degli italiani che raccontano la prima cosa che vogliono fare una volta che la quarantena dovuta al COVID-19 sarà finita.

Ascolta di nuovo l'audio: qual è il loro stato d'animo? Scrivi tutte le parole che ti vengono in mente.

Livello 2

a. Guarda il video (https://www.youtube.com/watch?v=848kapapk8I) e rispondi a queste domande–2 punti alla tua squadra per ogni risposta corretta:

a. Che tipo di video è?

- Una campagna politica;
- Il trailer di un film;
- Una pubblicità.

b. Qual è lo scopo del video?

- Far vedere la bellezza dei luoghi senza persone;
- Vendere i prodotti pubblicizzati negli ospedali;
- Ringraziare gli italiani per il lavoro che stanno facendo.

c. Perché il silenzio protegge le strade?

- Perché la gente è in casa per diminuire il rischio di contagio;
- Perché le strade sono libere e si evitano gli incidenti;
- Perché stare in silenzio riduce l'inquinamento acustico nelle strade.

d. Nella frase 'a chi è stremato, ma ci dà forza per sperare', cosa significa 'stremato'?

- Felicissimo;
- Stanchissimo;
- Pessimista.

e. Nella frase 'a chi è spaesato, ma si sente ancora un paese', con quale parola si può sostituire il termine 'spaesato'?

- Confuso;

– Apolide;
– Sicuro.

Livello 3

a. Qui sotto trovi la trascrizione del video, ma alcune parole sono nel posto sbagliato. Riesci a metterle in ordine? Attenzione: due delle frasi sono già nell'ordine corretto!
   5 punti alla tua squadra per ogni frase corretta:

A questo strade che silenzio le protegge nostre
e alla che balconi grida nei vita;
a muove chi è, si ma fermo;
chi dà nulla a senza tutto chiedere;
a chi è stremato, ma ci dà forza per sperare;
alla ricordarci che non bellezza di chi smette mai siamo;
paura coraggio che alla risveglia il
e sorriso senso ogni al fatica che dà a ogni;
a chi molla non stanco è, ma;
vicino a chi sa lontano, è ma starci
e a chi è spaesato, ma si sente ancora un paese.
All'ancora, che Italia volta una resiste.

Livello 4

a. (individuale) Leggi gli estratti dai primi discorsi sul COVID-19 di questi rappresentanti di Stato. Quale ti colpisce di più? Perché?

b. Segnala le parole chiave nel testo.—2 punti per ogni caratteristica culturale trovata che riesci a spiegare ai compagni.

c. Pensi che il discorso dei rappresentanti di Stato possa rispecchiare alcune caratteristiche culturali del Paese che rappresentano? Riusciresti ad aggiungere altre due caratteristiche per ogni Paese?

d. In che modo la quarantena dovuta al COVID-19 può aver influito sulla creazione o sullo sviluppo di un senso di comunità? Conosci esempi relativi ad altri paesi?

Livello 5

a. Scrivete un messaggio motivazionale per incoraggiare e ringraziare i vostri connazionali per l'impegno di questi mesi. Immaginate il contesto, scrivete le parole e descrivete le immagini che comporrebbero lo spot.

b. Pensate al messaggio realizzato. Di quali aspetti culturali avete tenuto conto per realizzarlo?

c. Condividete le vostre idee ed i vostri messaggi di ringraziamento con le altre squadre.
  Date 20 punti al discorso che ritenete più efficace e che più vi è piaciuto.

Notes

1. B1 students were selected as the target students of the present study because they are considered to have the necessary linguistic competence to address cultural differences, which are a cornerstone in second language learning.
2. Linguistic components: phonetic, morphosyntactic, textual, lexical, and semantic. Extra-linguistic components: kinesics, proxemics, objects, and clothing that define a person's status. Contextual components: sociolinguistic, pragmatic, and intercultural knowledge (Balboni 2015, pp. 34–35; Balboni and Caon 2015, pp. 21–22).
3. Organisation for Economic Co-operation and Development.
4. 'We build a virtual environment, but not less real, where the interaction takes place' (translated from Italian to English by the author).

5. For this reason, from now on the term *training* will be used instead of *teaching*.
6. Translated from Italian to English by author: 'Un processo di lifelong observation dei problemi di comunicazione interculturale'.
7. Obviously, intercultural education is not a project that can be carried out only in educational institutions and schools, but the entire society must be involved in it. If we teach respect for different cultures in the classroom, the same values presented to students should not be contradicted in everyday life. Using the words of Grant's preface (in Corner 1987, p. 3): 'One of the greatest educational challenges of our time—how to educate so that the identity and particular needs of diverse groups can be justly met within the framework both of the larger society and the international community of which it forms part. When looked at this way, multicultural education can no longer be relegated to the periphery, as something of minority interest only; it is as relevant to the majority as to minority communities, for in the international context we all belong to minority cultures. [...] From this standpoint, the diversity of our societies is an asset rather than a handicap, and multicultural education is an opportunity rather than a problem'.
8. Gamification can be applied in many other settings, such as business or health-care centres.
9. Adapted from Marczewski et al. (2016, pp. 231–232).
10. This, on the other hand, should be taken as a more general principle in teaching: whilst it is very difficult to identify and cater for the many and diverse learning styles within a lesson setting, especially of course when we deal with a large cohort, the most effective approach is always to make sure our teaching comprises a variety of activities and approaches—that, in other words, our teaching is inclusive, so as to cater for as many learning styles as possible.
11. See gamification user types in Sect. 2.4.
12. The didactic materials in Italian included two different videos, one for the warm-up activity and another one for the cultural and linguistic input.
13. It was adapted from the Konzai Group and their Intercultural Effectiveness Scale (https://www.kozaigroup.com/intercultural-skills/).
14. We would like to thank Patricia Falagán Carbajo for her help and support in the application of the activities in the Spanish module.

References

Abio, G. 2006. El modelo de «Flujo» de Csikszentmihalyi y su importancia en la enseñanza de lenguas extranjeras. *RedELE–Revista Eletrónica de Didáctica— Español Lengua Extranjera* 6.

Alm, A. 2016. Amateur online interculturalism in foreign language education. *EUROCALL*. https://doi.org/10.14705/rpnet.2016.eurocall2016.533. Accessed 26 December 2022.

Alsawaier, R.S. 2018. The effect of gamification on motivation and engagement. *International Journal of Information and Learning Technology* 35 (1): 56–79. https://doi.org/10.1108/IJILT-02-2017-0009.

Balboni, P.E. 2015. *Le sfide di Babele: insegnare le lingue nelle società complesse*. Torino: UTET Università.

Balboni, P.E., and F. Caon. 2014. A performance-oriented model of intercultural communicative competence. *Journal of Intercultural Communication* 35: 1–12.

———. 2015. *La comunicazione interculturale*. Venezia: Marsilio Editori.

Bartle, R. 1996. Hearts, Clubs, Diamonds, Spades: Players who suit MUDs. *Journal of MUD Research* 1: 19.

Bonfiglio, A. 2013. *Le nuove frontiere della didattica: e-learning, podcasting e Wikipedia per una didattica collaborativa in rete*. Rome: Aracne.

Cassany, D. 2004. Aprendizaje cooperativo para ELE. In *Actas del programa de formación para profesorado de español como lengua extranjera 2003–04*, 11–30. Munich: Instituto Cervantes de Múnich.

Celentin, P. 2007. *Comunicare e far comunicare in internet: comunicare per insegnare, insegnare per comunicare*. Venezia: Cafoscarina.

CERI. 1989. *One school, many cultures*. Paris: OECD.

Cohen, L., et al. 2017. *Research methods in education*. London: Routledge.

Cook, L., and M. Friend. 1995. Co-teaching: Guidelines for creating effective practices. *Focus on Exceptional Children* 28 (3): 10.17161/foec.v28i3.6852.

Csikszentmihalyi, M. 1988. The flow experience and its significance for human psychology. In *Optimal experience: Psychological studies of flow in consciousness*, ed. Mihaly Csikszentmihalyi, 15–35. New York: Cambridge University Press.

———. 1990. *Flow: The psychology of optimal experience*. New York: Harper-Row.

———. 1992. *Flow. The psychology of happiness*. London: Rider.

Dervin, F. 2009. Constructions de l'interculturel dans le deuxième programme à moyen terme du Centre Européen pour les Langues Vivantes (CELV): l'exemple de la communication interculturelle dans la formation des enseignants. *Synergies Pays Riverains de la Baltique* 6: 77–88.

———. 2010. Assessing interculture in language learning and teaching: A critical review of current effort. In *New approaches to assessment in higher education*, ed. F. Dervin and E. Suomela-Salmi, 157–173. Bern: Peter Lang.

———. 2016. *Interculturality in education: A theoretical and methodological toolbox*. London: Palgrave Macmillan.

Deterding, S., et al. 2011. From game design elements to gamefulness: Defining 'gamification'. *Proceedings of the 15th International Academic MindTrek Conference: Envisioning Future Media Environments*, Tampere, Finland, pp. 9–15. https://doi.org/10.1145/2181037.2181040.

Díaz Antillanca, O.F. 2016. Niño, juego y dimensión lúdica: Primeros niveles bio-epistémicos de limitación. *Revista infancia, educación y aprendizaje* 2: 94–105.

Foncubierta, J.M., and C. Rodríguez. 2014. *Didáctica de la gamificación en la clase de español*. Madrid: Programa de Desarrollo Profesional. Editorial Edinumen.

Grant, N. 1984. Education for multicultural society. In *Education in multicultural societies*, ed. Trevor Corner, 7–28. New York: St. Martin's Press.

Keyser, W., et al. 2022. Empathy in action: Developing a sense of belonging with the pedagogy of 'real talk'. *Journal of University Teaching & Learning Practice* 19 (4): 1–27. https://ro.uow.edu.au/jutlp/vol19/iss4/10.

Lee, J., and J. Hammer. 2011. Gamification in education: What, how, why bother? *Academic Exchange Quarterly* 15: 1–5.

Marczewski, A. 2015. *Even ninja monkeys like to play: Gamification, Game thinking and motivational design*. London: Blurb.

Marczewski, A., et al. 2016. The gamification user types hexad scale. *Proceedings of the 2016 Annual Symposium on Computer-Human Interaction in Play*, Austin, TX, pp. 229–243.

Ming, L.E. 2004. La piattaforma E-learning Moodle per la formazione di apprendenti sinofoni. In *Tecnologie per l'insegnamento delle lingue*, ed. I. Fratter, 257–286. Rome: Carocci.

Pujolà, J.T., and F.J. Herrera Jiménez. 2018. Gamificación: (Gamification). In *The Routledge handbook of Spanish language teaching*, 583–595. London: Routledge.

Redondo Juárez, P. 2021. Innovación en el aula. Profundización en el elemento lúdico: Factores y aplicación didáctica. In *Internacionalización y Enseñanza del Español como Lengua Extranjera: Plurilingüismo y Comunicación Intercultural*, ed. M. Saracho-Arnáiz and H. Otero-Doval, 1193–1211. Oporto: ASELE.

Troncarelli, D. 2004. L'Insegnamento dell'italiano per scopi specifici con le tecnologie di rete. In *Tecnologie per l'insegnamento delle lingue*, ed. I. Fratter, 99–131. Rome: Carocci.

Tulloch, R. 2014. Reconceptualising gamification: Play and pedagogy. *Digital Culture & Education* 6: 317–333.

Part IV

Conclusions

9

The Future of Assessment in Language Education: What Have We Learnt from the Pandemic?

Marion Coderch

1 Introduction

The restrictions on face-to-face activities brought about by the coronavirus pandemic in early 2020 made language teaching professionals question their conventional practices in order to adapt quickly to the demands of remote teaching. While authentic online learning curricula could take several months or years to design and develop, language professionals in higher education were compelled to restructure their whole programmes in a matter of weeks. Teachers attempted to strike a balance between the high standards of teaching expected by their institutions and their students, on one hand, and the practical and logistical constraints imposed by unforeseen working conditions, on the other. In this context, the

---

M. Coderch (✉)
Durham University, Durham, UK

Facultad de Filología, Universidad Nacional de Educación a Distancia, Madrid, Spain
e-mail: mjcoderch@flog.uned.es

nature and place of assessment in language modules was, inevitably, one of the main objects of discussion.

Despite the central role of assessment and feedback in the organisation of courses and in the workload of staff and students, there is consistent evidence of the dissatisfaction students have experienced with these procedures (Ferrell and Knight 2022b). Prior to the pandemic, innovation in assessment practices had been hindered by different factors: the universities' conservative stance towards assessment (Sambell 2016), lack of institutional support for staff who wished to innovate (McLean 2018), and limitations on teachers' freedom imposed by institutional patterns and regulations (Carless 2015). From March 2020 onwards, the need to think creatively about assessment lifted some of these barriers. The reflection on assessment procedures that took place later expanded beyond the mere rethinking of activities with a view to adapting them to the virtual environment: it also involved questioning the nature of assessment tasks and the role of assessment in the curriculum. The following paragraphs summarise the aspects that have acquired prominence in discussions about assessment since then: the role of continuous assessment; holism, flexibility and choice; inclusivity, equity and academic integrity. The chapter concludes with several recommendations aimed at guiding the implementation of these principles in teaching and learning practice.

2   The Notion of Continuous Assessment

As a result of the disruption faced by staff and students in the spring of 2020, the need to embed assessment firmly in teaching became obvious as a means to clarify the connection between the everyday development of the modules and assessment activities. Embedding assessment in teaching contributes to student motivation and engagement, steering away from the notion of final exams as a standalone piece of work with the only purpose of awarding credit. Continuous assessment systems emerged, then, as the obvious solution for integrating assessment activities in the teaching flow—as Giacosa has observed in Chap. 2.

One of the benefits of continuous assessment systems is the fact that they give students multiple opportunities to engage with feedback and to act upon it (Carless 2015; Hernández 2012). In addition, they are more inclusive of students with different learning preferences or needs (Padden and O'Neill 2021; Sambell et al. 2017). Continuous assessment does not necessarily mean asking students to complete summative tests continuously nor spreading summative assessment tasks throughout the teaching schedule so that no more than a few weeks pass without students sitting some kind of test. It does not involve taking one final exam and shredding it into bite-size mini-exams worth only a small fraction of the final mark (10%, 15%, etc.). These methods risk leading to the accumulation of assessment, which could reduce opportunities to engage in formative tasks and may moreover end up promoting a strategic approach on behalf of students, potentially limiting the development of broader skills and independent learning (Elkington 2021).

Ideally, a continuous assessment system for language modules would allow students to document their progress and to work consistently towards a final product. In practice, though, this goal is difficult to attain. To be meaningful, it requires close monitoring of every single student's individual project, giving feedback and having conversations about it with each student. The amount of time necessary to keep track of every individual student's progress makes this assessment method inadequate for large cohorts since it would add exponentially to the teachers' workload. The issue of lack of time was accentuated after the move to online teaching and learning: teaching staff saw increases in workloads that were already remarkably high. In a survey conducted by the University and College Union (2022), more than 50% of teachers in UK universities reported that time spent on administration (departmental as well as student-related), class preparation and pastoral care had increased significantly since 2016 when the last workload survey had been carried out. If giving frequent, personalised feedback to large groups of students was difficult before 2020, the new context makes this prospect seem even more unrealistic.

The key is, then, to find a model of continuous assessment that is inclusive and offers quality feedback, as well as opportunities to act on it while being cost- and time-effective—in other words, a system that generates student engagement without creating an excessive marking load

(Brown 2005; Gibbs and Simpson 2005). A holistic approach to assessment provides a possible answer to this conundrum.

3 A Holistic Approach to Assessment

Assessment can be approached holistically in two ways: through the integration of different types of assessment (formative and summative) and through the integration of different language skills in one single task (i.e. testing integrated skills rather than skills in isolation).

Traditionally, the distinction between formative and summative assessment has implied that formative activities were seen as a number of low or no-stakes tasks, a sort of mock practice set of activities that were only useful in so far as they could help students develop strategic skills for success in the final exam. The strong focus on one final piece of summative assessment led students to perceive formative tasks as activities that 'didn't count' (because the marks awarded carried no weight for the final grade of the module), as opposed to the tasks that 'count' (i.e. exams). Nevertheless, if assessment is thought of holistically, the distinction between formative and summative assessment loses meaning. In the separation between formative and summative assessment, the goal of doing well in the final exam overwhelms the intrinsic aim of studying a language: to learn how to use it to communicate effectively. Conversely, blurring the boundaries between formative and summative tasks shifts the focus from performing well in the final exam to learning and improving throughout the year: every task is an opportunity to learn, rather than a hoop to jump through in order to get a mark.

The merging of formative and summative assessment is in line with the principles of assessment for learning and assessment as learning. In assessment for learning, tasks furnish opportunities to receive feedback and feed forward (Carless 2007): students obtain information about the progress they have made so far, as well as about the actions they need to undertake to enhance their learning (Sadler et al. 2022). In assessment as learning, formative and summative tasks are part of a continuum where students have the chance to discuss their progress and the expectations placed on them (Ferrell and Knight 2022a, b). Assessment must be a learning experience in itself rather than something that students do to get marks (Nordmann et al. 2020). When the boundaries between formative and summative assessment are blurred, final exams are no longer the main event of the year: every single task matters.

The integration of formative and summative assessment may be achieved by designing tasks that students would need to complete during the year as part of their learning process, regardless of whether these would be formative or summative. Once the schedule of tasks has been completed, a decision can be made about which of these tasks would account for the attainment of learning outcomes. These tasks can then be taken as summative at the end of the year for accreditation purposes. Liberating assessment from the dichotomy of formative/summative tasks would increase the flexibility and resilience of assessment schedules in a way that would make them more adaptable to unforeseen changes in circumstances.

Given the resistance to change in assessment practices that characterises the sector, this development is likely to find some opposition among departmental regulators and quality assurance officers. In these cases, it would be necessary to highlight the fact that the distinction between the two types of assessment (formative and summative) is not being scrapped. Students will still have the opportunity to complete tasks that will contribute to their progress, as well as others that will be used for accreditation purposes. The main difference from the traditional system is the timing of the decision to distinguish between formative and summative work: while, traditionally, the nature of every task is determined in advance at the start of the academic year, the holistic approach would initially view all tasks as opportunities to develop the students' skills, postponing the selection of tasks that count towards accreditation until the end of the year. This change would not hinder the normal implementation of quality assurance procedures, such as internal and external moderation: if students have been submitting work throughout the year, all the tasks, including those that will be considered for accreditation, will be completed and marked at, or shortly after, the end of teaching. Online assessment facilitates the application of this model, in that several tasks and submission points can be scheduled during the academic year without the need to free up contact time to hold in-class assessments or to find an additional time slot outside the teaching schedule where everyone is available to complete the test in person.

The strategy of integrating skills into one task would effectively reduce the assessment load for staff and students alike. The combination of receptive and productive skills (reading and writing/reading and speaking/listening and writing/listening and speaking) lends itself to a rich variety of task designs. These could account for the acquisition of more than one skill so that more weighting could be granted to every task. In addition, students would need to complete fewer tasks to demonstrate the achievement of learning outcomes, which would contribute to avoiding assessment overload. It is pertinent to highlight that assessing integrated skills does not mean simply assessing two or more skills in one single test (e.g. by preparing a reading comprehension activity and, then, a writing task that is completely independent of the former). Testing integrated skills requires students to use the input they get through their receptive skills to produce something new: a reply to an email, a commentary on an opinion piece, a discussion on some source of written or audiovisual input and so forth.

4   Flexibility and Choice

As noted above, blurring the boundaries between formative and summative assessment would allow for a greater flexibility in practice, leaving a certain margin to cater for changes at short notice. Flexibility has benefits from the point of view of diversity and inclusion too: it allows for the personalisation and adaptation of assessment tasks to individual students' paces and needs (Nicol 2009). Moving assessment tasks online has opened up avenues for the implementation of adaptable practices which take into consideration the different circumstances that students can find themselves in: it has made it easier to give all students equal opportunities to showcase their knowledge without the need to request individual adjustments. This section and the next describe several ways in which online assessment can be used to promote inclusive practices.

Flexibility in assessment goes hand in hand with choice. Giving students the possibility to make decisions about their own assessment increases their autonomy and enhances their personal investment in tasks. Students can be given choices about different aspects of assessment, such as the timing, the weighting or the character: for example, in a system where there is no initial distinction between formative and summative tasks, students could be given the choice to select which of the tasks completed during the year they want to be taken into consideration as summative, in line with a model that Sobhanzadeh and Zizler have called 'selective assessment' (2021).

Cook (2001) and Jopp and Cohen (2020) describe and discuss experiences of the implementation of flexibility and choice in assessment: from giving the option to take different combinations of tasks with variable weightings (Cook 2001) to providing different types of tasks for every assessment component (Jopp and Cohen 2020). The assessment of language proficiency, though, has some particular features that need to be taken into consideration: diversity in assessment is already guaranteed by the nature of the tasks required to test the different skills since students would need to complete at least two types of tests—up to four if skills are tested separately. On the other hand, when designing different types of tasks to test the same skill, attention must be paid to potential perceptions of irregularities in the difficulty of the various tasks: while diversity in task design is positive in that it allows students with varied learning styles to demonstrate their progress, every student should have the choice of participating in all different types of tasks to maximise inclusion and chances of success.

5   Inclusive Assessment

Diversity and choice of assessment feature as two of the principles of inclusive task design, together with clarity of assessment strategy and goals, reduction of assessment load, scaffolded assessment and self-assessment (Padden and O'Neill 2021). On a wider scale, inclusive assessment must consider issues of equity, digital and otherwise—especially in the current landscape, where a significant proportion of assessment tasks have been moved online for good.

Digital equity, defined as 'a condition in which all individuals and communities have the information technology capacity needed for full participation in our society, democracy and economy' (Willems et al. 2019), has long been considered a social justice goal, in so far as it can contribute to bridging the knowledge divide (Resta and Laferrière 2008). The absence of digital equity implies that some individuals suffer from digital poverty. In 2020, the Office for Students coined a definition of digital poverty which is inclusive in that it considers not only the need to have access to reliable digital equipment, but also appropriate guidance and working environments (Maguire 2020). Issues of digital poverty inevitably surfaced with vigour in 2020, with the move to online teaching: in fact, a survey run in September 2020 by the Office for Students revealed that 'during the lockdown 52% of students said their learning was impacted by a slow or unreliable internet connection and 18% were affected by lack of access to a computer, laptop or tablet device' (Maguire 2020).

These challenges were exacerbated by the fact that enjoying appropriate conditions for academic work requires more than having access to a computer and an internet connection. A quiet space to work for extended periods of time is also indispensable, as well as sufficient skills for independent study. As a consequence, there are a number of possible scenarios that teachers would need to bear in mind when planning technology-based activities: one can never assume that all the students will have the optimal degree of quality, reliability and availability of technology and study spaces; access to adequate technology equipment and study conditions often depend on a range of factors beyond the students' control.

In making decisions about technology-based assessment, the focus should be placed on establishing a gradation that includes students with different working equipment and in varying conditions (e.g. their physical study space). This implies setting up an assessment regime where no student could be disadvantaged for having an unreliable internet connection, a slow laptop or an unsuitable space to work. For tests that students need to complete and submit remotely, these conditions can be achieved by avoiding time-limited tasks. In time-limited conditions (whether the time window is 2 or 24 hours), students who enjoy a reliable and fast internet connection will be more relaxed and less likely to experience pressure, whereas those who cannot rely on the connectivity of their own resources might be forced to find an alternative physical space (e.g. a library) where they would need to complete the task in surrounding conditions that are not totally under their control.

In addition, timed assessment tasks, whether they are online or in-person, may entail difficulties for students with disabilities who require reasonable adjustments (Padden and O'Neill 2021). While special arrangements can be made for these individuals, the focus of inclusive assessment should be not on making distinctions between students with and without disabilities but on making assessment tasks accessible and fair to all so that no exceptional arrangements have to be made for particular cases (Delaney and Hata 2020). In fact, assessment plans that compare students with disabilities to their peers can exacerbate feelings of anxiety, affecting performance and motivation negatively (Tolbert 2017). The practice of making exceptional arrangements for students with a disability stems from an ableist mindset where disabilities are seen as 'deficits that need to be accommodated' (Nieminen 2022), thus othering a group of students who do not fit into what is seen as the norm.

In a face-to-face setting, the needs of students with disabilities are normally accommodated through the application of reasonable adjustments (additional time, different physical spaces). Given the undesirable effects of these practices described above, it cannot be argued that these arrangements provide equitable access to assessment tasks for all individuals. Instead, untimed online submissions offer the degree of flexibility required to accommodate the needs of all students (Mahoney and Hall 2017): submission points can be available for weeks or even months so that all students can showcase their knowledge in parity of conditions and with no pressure. This practice gives everyone the freedom to choose the time and space that best suits them to complete and submit assessment tasks, maximising performance and chances of success.

The awareness of the different conditions in which students might need to complete assessment tasks is fundamental to assessment design and planning. Inclusive practices mean that no student can be disadvantaged by a particular task requirement. Equality impact has to be embedded in decision-making: rather than planning assessments and waiting for individual students to tell us they have special needs so that we can make adjustments exclusively for them, teachers need to foresee the potential diversity in needs and circumstances of students and plan assessment tasks with these in mind. Inclusive educational design is a powerful mechanism to make sure that no student is marginalised or excluded due to circumstances beyond their control (Moody 2020).

6 Academic Integrity in the New Landscape

The adoption of technology for teaching and learning has implications beyond the mode of class delivery or submission of assessment tasks. It requires a reconsideration of conventional, well-established procedures to assess whether they need any changes in light of the new landscape. It is acknowledged that teachers who newly adopt technologies for their work often tend to apply these tools to reproduce their previous practices: 'doing the same thing as before, but a little more quickly, a little more frequently, or a little better' (Resta and Laferrière 2008). This approach seems to have been replicated, to a certain extent, in the assessment practices adopted in response to the COVID-19 emergency situation. As Jan McArthur says, the fundamental principles of assessment have not been deeply rethought, even though practitioners had a unique opportunity to do so: 'many universities have pursued technocratic solutions that reproduced the trusted orthodoxy of the time-limited, unseen exam as closely as possible'. In effect, the time-limited, unseen exam remains the gold standard of assessment (McArthur 2021).

A survey carried out by Jisc in 2021 revealed that staff resistance to change and to the need to rethink patterns of assessment design were among the main challenges to innovation in assessment practices (Ferrell and Knight 2022a). In the field of language teaching, a considerable proportion of staff who resist change appeal to concerns over academic integrity: it is frequently argued that if timed assessments are replaced with time-unlimited open-book exercises, students will have more opportunities to cheat using online tools. Concerns centring on students' use of technology-based solutions in language assessments have been the object of debate for language practitioners over the last 15 years. A prominent topic of discussion is the use of machine translation tools to complete writing assessment tasks (i.e. where students are expected to demonstrate their linguistic competence without external aid, as opposed to translation tasks where students would need to prove that they can use the tools commonly employed by professional translators). While it was widely assumed that markers and moderators could easily detect machine-generated translations thanks to their artificiality and clunkiness, these expectations were defied after Google introduced Neural Machine Translation technology in 2016. Some of the improved features of the new system were the use of syntax and context recognition, which made detection of the use of these tools virtually impossible in some cases.

After the move to online teaching and assessment in the spring of 2020, these concerns resurfaced with extraordinary strength. Since there were no language assessments taken in traditional exam conditions (i.e. in large halls on university premises, with limited time and invigilators), all assessment tasks were virtually susceptible to being completed with the assistance of translation tools. It became clear that universities were unprepared to deal with potential cases of academic misconduct where the work submitted by students could not be considered their own production. The question of whether students should be allowed to use online resources to complete writing tasks is still the object of much debate among language-teaching communities.

Nevertheless, the fact is that cheating in assessment tasks is part of academic life, in languages as in any other discipline, and practitioners must accept it and live with it (Dyer et al. 2020). The solution to cheating in assessment tasks is not to try to avoid it because there will always be some kind of advanced technology that will win (Pauli 2021). In addition, if students are determined to cheat, they will do it regardless of whether they have one hour, two, or even a day. Seeing all students as potential culprits in the game of academic malpractice has no place in the relationship we wish to develop with them based on mutual trust and respect.

On the other hand, the use of online sources is a skill that students will need to master in their professional life. Allowing them to use these resources in assessment tasks adds authenticity and context validity (McLelland 2017; Jisc 2020; Andrews and McVitty 2022; Bearman et al. 2022). Online translation tools, dictionaries and thesauri are routinely used by linguists in their everyday work. If these tools are available, students will take advantage of them. They would obviously be expected to use these resources in assessment tasks designed to test translation skills, but they might as well employ them in writing expression and interaction assignments. The mere availability of these tools does not guarantee that students who access them will achieve an unjustified higher mark: students need to be able to apply a range of critical and analytical skills to make the most of the tools within their reach. These are resources students would also be likely to use in real life when they need to communicate in the target language.

Other methods that have gained popularity in the drive to avoid cases of academic malpractice, such as automated proctoring, have proven to be problematic: the use of artificial intelligence software to invigilate exams can be inherently biased since it might fail to recognise racial and gender differences, as well as disabilities. It has raised concerns about students' privacy (Jisc and Emerge Education 2020; Padden and O'Neill 2021) and about exacerbated anxiety among students who are invigilated (Bearman et al. 2022). All in all, it is evident that the solution to the challenges posed by academic malpractice does not lie in trying to avoid such malpractice, but in redesigning assessment tasks to make fraudulent behaviour irrelevant. Besides the difficulty posed by the need to rethink assessment tasks, the process requires a significant investment of time and resources. For this reason, the fight against academic malpractice would require institutional support. Senior management would need to make the cause a priority and provide academic departments with the resources necessary to redesign assessment in line with the demands of the post-COVID era (Pauli 2021).

7   Practical Recommendations

This final section of the chapter summarises the suggestions offered above to help teachers and examiners to put into practice the principles previously outlined. It finishes with some thoughts on the role of online assessment in the new landscape.

Integrate assessment tasks in the day-to-day progress of the module. Make explicit the connection between the work that students do every day and the work that will be assessed. Avoid making a distinction between the everyday tasks and 'exams'. In this way, students will realise that everything they do is relevant because everything is related to assessment.

Keep it simple. Avoid setting tasks worth only small percentages, as well as excessive divisions into components and subcomponents. The more tasks students will have to complete, the greater the chance that something will go wrong: missed deadlines, lost submissions, technical problems or requests to reschedule due to health issues or other reasons. In addition, a complicated assessment system with many sections and sublevels might look confusing or be difficult for students to understand. It is advisable to keep tasks and instructions as simple as possible to avoid confusion and misunderstandings.

Aim for fewer tasks by integrating skills and allocating a higher percentage to assessment tasks (e,g. combining receptive and productive skills). The integration of skills also reduces the risk of grade inflation, particularly in comparison with tasks where only receptive skills would be tested. If students could complete these unintegrated tasks remotely, even with limited time, their marks would be likely to be high and they might not necessarily be an accurate reflection of their level of competence.

Blur the boundaries between formative and summative assessment. Give students the opportunity to decide what part of the work they have completed will be taken as summative. Another option would be to only decide which tasks will hold summative status at the end of the year once all the assessments have been completed. For example, the tasks where a student has achieved the highest scores for every component could be chosen as summative.

Streamline the feedback process as much as possible. Take advantage of the rubric tools in your virtual learning environment. In this way, personalised feedback can be limited to a few additional statements for every student—this can also be delivered during individual, face-to-face (in-person or online) sessions. Consider, too, giving feedback orally through audio or video recordings: recent evidence suggests that students perceive these methods as more personalised and engaging (Pitt and Quinlan 2022).

Prepare materials and tasks that students can access in advance. In online assessment, this measure will minimise the risks associated with students not being able to access the instructions on the day of the test. In addition, giving students the opportunity to access the input in advance facilitates the integration of receptive and productive skills: they could be asked to carry out some comprehension or research tasks to be able to produce a piece of work based on the resources provided.

Design tasks that require students to engage with the target language critically and analytically. This recommendation affects mostly the assessment of receptive skills. Move away from superficial activities that could be easily completed in an unlimited period of time so that, without time constraints, most students would achieve a mark of 100%. Avoid using time limits as an added challenge to make up for the simplicity in task design. Below are some types of tasks that require a deeper level of engagement with the textual or audiovisual source:

- Offering a number of statements about the content of the input and asking students to select only those that are true (for lower levels) or those which best reflect the contents of the source (for higher levels).
- Offering a list of definitions and asking students to locate in the input the words or expressions that correspond to them (students will need to understand not only the relevant word or expression but also the context).
- Giving students a text with gaps to complete, choosing options from a list (according to the level, the items can be offered in multiple-choice form or simply as a list with some distractors mixed in); this activity can be used to test several language skills at the same time, besides reading comprehension: vocabulary, syntax and grammar.
- Giving students a text in fragments and asking them to put them in the correct order to reconstruct the original source.
- Asking students to complete a piece of input using given sentences or paragraphs (with or without distractors), inserting these in the right space.
- Selecting words or expressions from a piece of input and asking students to write sentences, a paragraph or a short text where these are contextualised and their meaning is clear.

9 The Future of Assessment in Language Education: What Have…

The true role of the advice outlined above is to allow practitioners to gather faithful and reliable pieces of evidence that the students have achieved the learning outcomes for accreditation purposes. There is nothing preventing teachers and examiners from using these pieces of assessment as opportunities to learn. Instead of viewing every assessment task as a power game where the examiner holds the students' destiny in their hands, language professionals should aim for a richer notion of assessment: an opportunity for teachers and students to cooperate and work together towards the shared goal of supporting learning.

Technologies will play a crucial role in the implementation of these measures. As noted above, online submissions open up an array of possibilities to adopt flexible practices that benefit all students, not only those in need of reasonable adjustments. Ensuring equal and equitable access to assessment tasks promotes feelings of belonging and integration as the distinctions between students with and without disabilities are removed. In addition, it reduces the anxiety and stress associated with having to complete exams under controlled conditions. It is also aligned with the principles of the Universal Design for Learning (UDL) framework, according to which 'all students can learn and teachers should plan and prepare for each individual difference of the diverse classroom' (Mahoney and Hall 2017).

As teaching and learning in higher education slowly return to a semblance of normality, the debate around assessment practices considers whether the changes brought about by the pandemic should be kept or whether practitioners should default to the previous order. The circumstances experienced during the last two years have allowed teachers and assessors to innovate and experiment with methods of online assessment that might not have been trialled otherwise. As a consequence, the opportunity to make assessment more authentic, more relevant and more aligned with the practical needs of students has been revealed. Regardless of the mode of teaching and learning that prevails in the future, practitioners and policy makers should acknowledge the value of these changes to traditional modes of assessment and embed them in their practices before the old habits set back in and take the place of innovation.

Acknowledgements I would like to thank the editor and the anonymous reviewers of this chapter for their valuable and insightful comments.

References

Andrews, M., and D. McVitty. 2022. Changing assessment: Embedding pedagogic innovation in a post-pandemic world. https://www.adobe.com/uk/creativecloud/buy/education/webinars/1-changing-assessment.html. Accessed 23 June 2022.

Bearman, M., et al. 2022. Designing assessment in a digital world: An organising framework. *Assessment & Evaluation in Higher Education* 48: 291. https://doi.org/10.1080/02602938.2022.2069674.

Brown, S. 2005. Assessment for learning. *Learning and Teaching in Higher Education* 1: 81–89. https://eprints.glos.ac.uk/3607/7/LATHE%20Contents%201.pdf. Accessed 7 April 2022.

Carless, D. 2007. Learning-oriented assessment: Conceptual bases and practical implications. *Innovations in Education and Teaching International* 44 (1): 57–66. https://doi.org/10.1080/14703290601081332.

———. 2015. Exploring learning-oriented assessment processes. *Higher Education* 69: 963–976. https://doi.org/10.1007/s10734-014-9816-z.

Cook, A. 2001. Assessing the use of flexible assessment. *Assessment and Evaluation in Higher Education* 26 (6): 539–549. https://doi.org/10.1080/02602930120093878.

Delaney, T.A., and M. Hata. 2020. Universal Design for Learning in assessment: Supporting ELLs with learning disabilities. *Latin American Journal of Content & Language Integrated Learning* 13 (1): 79–91. https://doi.org/10.5294/laclil.2020.13.1.5.

Dyer, J. et al. 2020. Want to stop student cheating? Then stop giving tacit permission. *Times Higher Education*. https://www.timeshighereducation.com/opinion/want-stop-student-cheating-then-stop-giving-tacit-permission. Accessed 8 April 2022.

Elkington, S. 2021. Scaling up flexible assessment. In *Assessment and feedback in a post-pandemic era: A time for learning and inclusion*, ed. P. Baughan, 31–39. York: Advance HE. https://www.advance-he.ac.uk/news-and-views/assessment-and-feedback-post-pandemic-era-time-learning-and-inclusion. Accessed 29 July 2022.

Ferrell, G., and S. Knight. 2022a. Assessment and feedback higher education landscape review: Survey outcomes. Jisc. https://www.jisc.ac.uk/reports/assessment-and-feedback-higher-education-landscape-review-survey-outcomes. Accessed 8 April 2022.

———. 2022b. Principles of good assessment and feedback: How good learning, teaching and assessment can be applied to improving assessment and feedback practice. Jisc. https://www.jisc.ac.uk/guides/principles-of-good-assessment-and-feedback. Accessed 29 July 2022.

Gibbs, G., and C. Simpson. 2005. Conditions under which assessment support students' learning. *Learning and Teaching in Higher Education* 1: 3–31. https://eprints.glos.ac.uk/3609/. Accessed 7 April 2022.

Hernández, R. 2012. Does continuous assessment in higher education support student learning? *Higher Education* 64: 489–502. https://doi.org/10.1007/s10734-012-9506-7.

Jisc. 2020. *The future of assessment: Five principles, five targets for 2025.* http://repository.jisc.ac.uk/7733/1/the-future-of-assessment-report.pdf. Accessed 8 April 2022.

Jisc & Emerge Education. 2020. *Assessment rebooted: From 2020's quick fixes to future transformation.* https://www.jisc.ac.uk/reports/assessment-rebooted. Accessed 29 July 2022.

Jopp, R., and J. Cohen. 2020. Choose your own Assessment: Assessment choice for students in online higher education. *Teaching in Higher Education*. https://doi.org/10.1080/13562517.2020.1742680.

Maguire, D. 2020. Learning and teaching reimagined: A new dawn for higher education? Jisc. https://www.jisc.ac.uk/reports/learning-and-teaching-reimagined-a-new-dawn-for-higher-education. Accessed 29 July 2022.

Mahoney, J., and C. Hall. 2017. Using technology to differentiate and accommodate students with disabilities. *E-Learning and Digital Media* 14 (5): 291–303. https://doi.org/10.1177/2F2042753017751517.

McArthur, J. 2021. For assessment to count as authentic it must mean something to students. Wonkhe, March 3. https://wonkhe.com/blogs/for-assessment-to-count-as-authentic-it-must-mean-something-to-students/. Accessed 8 April 2022.

McLean, H. 2018. This is the way to teach: Insights from academics and students about assessment that supports learning. *Assessment & Evaluation in Higher Education* 43 (8): 1228–1240. https://doi.org/10.1080/02602938.2018.1446508.

McLelland, N. 2017. *Teaching and learning foreign languages: A history of language education, assessment and policy in Britain*. Abingdon: Routledge.

Moody, J. 2020. Keeping student engagement inclusive: Reflections for 2021. Advance HE. https://www.advance-he.ac.uk/news-and-views/Keeping-student-engagement-inclusive. Accessed 8 April 2022.

Nicol, D. 2009. Transforming assessment and feedback: Enhancing integration and empowerment in the first year. The Quality Assurance Agency for Higher Education. https://www.enhancementthemes.ac.uk/docs/ethemes/the-first-year/transforming-assessment-and-feedback.pdf?sfvrsn=c62f981_12. Accessed 7 April 2022.

Nieminen, J.H. 2022. Assessment for inclusion: Rethinking inclusive assessment in higher education. *Teaching in Higher Education*. 2022: 1. https://doi.org/10.1080/13562517.2021.2021395.

Nordmann, E., et al. 2020. Ten simple rules for supporting a temporary online pivot in higher education. *PLoS Computational Biology* 16 (10): e1008242. https://doi.org/10.1371/journal.pcbi.1008242.

Padden, L., and G. O'Neill. 2021. Embedding equity and inclusion in higher education assessment strategies: Creating and sustaining positive change in the post-pandemic era. In *Assessment and feedback in a post-pandemic era: A time for learning and inclusion*, ed. P. Baughan, 138–147. York: Advance HE. https://www.advance-he.ac.uk/news-and-views/assessment-and-feedback-post-pandemic-era-time-learning-and-inclusion. Accessed 6 April 2022.

Pauli, M. 2021. Rethinking assessment. From fixes to foresight: Jisc and emerge education insights for universities and startups. Jisc. https://www.jisc.ac.uk/reports/rethinking-assessment. Accessed 6 April 2022.

Pitt, E., and K.M. Quinlan. 2022. *Impacts of higher education assessment and feedback policy and practice on students: A review of the literature 2016–2021*. York: Advance HE. https://www.advance-he.ac.uk/knowledge-hub/impacts-higher-education-assessment-and-feedback-policy-and-practice-students-review. Accessed 23 May 2022.

Resta, P., and T. Laferrière. 2008. Issues and challenges related to digital equity. In *International handbook of information technology in primary and secondary education: Part one*, ed. J. Voogt and G. Knezek, 765–778. New York: Springer Science.

Sadler, I., et al. 2022. Feedforward practices: A systematic review of the literature. *Assessment & Evaluation in Higher Education* 48: 305. https://doi.org/10.1080/02602938.2022.2073434.

Sambell, K. 2016. Assessment and feedback in higher education: Considerable room for improvement? *Student Engagement in Higher Education* 1(1): 1–14. https://193.60.48.124/index.php/raise/article/view/392/350. Accessed 7 April 2022.

Sambell, K., et al. 2017. *Professionalism in practice: Key directions in higher education learning, teaching and assessment*. London: Palgrave Macmillan.

Sobhanzadeh, M., and P. Zizler. 2021. Selective assessment in introductory physics labatorials. *The Physics Teacher* 59 (2): 114–116. https://doi.org/10.1119/10.0003465.

Tolbert, J.B.L. 2017. Foreign language assessment: Instructional considerations for students with specific learning disabilities. *Journal of Language Teaching and Research* 8 (3): 441–446. https://doi.org/10.17507/jltr.0803.01.

University and College Union. 2022. Workload survey 2021: Data report. https://www.ucu.org.uk/media/12905/WorkloadReportJune22/pdf/WorkloadReportJune22.pdf. Accessed 22 June 2022.

Willems, J., et al. 2019. The increasing significance of digital equity in higher education: An introduction to the digital equity special issue. *Australasian Journal of Educational Technology* 35 (6): 1–8. https://doi.org/10.14742/ajet.5996.

Index[1]

A

Assessment, 1, 2, 5–14, 17, 18, 19n4, 19n5, 30–36, 38–40, 42–49, 51–53, 61–64, 66–80, 81n3, 89–92, 98, 101, 110, 111, 115, 117, 119, 123–125, 133, 139, 141, 142, 145, 146, 154, 164–168, 170–173, 192, 194, 196, 199–201, 225, 268–281

Audiovisual, 110, 120, 132, 222, 272, 280

Autonomous learning, 4, 13, 44, 208, 217, 225

B

Blended, 3, 7, 30, 94, 98, 104, 110, 118, 121, 122, 124, 152, 176, 212, 216

C

Common European Framework of Reference (CEFR), 14, 99, 111, 115–117, 119, 120, 122

Community, 1, 3–6, 9–11, 14, 16, 17, 18n2, 40, 43, 62, 63, 67, 68, 70, 71, 74, 78, 80, 90, 93, 98, 104, 105, 111, 113, 114, 117, 123, 125, 126, 135, 141, 143–145, 207–211, 214, 216–218, 222–225, 226n1, 226n5, 234, 235, 240, 241, 246–250, 252, 253, 261n7

Creativity, 2, 15, 40, 113, 121, 124, 153

---

[1] Note: Page numbers followed by 'n' refer to notes.

© The Author(s), under exclusive license to Springer Nature Switzerland AG 2023
W. Fiorucci (ed.), *Language Education During the Pandemic*,
https://doi.org/10.1007/978-3-031-35855-5

D

Distance learning, 62, 89, 237
Diversity, 63, 68, 253, 261n7, 272, 273, 276

E

Emergency remote teaching (ERT), 1–3, 5, 6, 8, 10–12, 14, 16, 18n3, 19n5, 29–31, 35, 36, 39, 41, 42, 46, 51, 52, 54n1, 89, 93, 98, 110, 118, 151, 152, 223, 250
Employability, 42, 125, 137–140
Engagement, 1, 3, 5, 9–12, 16, 18n2, 33, 40, 45, 62, 98, 101, 102, 104, 105, 110, 119, 122, 123, 125, 126, 151, 156, 208, 209, 215, 217, 218, 222, 225, 226n1, 234, 239, 241, 245, 247, 253, 268, 269, 280
English as a foreign language (EFL), 5, 6, 12, 16, 18n3, 31, 32, 34–36, 52, 53, 54n1, 80n1, 94, 95
Equality, 275
Essay, 40, 124, 152, 226n1, 227n5
Exams, 2, 8, 9, 19n5, 30, 31, 34, 39, 40, 47, 50, 52, 53, 68, 71, 74, 79, 99, 268–271, 278, 279, 281

F

Feedback, 7–9, 11, 13, 16, 34, 43, 46–48, 62, 68, 74, 76, 78, 88–90, 95, 97–104, 122, 126, 136, 140, 143, 144, 146, 154, 175, 210, 216–218, 246, 248, 249, 251, 268–270, 279
Fluency, 15, 64, 100, 104, 158, 160, 162
Formative, 8, 9, 17, 30, 34, 47, 89–92, 95, 97, 98, 100, 101, 104, 122, 133, 140, 146, 154, 164, 165, 168, 172, 217, 269–273, 279

G

Gamification, 16, 234, 235, 239–244, 247, 249, 252, 253, 261n11
Grammar, 13, 14, 66–69, 74, 79, 87, 95, 99, 100, 104, 109, 110, 112, 113, 116, 121, 124, 129, 138, 143, 237, 280

H

Higher Education, 2, 8, 11, 16, 18n2, 19n5, 32, 114, 169, 211
Hybrid, 31, 37, 50, 121, 151, 155, 212, 215, 216

I

Innovation, 2, 8, 13, 87, 93, 212, 268, 276, 281
Intercultural communication, 5, 16, 209, 210, 216, 221, 225, 233
Intercultural competence, 16, 78, 117, 210, 221, 233, 234, 242, 247, 249, 252

Index

L

Language education, 3, 5, 13, 16, 87, 207, 209, 237
Language lab, 13, 87–94, 96, 104
Language learning, 4, 5, 13, 16, 63–65, 67, 88–91, 93, 103, 105, 109–111, 114–116, 118, 120, 122, 169, 207, 209, 210, 220–222, 226n1, 233, 260n1
Language production, 89, 90, 96, 101, 104
Learning and teaching, 3, 5, 6, 63, 94, 98, 110, 209

M

Motivation, 1, 3–5, 9, 11–13, 16, 18n2, 30, 33, 45, 63, 67, 68, 98, 101, 102, 104, 105, 139, 143, 151, 156, 173, 207–209, 211, 213, 215, 216, 221, 225, 226n1, 234, 241, 244, 245, 253, 268, 275
Multicultural, 63, 214, 234, 236, 253, 261n7

O

Online delivery, 3, 18, 89, 142, 250
Online learning, 3, 6, 12, 14, 18n2, 61, 89, 92, 122, 152, 207, 208, 223, 224, 237, 267
Oral, 19n5, 49, 64, 97, 99, 104, 115, 121, 154, 160, 161, 164–167, 170, 171, 173, 175, 176, 192, 194, 196, 199–201

R

Reading, 6, 41, 47, 69, 112, 114, 119, 140, 156, 174, 216, 217, 226n1, 272, 280
Remote, 1, 3–7, 9, 12, 13, 18, 29, 30, 32, 38, 42, 46, 47, 87–89, 91, 110, 212, 250, 252, 267
Remote learning, 4, 7, 13, 91, 250

S

Secondary school, 20n5, 66
Summative, 2, 7, 17, 30, 33, 35, 44, 63, 99, 100, 103, 123, 140, 154, 164–168, 170, 171, 173, 176, 199–201, 269–273, 279
Syntax, 124, 131, 138, 277, 280

T

Technology, 3, 7, 14, 15, 43, 51, 87, 88, 91–94, 97, 116, 118, 143, 152, 209, 214, 222, 223, 238, 274, 276, 277
Translation, 14, 15, 41, 87, 99, 109–113, 115–117, 119, 120, 122, 123, 125–146, 152, 276, 277

V

Virtual, 11, 15, 16, 40, 61, 89, 102, 104, 152, 176, 212, 213, 222, 226n5, 245, 247, 260n4, 268, 279

290 Index

Vocabulary, 64, 65, 99, 100, 104, 124, 127–129, 133–135, 137, 138, 153, 175, 177, 218, 225, 226n1, 245, 249, 280

W

Writing, 40, 47, 65, 112, 114, 116, 119, 137, 226n1, 272, 277, 278

Printed in the United States
by Baker & Taylor Publisher Services